A YEAR IN

THE LIFE OF THE

SUPREME COURT

CONSTITUTIONAL CONFLICTS

A SERIES BY THE INSTITUTE OF BILL OF RIGHTS LAW

AT THE COLLEGE OF WILLIAM AND MARY

EDITED BY RODNEY A. SMOLLA AND NEAL DEVINS

A YEAR IN

THE LIFE OF THE

SUPREME COURT

BY PAUL BARRETT, RICHARD CARELLI, MARCIA COYLE,

LYLE DENNISTON, AARON EPSTEIN, KAY KINDRED,

TONY MAURO, DAVID SAVAGE, AND STEPHEN WERMIEL

EDITED BY RODNEY A. SMOLLA

DUKE UNIVERSITY PRESS *Durham and London 1995*

The author of Chapter Three requests the following clarifi-
cation. Lyle Denniston is not responsible for the concluding
material in Chapter Three, beginning with the paragraph on
page 94 that opens with the phrase: "Indeed, as this book was
being prepared. . . ." The material through the end of the chapter was added without his knowledge or concurrence and does
not reflect his own perception of the events described in that
addition. The middle three paragraphs on page 92 were also
added without any consultation with the author. In addition,
Mr. Denniston does not concur with the editor's remarks in the
book introduction and in the introduction to Chapter Three
purporting to describe Mr. Denniston's personal views.

Second printing, 1997
© 1995 Duke University Press   All rights reserved
Printed in the United States of America on acid-free paper ∞
Typeset in Berkeley Medium by Tseng Information Systems, Inc.
Library of Congress Cataloging-in-Publication Data appear on
the last printed page of this book.

THE ANNENBERG WASHINGTON PROGRAM

IN COMMUNICATIONS POLICY STUDIES

OF NORTHWESTERN UNIVERSITY

THE INSTITUTE OF BILL OF RIGHTS LAW

COLLEGE OF WILLIAM AND MARY

MARSHALL-WYTHE SCHOOL OF LAW

CONTENTS

ACKNOWLEDGMENT

THIS BOOK WAS MADE POSSIBLE

BY THE GENEROUS SUPPORT OF

THE ANNENBERG WASHINGTON PROGRAM

IN COMMUNICATIONS POLICY STUDIES

OF NORTHWESTERN UNIVERSITY

CHAPTER ONE

Introduction: Personality and Process

RODNEY A. SMOLLA

The Reporters

This book, by Paul Barrett, Richard Carelli, Marcia Coyle, Lyle Denniston, Aaron Epstein, Kay Kindred, Tony Mauro, David Savage, and Stephen Wermiel, profiles a year, 1992–93, in the life of the Supreme Court of the United States. Included among these contributors are many of the most significant "Court watchers" in the nation, journalists who have made observing and reporting on the Court their lives' avocation. Chances are, indeed, that the reports of writers who cover the Court for the nation's major news organizations are the source of much of the information most Americans have on the decisions of the Court over the years. Outside a relatively small group of lawyers, judges, students, and academics, few Americans ever have the opportunity to observe a Supreme Court argument, or take the time actually to read the text of a Supreme Court opinion. Journalists are the eyes and ears of the American people on the actions of the Supreme Court, and in that sense, are the eyes and ears of the people on the Constitution itself.

The Stories of Real People

This book is intended to give readers a sense of the richness of Supreme Court litigation. The cases heard by the Court are, first and foremost, *cases,* disputes involving real people with real stories. The accidents and twists of circumstance that propelled their lives into the rarefied arena of the Supreme Court are often compelling drama.

Walter Biggins just wanted "a damn raise." Thomas and Robert Hazen, who employed Biggins in their family-owned business in Holyoke, Massachusetts, did not think Biggins deserved as big a raise as he wanted, and as negotiations embittered, relations deteriorated. Biggins was fired. He sued. His suit reached the Supreme Court.

Jayne Bray, a homemaker from Bowie, Maryland, just wanted to register her moral outrage at abortion. She participated in an abortion clinic blockade as part of the civil disobedience efforts of Operation Rescue, one of the nation's most vocal and aggressive anti-abortion groups. The National Organization for Women simply wanted peace for abortion clinics, for doctors who provide abortions, and for women who attend such clinics to exercise their recognized constitutional right of privacy to obtain abortions. It sponsored a lawsuit against Operation Rescue and Jayne Bray, claiming that their aggressive protest tactics violated the civil rights of women attending abortion clinics. The suit reached the Supreme Court.

Tim Dickerson was twenty-three, and had never been in trouble with the law. But one day, two seasoned police officers, Vernon Rose and Bruce Johnson, spotted Dickerson walking down the street in Minneapolis, and thought he looked suspicious. The officers stopped Dickerson and subjected him to a patdown. Officer Rose says he felt what seemed to be "a lump of crack cocaine in cellophane" in the front pocket of Dickerson's nylon jacket. It turned out to be one-fifth of a gram of cocaine. Dickerson claimed that the officers had no right to stop him and search him and that his conviction for cocaine possession should be overturned. He brought his case to the Supreme Court.

James Zobrest, a teenager who had been deaf since infancy, wanted to attend Salpointe Catholic High School in Tucson. He and his parents wanted the public school district to pay the costs of a sign language interpreter, just as the school district would pay if James had gone to the public high school. They sued the school district; the case found its way to the Supreme Court.

Leonel Herrera claimed he was an innocent man. Herrera was convicted by the state of Texas of killing a cop, he claimed that the state got the wrong man and that he deserved a new trial to attempt to prove that. But Herrera was sentenced to death by the state of Texas, and all his normal avenues of appeal and redress had run out. He wanted the federal courts to intervene and filed a federal writ of habeas corpus, claiming that it would violate the United States Constitution to execute an innocent man. With his life hanging in the balance, hours before the scheduled execution, his case was brought to the Supreme Court.

In St. Paul, Minnesota, Russ and Laura Jones were finding it difficult to make peace with their neighbors. Russ and Laura, African Americans, had moved with five children into a predominately white working-class neighborhood on Earl Street in St. Paul, and had been besieged with race hate: slashed tires, a smashed station wagon window, and racist slurs directed at the kids. One night a group of teenage skinheads, including Robert A. Victora, set fire to a makeshift cross in the Jones's backyard. The City of St. Paul prosecuted the teenagers under a city "hate crimes" ordinance, a law that made it a crime to burn a cross or display a Nazi swastika to cause anger, alarm, or resentment in others on the basis of their race, color, creed, religion, or gender. Victora claimed that the law violated his rights of freedom of speech under the First Amendment, in a case that reached the Supreme Court.

Jake Ayers was a former sharecropper in Mississippi. What he and his wife, Lillie Ayers, wanted was a chance for a quality college education in Mississippi for their nine children. In 1975 Ayers filed suit against the state of Mississippi, claiming that it had systematically underfunded the historically black state colleges and universities and that decades after the Supreme Court's historic desegregation decision in *Brown v. Board of Education* the state of Mississippi still ran a discriminatory higher education system. Ayers died in 1986, but his suit lived on after him and reached the Supreme Court.

Christine Franklin was a high-school student at North Gwinnett High School, a suburban high school north of Atlanta, in Gwinnett County, Georgia. Andrew Hill was the high-school football coach, athletic director, and economics teacher. Franklin claimed that Hill sexually harassed her and had sexual intercourse with her on several occasions, and when her complaints failed to draw what she believed was a meaningful and appropriate response from the high school's officials, she sued the school district for damages arising from her claim of sexual harassment in a case that was eventually ruled on by the Supreme Court.

The Issues

These chapters tell interesting stories, but they do far more than that, for these are not just any stories, or any set of cases. These are, rather, disputes that take on a larger meaning, that are enveloped by the great social issues of the day, disputes that reach to the heart of the meaning of the Constitution and the fabric of American law: abortion, separation of church and state, freedom of speech, the right of privacy, crime, violence, police misconduct, race discrimination, sex discrimination, age discrimination, the death penalty. These are the issues that Americans think, talk, fight, vote, and sue about. These are the issues on which elections turn, on which senators grill nominees to the Supreme Court, and on which Supreme Court Justices in turn grill the lawyers who argue before them.

The Justices

The personalities and jurisprudential leanings of the nine Justices who served on the Court during its 1992–93 term are always brightly in evidence in the chapters that follow. That is partly because those who watch the Court regularly come to see it not as mystical and mythical, an oracular institution pronouncing the sacred truths of the republic from on marble high, but rather as a collection of nine quite distinct individuals, men and women who often squabble and snarl and struggle as they wrestle each other for the votes necessary to resolve many of the deepest conflicts of our national identity.

The decisions of the Court are generally announced in written opinions, in which the decision and supporting rationales are explained. As the terms are used throughout this book, a "majority opinion" is an opinion in which at least five of the nine Justices on the Court join. An individual Justice will write this majority opinion, and is referred to as writing "for the Court." Justices who agree with the outcome of the majority opinion, but who reach that result through some other line of reasoning, or who wish to append certain individual remarks regarding the case, may file separate "concurring opinions." Justices who disagree with the outcome reached by the majority file "dissenting opinions," explaining why they would reach some other result. Sometimes no single rationale will command a five-Justice majority; then the result of the case is determined by piecing together enough concurring opinions to come up with at least five Justices who agree on the appropriate outcome, even if they cannot reach consensus on the reasoning. In such a case the concurring opinion commanding the most votes (at least two votes but less than five) is called a "plurality opinion."

The decisions of the Court are often decided by one vote, and predicting the "direction" of the Court, whether more liberal or more conservative, more activist or more restrained, is a capricious science.

The individual Justices are in many ways a cross-section of the political landscape of the nation.

Farthest to the right is Justice Antonin Scalia, the most colorful and intellectually interesting Justice on the contemporary Supreme Court, and one of the most colorful in the Court's history. His strongly held conservative views on substantive issues, his fiery temperament, his distinctive approach to interpreting the Constitution, and his brilliant writing ability combine to make him one of the most formidable persons ever to sit on the Court. His views are worth detailed examination by any serious student of the Constitution and the role of the Court, for he has staked out a conservative jurisprudence of unique purity; if one understands Scalia's thought, and the thought of those who passionately despise Scalia's thought, one pretty much understands the full tonal range of modern constitutional debate.

Justice Scalia's substantive views of constitutional law are "conservative," as that term is usually used in popular discourse, and by most measures he is indeed the most conservative member of the modern Court. He believes in strict separation of powers among the various branches of the federal government; he favors increasing protection for private property under the Takings Clause; he does not believe that affirmative action should be permitted as a remedy for race discrimination; he favors overruling *Roe v. Wade* and holds that the Constitution does not protect abortion; he does not believe that other "unenumerated rights," such as a right to die with dignity, should be read into the Constitution; he believes that the death penalty is constitutional; he would relax the line of separation between church and state under the Free Exercise Clause and Establishment Clause of the First Amendment; and he would permit the government to limit the free speech rights of persons who receive government benefits by placing conditions restricting the exercise of those rights on the receipt of those benefits.

Yet to say that Justice Antonin Scalia is a conservative is to say that an eagle is just a bird. For Scalia is not just a conservative, he is a magnificent conservative, often soaring alone above friends and foes with a power and style that are his alone. He is, in short, not just *any* conservative. There is, for example, a libertarian streak to his conservatism that at times places him in alliance with liberals. In the First Amendment area, for example, Scalia has adopted a virtually absolute rule against discrimination against speech on the basis of its viewpoint.

This caused Scalia to join with liberal Justices like William Brennan and Thurgood Marshall in voting to strike down laws against flag desecration. It also lead Scalia to write a far-reaching opinion for the Court in *R.A.V. v. City of St. Paul,* striking down laws targeted at racist "hate speech," a decision profiled in the chapter written by David Savage.

Scalia's distinctive mark, however, is not so much captured by cataloguing his substantive views as it is by examining his judicial personality itself—his zest for intellectual combat, his unique views on constitutional interpretation, and his incisive writing style.

Scalia has a gregarious, exuberant personality. He is loquacious in oral argument, loving to put difficult hypotheticals and stinging questions to advocates. At times his style in oral argument appears more that of the law professor strutting his stuff before a class than the conventional image of the staid and sober jurist.

In his approach to interpreting the Constitution, and indeed in his approach to the task of judging itself, Scalia has adopted three positions that work together to set him apart from most of his colleagues on the Court. These three views of Justice Scalia can for convenience be labeled (1) a skepticism of the value of stare decisis, (2) a preference for textualism over the use of legislative history, and (3) a belief in the primacy of clear-cut rules over amorphous standards.

First, Justice Scalia does not place a high value on the notion of stare decisis (adherence to precedent from prior cases). The traditional view of stare decisis is that once an important issue has been settled by the Court, it should remain settled, unless there are strong reasons for reconsidering the issue and changing the law. The conventional wisdom is that this value of adherence to precedent is laudable because it promotes stability in the law and respect for the Court as an institution. A constitutional system in which the rules are constantly being changed by the Court, the theory goes, is disruptive, weakens the fabric of the law, and creates the appearance that constitutional law is largely a political game, in which the rules change whenever the personnel of the Court changes.

Justice Scalia has largely eschewed these traditional views about stare decisis. He believes that as a Supreme Court Justice, it is more important that issues be decided correctly than that the Court honor such abstract notions as "stability" and "respect" in order to preserve a legal rule that no longer commands a majority of the Court. While Scalia is often criticized fiercely for his views, often chastised (particularly by liberal critics) as a shrill and strident conservative, his views on stare decisis mark one sense in which it should be said that Scalia is the most open-minded of all the Justices on the Court. As a Justice who does not believe strongly in honoring precedent, nothing is ever finally decided, and lawyers have the freedom to invite Justice Scalia to take a fresh look at virtually anything. For Justice Scalia, if it has not been decided right, it hasn't been decided.

Justice Scalia's second striking approach to constitutional interpretation is his strong preference for using the language of the text itself in interpreting a provision of the Constitution or a statute, rather than the "legislative history" of that provision. Once again, this approach sets Scalia apart from most of his colleagues and from traditional practice.

In the American legal system it is common for lawyers and judges to invoke "legislative history" to explain the meaning of a law. The traditional justification for this is that the "law" is not the literal words written down on paper, but rather the "intent" or "meaning" of the persons who enacted those words. Because language is inherently ambiguous, and because those who write laws can never cover every conceivable detail or potential application, judges must have the flexibility to "interpret" the language in light of the actual intent of those who wrote it. For a Supreme Court Justice, interpreting the meaning of a statute is often critical, for two quite different reasons. When there is no constitutional issue at stake and the Court is merely interpreting a federal law in order to decide a case brought under that law, it is obviously important to interpret the meaning of the law, so that the case can be decided. If an employee sues an employer for discrimination under a particular federal civil rights law, for example, it is important to know whether that civil rights law "covers" that type of alleged discrimination. Traditionally, the Supreme Court has been willing to examine the legislative history of the law, including such things as reports prepared by congressional committees leading up to the passage of the bill, or remarks by members of Congress during floor debates, to shed light on what the law means.

Statutory interpretation is also critical to the task of a Supreme Court Justice in a second circumstance—when the law at issue is challenged as unconstitutional. In many areas of modern constitutional law, the constitutionality of the law may in fact turn on the legislature's reasons for enacting it. When a legislature acts with intent to discriminate against religion, for example, it is well established under current doctrines that the law violates the Free Exercise Clause of the First Amendment. Most Justices on the Supreme Court are willing to examine the legislative history of a law to determine the legislature's intent in passing it, so that the law may be struck down if that intent proves to be invidious or discriminatory.

Justice Scalia disagrees with both of these uses of legislative history, a disagreement that places him at odds with a majority of his colleagues. To put it bluntly, Scalia believes that legislative history is hokum. Committees prepare elaborate reports and members of Congress make fancy speeches, all for the purpose of exerting "spin control" on the meaning of a new law. Congress is a partisan body buffeted by many different ideologies and interest groups, all of whom want to influence how courts will decide the meaning of the law in the future. Liberals want to make the language of a bill seem more liberal, conservatives more conservative. At the same time, all concerned must be careful not to put too much partisan spin on the language of a bill, particularly when compromise is crucial to passage, for fear that votes might be scared away. Justice Scalia takes the view that in light of all this political reality, it is simply wrong for judges to look into legislative history at all, because it is entirely unreliable. In Scalia's view, the only thing that the legislative body actually enacts as a whole is the final language of the law itself, and Justices should confine themselves to that language when construing it. Using "objective" tools for discerning the meaning of language and traditional canons of interpretation, the judge should focus on what a law says, not what others claim it meant to say.

Similarly, Justice Scalia is unwilling to look at legislative history to determine the intent behind a law to decide whether it is unconstitutional, except to the extent that such intent is revealed "objectively" through the actual language of the law, or the effects of the law in operation. A good recent example of this was the case *Church of the Lukumi Babalu Aye v. City of Hialeah,* decided in 1993. At issue was an ordinance passed by the City of Hialeah, Florida, forbidding the ritual sacrifice of animals. A church in the Santería religion, an ancient religion with roots in Africa and Cuba that includes the ritual sacrifice of animals as part of its religious practice, challenged the ordinance. The Court struck down the ordinance as a violation of the Free Exercise Clause. A majority of the Justices, in an opinion written by Justice Anthony Kennedy, explored in detail the legislative history behind the passage of the ordinance, including speeches made by city officials, to reach the conclusion that Hialeah had passed this ordinance largely out of an intent to discriminate against the Santería religion. Justice Scalia agreed with the majority of his colleagues that the law was unconstitutional, but he sharply parted company with them on their use of legislative history. "The First Amendment does not refer to the purposes for which legislators enact laws, but to the effects of the laws enacted," Scalia argued. "This does not put us in the business of invalidating laws by reason of the evil motives of their authors." Scalia maintained that if the Hialeah officials had *intended* to discriminate against the Santería religion, but through "ineptness" had failed to do so, the law would not be unconstitutional. Nor, he claimed, would it matter if "a legislature consists entirely of the pure-hearted, if the law it enacts in fact singles out a religious practice for special burdens."

The third defining characteristic of Justice Scalia's jurisprudence is his preference for clear-cut legal rules over more amorphous and flexible tests and standards. In many areas of contemporary constitutional law, the Supreme Court has not adopted absolute or clear-cut rules as to what is or is not constitutional, but has instead announced a "standard" or "test," usually requiring the balancing of multiple "prongs" or "factors," that are applied to different situations case by case. These multifactor balancing tests and standards so permeate existing constitutional doctrine that it is virtually impossible for any Supreme Court Justice to avoid using them, and even Justice Scalia at times invokes them and applies them. But these flexible balancing tests reflexively rankle Scalia, and he pushes hard, whenever he can, to replace them with more pristine all-or-nothing rules that create much brighter and sharper lines separating the dos and don'ts of the Constitution.

There are many examples of this proclivity of Scalia's for rules over standards. In the separation of powers area, for example, many Justices opt for a "functional" approach to such questions as whether Congress may place limits on the power of the president to remove executive officials from office. In *Morrison v. Olson,* for example, a case involving a constitutional challenge to the law that created the office of the "independent counsel," a majority of the Court, led by Chief Justice Rehnquist, upheld the law. Chief Justice Rehnquist wrote that the critical question was whether the "removal restrictions are of such a nature that they impede the President's ability to perform his constitutional duty." Justice Scalia dissented, with an acerbic attack on Chief

Justice Rehnquist's invocation of such an uncertain standard. At one point in Scalia's attack on the Rehnquist opinion, he opined, "This is not the government of laws that the Constitution established; it is not a government of laws at all."

Justice Scalia's penchant for clear rules appears throughout his jurisprudence. He would, for example, replace the intricate abortion jurisprudence of *Roe v. Wade* and the landmark 1992 opinion in *Planned Parenthood v. Casey,* which reaffirmed the core of *Roe,* by a flat-out ruling that the Constitution does not protect abortion at all. Similarly, in the affirmative action area, Justice Scalia favors adoption of an absolute rule of color blindness, which abolishes all use of race by government to distribute benefits, and thus all affirmative action. In contrast, the majority of Justice Scalia's colleagues on the Court employ the "strict scrutiny" test, requiring that racial classifications be supported by "compelling governmental interests" and be "narrowly tailored" to achieve those interests. Although the strict scrutiny test sets a high standard, resulting in the rejection of many affirmative action programs, it is less draconian than Justice Scalia's proposed rule of absolute color blindness, for under the strict scrutiny test affirmative action programs are still examined by the Court on a case-by-case basis, with some struck down and others upheld.

So too, in the religion field, Scalia supports the simple proposition that laws of "general applicability" which do not single out religion for disfavorable treatment should not be struck down merely because they happen to penalize the exercise of a religious belief. In one of his most famous opinions, for example, *Employment Division v. Smith,* the Court was faced with the issue of whether a law that banned the use of the drug peyote could be constitutionally applied to the ingestion of small amounts of peyote by Native Americans as part of the sacramental rituals of the Native American church. Scalia, writing the majority opinion for the Court, upheld the law, ruling that the legislature was not compelled by the First Amendment to make an exception for religious use of the drug. Since the law was "neutral" and of "general applicability," he reasoned, there was no constitutional violation.

Perhaps no multifactor test used by the modern Court draws more ire from Justice Scalia, however, than the "three-pronged test of *Lemon v. Kurtzman,*" which the Court has used for years to determine whether a law violates the Establishment Clause. Under the "*Lemon* test," a law must have a primarily "secular purpose," must not "advance or inhibit religion," and must not foster "excessive entanglement" with religion. Justice Scalia's bulldog hatred for *Lemon* is well illustrated by a colorful passage from a 1993 case, *Lamb's Chapel v. Center Moriches School District,* in which he wrote: "Like some ghoul in a late-night horror movie that repeatedly sits up in its grave and shuffles abroad, after being repeatedly killed and buried, *Lemon* stalks our Establishment Clause jurisprudence once again, frightening the little children and school attorneys of Center Moriches Union Free School District." (To this, Justice White's majority opinion wryly responded: "While we are somewhat diverted by Justice Scalia's evening at the cinema, we return to the reality that there is a proper way to inter an established decision and *Lemon,* however frightening it might be to some, has not been overruled.")

A portrait of Justice Scalia would not be complete without discussion of his extraordinary ability as a writer. There simply has not been a writer on the Supreme Court with the imagination, wit, and tenacity of Antonin Scalia since Oliver Wendell Holmes. There is, indeed, a stylistic kinship between Scalia and Holmes. Scalia, like Holmes, is at his best when writing in dissent. When Scalia can scratch and claw derisively at the perceived backings and filings of the majority, Scalia is at his most venomous, and most eloquent. Scalia, like Holmes, is a master of the sound bite. There may someday be books collecting the quips and jabs and aphorisms of Scalia opinions, just as such books abound for Holmes. Wholly aside from the substance of his positions, the freshness and creativity with which he experiments with words and phrases bring a vibrancy to his writing rarely seen in judicial opinions. As part of his attack on legislative history, for example, he once made reference to the futility of parsing the "dimmy past."

In the end, his color and candor may at once define Justice Scalia's strengths and limitations. He does not appear to build coalitions easily among his colleagues. With the possible exception of Justice Clarence Thomas, who often does join with him, Scalia has not formed lasting or consistent alliances with others on the Court who might be thought to share his general inclination toward conservatism, such as Chief Justice Rehnquist or Justice Kennedy. His willingness to attack his colleagues in dissenting opinions with bitter derision might, some Court watchers argue, interfere with his ability to work behind the scenes to create solid voting blocs on the Court.

The building of coalitions, however, would not appear to be Justice

Scalia's agenda, and indeed, seems basically inimical to his temperament. It is not what he is about. Scalia's role on the Court is rather that of provocateur, gadfly, agitator, conscience. (Not a conscience to everyone's liking, to be sure, but a conscience all the same.) Antonin is likely always to remain the aggressive conservative that liberals love to hate—a hatred, one senses, at which he most delights.

At the opposite extreme from Scalia is Harry Blackmun. After the retirement of Justices Thurgood Marshall and William J. Brennan, Blackmun was the sole remaining "traditional liberal" on the Court. As Lyle Denniston explains in his chapter on abortion and abortion protests, even Blackmun did not vote a liberal line all of the time; he tended toward conservatism on criminal law matters and until recently was not opposed to the death penalty. Blackmun is perhaps the most famous example in modern times of a Justice making a distinct ideological migration. He began as a conservative jurisprudential soul mate of Chief Justice Warren Burger. He had a reputation for working in a tedious, plodding style and for procrastination in reaching a decision in big cases.

All that would gradually change, however, as Blackmun emerged as a champion of the rights of women, minorities, and the poor. He will be forever remembered as the Justice who wrote the majority opinion in the most controversial Supreme Court ruling of this century, the abortion rights decision in *Roe v. Wade*. And as Lyle Denniston's portrait so poignantly reveals, Blackmun's tenure on the Court would be largely marked by his tenacious defense of *Roe* against what he perceived as a relentless effort by the Reagan and Bush administrations to ravage what he regarded as a cornerstone of American individual freedom.

Between Scalia on the right and Blackmun on the left were seven Justices with diverse ideologies and personalities moving about in shifting coalitions and voting patterns. Closest to Harry Blackmun on the "liberal wing" was John Paul Stevens. In his early years on the Court, John Paul Stevens was widely viewed as an enigmatic, independent centrist, a Justice with pragmatic views who defied easy ideological labels. Justice Byron White nicknamed him "One-eyed Jack," both for his penchant for playing cards and his tendency to file individual opinions that embraced neither the liberal nor conservative viewpoint. The story is told of a conference session in which the conservative Bill Rehnquist and the liberal Bill Brennan expressed diametrically opposing views of a case. When the time came for Stevens to talk, he simply cracked, "I agree with Bill."

Stevens began as a centrist, perhaps even a centrist with slightly conservative leanings, but as the Court moved gradually to the Right over the years, with stalwart liberals such as William Brennan and Thurgood Marshall resigning, Stevens began to look more and more like one of the Court's habitual liberals. By the 1990s, Stevens was as liberal in his voting patterns as Harry Blackmun.

At the other end of the spectrum, nearest to Scalia on the "conservative wing" of the Court were newly appointed Justice Clarence Thomas and Chief Justice William Rehnquist.

The cases contained in this volume were from Clarence Thomas's second term. Even into his second year, his confirmation remained as much in the consciousness of the public as anything he had yet accomplished on the bench, for no Justice in recent memory had ascended to the Court amid so much controversy.

As Richard Carelli explains in his chapter, Thomas had distinguished himself in his years of government service as "a new breed of politically active and outspoken black man, a social conservative most noted for opposing conventional affirmative action and welfare programs." But Carelli notes that Thomas's "embrace of black self-help did not make him blind to the sometimes frightening realities of being black in a white-dominated society." Talking about his life in the nation's capital, Thomas once complained, "In my own neighborhood, I used to get stopped by the cops."

President Bush was impressed with Thomas and nominated him to fill the spot vacated by Thurgood Marshall. The rest is history. After a contentious effort by many civil rights and civil liberties groups to derail the nomination, the Senate Judiciary Committee initially split seven to seven on whether to send his nomination to the full Senate with approval. As the vote by the full Senate approached, the sexual harassment allegations of a University of Oklahoma law professor, Anita Hill, were made public. The Senate Judiciary Committee reopened the hearings for one of the most riveting episodes of national political drama ever broadcast on television. As Carelli observes, never before "had pubic hairs and a pornographic movie star named Long Dong Silver been part of a Supreme Court confirmation process."

In an impassioned and angry statement at the end of the hearings, Thomas stated to the senators, and a national television audience:

"In my forty-three years on this earth I have been able with the help of others and with the help of God to defy poverty, avoid prison, overcome segregation, bigotry, racism, and obtain one of the finest educations available in this country, but I have not been able to overcome this process. This is worse than any obstacle or anything that I have ever faced.

"I am proud of my life, proud of what I have done and what I have accomplished, proud of my family. And this process, this process is trying to destroy it all. No job is worth what I have been through. No job. No horror in my life has been so debilitating. Confirm me if you want. Don't confirm me if you are so led, but let this process end. Let me and my family regain our lives."

Thomas won confirmation by a fifty-two to forty-eight vote; but the entire episode raised profound questions about how the nation chooses Supreme Court Justices. In reflecting on the Thomas nomination and setting aside the still-contested credibility contest between Thomas and Hill, certain truths about the Thomas nomination and the bonfire of the vanities that followed it appear to be self-evident: that Clarence Thomas was a black conservative, that he was nominated to the Court by President Bush because he was a black conservative, and that *some* of the organized opposition to his nomination was the result of his being a black conservative. (I say *some* because I believe that *most* of the opposition was the result of his being conservative, period—without regard to his race.)

The philosophical questions posed are whether it was legitimate for President Bush to nominate Thomas because he was either black or conservative or both, and conversely, whether it was legitimate to oppose him for those reasons.

We can analyze the president's choice by first breaking it down to its component parts. Is it legitimate for the president to nominate a conservative? The consensus answer is surely yes.

The argument is made, of course, that presidents should appoint "distinguished" lawyers to the Supreme Court on the basis of anti-septic and neutral "professional qualifications." Since this is so wildly out of touch with what presidents in fact do, this argument is seldom pressed in its pure form. In healthy deference to reality, nearly everyone concedes that presidents may take ideology into account. One usually hears, however, the platitude that a nominee should be approved by a senator, even when the senator disagrees with the nominee's ideo-logical positions, as long as the nominee is "within the mainstream." But this tradition is itself more a matter of convenience and politics than principle. The width of the "mainstream" increases and decreases with the importance of the nomination and the caprices of politics. This tug and pull is itself within the mainstream of the constitutional tradition—there is nothing unnatural or wrong with the confirmation testimony of some nominees lasting two weeks, and others (like the testimony of Lewis Powell) lasting two hours.

A president is thus well within constitutional tradition in seeking to place persons on the Court with whom he or she is in ideological harmony. The president is checked only by the political will of the Senate. There is no question of moral or constitutional legitimacy here, only raw politics: the president is entitled to appoint persons as conservative or liberal as he or she can get away with, given the political mood of the moment.

Is it legitimate for a president to use race, ethnicity, religion, or sex in choosing a nominee? Here, serious students of the Constitution differ. There will be colorblind and sex-blind individualists who will insist that the only valid criteria are "professional qualifications," which may include, presumably, harmony with the president's ideological views, but never such matters as race or sex. Thus it is said that there should not be a "black seat" or "Jewish seat" or "woman's seat" on the Court. President Bush paid half-hearted and unconvincing lip service to this colorblind view in insisting repeatedly that he was merely looking for the "best qualified" person to fill Thurgood Marshall's vacancy.

President Bush did the nation a disservice by failing to be candid with the American people, in not openly admitting that Clarence Thomas's race was a dominant factor in his selection. The president should not have been ashamed of it. Racial, ethnic, sexual, and religious diversity on the Court is vital to the constitutional process in modern times. While a president should never make specific racial or sexual identity a *requirement* in filling vacancies (and should never be so crass and mechanical as to insist on the maintenance of a "black seat"), treating the pursuit of diversity as a significant "plus factor" in shaping the *aggregate* makeup of the Court is not only permissible but necessary. To put the matter bluntly, the Supreme Court and the nation benefited enormously from the service of Justice Thurgood Marshall and Justice Sandra Day O'Connor (and later, Justice Ruth Bader Ginsburg) in both substance and symbol, not merely because they are talented lawyers and leaders, but because their race and sex brought experiences and insights to the Court that enriched and improved its decision making.

If President Bush could act legitimately in nominating a conservative or a black, did this nomination somehow forfeit its legitimacy
because Thomas was both conservative and black? It should be said
here that many liberal senators and public interest groups who opposed
Thomas opposed him because he was conservative and/or because
they regarded him as professionally unqualified—race was not a factor.
Many of those same senators and groups also opposed Robert Bork,
and in some instances David Souter, on the same ideological grounds.
That opposition was perfectly legitimate—every bit as legitimate as the
president's invocation of ideology in selecting the candidate in the first
place. This is, again, simply a matter of political struggle: the president
is entitled to push as hard in one direction as he or she can, and political opponents are entitled to push back as hard as they can, with each
side left to its own devices in calculating the net long-term political
pluses and minuses.

But there was a sense at large in the nomination debate from some
quarters that if a nominee is to be African American, he or she must
be a liberal African American, a Thurgood Marshall African American.
The defense offered is that if one wants an African American nominee to represent the "African American viewpoint" as defined by the
civil rights leadership in the nation, then it is perfectly fair to oppose
a presidential nomination that fails to vindicate that goal. Under this
view, President Bush should have appointed another white Anthony
Kennedy or David Souter and spared the nation the "tokenism" of
Thomas.

From the perspective of Clarence Thomas, however, this must seem
the height of arrogance, for it might be understood as effectively com-
municating to Thomas, "Because you were born black, you should not
aspire to the Supreme Court of the United States unless you agree to
embrace moderate-to-liberal ideological positions."

Against this tempestuous backdrop, Thomas's first term was closely
watched; and, indeed, he would be called upon to rule on many issues
deeply connected to the philosophical debates that surrounded his own
nomination. As explained in the chapter by Kay Kindred, one of these
involved the vexing question of how states should treat historically
black state colleges and universities in light of the mandate of *Brown v.
Board of Education* to dismantle all vestiges of discrimination in education.

Rounding out the conservative wing of the Court was Chief Justice William Rehnquist. As Marcia Coyle's chapter explains, in his early years on the Court, prior to becoming Chief Justice, William Rehnquist was widely perceived as the lonely voice of the extreme ideological right. Harvard Law School professor David Shapiro nicely summarized Rehnquist's philosophy as one of siding with the government whenever conflicts between the government and individuals arise, as siding with states in conflicts between state and federal authority, and as disfavoring, as a general matter, the exercise of federal judicial jurisdiction. As Coyle relates, in his early days Rehnquist was the "Lone Ranger," marked by his persistent one-Justice dissents against liberal rulings. As Presidents Reagan and Bush were able to appoint many more moderate and conservative jurists to the Court—ultimately elevating Rehnquist himself to the position of Chief Justice—he became less a Lone Ranger and more a commander in chief, often able to commandeer a majority of the Court in moving the law toward more conservative principles. Chief Justice Rehnquist was motivated in all of this by an abiding conviction that in a democracy it is the political process, not the judicial process, that should set social policy.

But neither more liberal Justices like Blackmun and Stevens nor the more conservative Justices like Rehnquist, Scalia, and Thomas were ever able to dominate the Court; the fulcrum of power stood with the Justices in the middle: Byron White, Sandra Day O'Connor, Anthony Kennedy, and David Souter. These Justices tended to be liberal in some areas and conservative in others, and the shifting coalitions among them resulted in an overall jurisprudence that could not be characterized easily as predominately one or the other, and that often led to splintered decisions in which it was difficult to tell exactly what the Court had held, or in compromise positions in which the Court seemed to try to give a little something to everyone.

The veteran of this middle group was Byron "Whizzer" White. (As this book was being prepared, Justice White announced his resignation, and he has now been replaced by Justice Ruth Bader Ginsburg.)

White is perhaps emblematic of the difficulty of pinning stripes to a centrist. He is often described as conservative—and certainly in his later years on the Court he *was,* more often than not; yet throughout his thirty-one years on the Court, White often authored moderate and even liberal opinions. As Kay Kindred explains in her chapter, Byron White was perhaps not an ideological Justice at all. He seemed to eschew any overarching judicial philosophy for a case-by-case pragmatism that was never much tied to dogma.

Another "centrist" on the Court was Sandra Day O'Connor, the first woman to serve on the Court. Like a number of the other centrist Justices, she often appears to approach cases one at a time, avoiding unnecessarily broad philosophical pronouncements. As described in the profile by Paul Barrett, Justice O'Connor is highly regarded in many circles for her common sense and independence, even though she has never developed a clearly defined judicial philosophy. She has been cognizant of the importance of her role as the Court's first woman, but at the same time has carried herself with a certain reserved dignity and humility that has downplayed the importance of her gender. Yet O'Connor, who had herself experienced firsthand sex discrimination as a lawyer, has been sensitive to gender issues while on the Court.

Somewhat like O'Connor in philosophy and style is Anthony Kennedy, yet another restrained, pragmatic conservative lacking any global legal ideology or philosophy. And also somewhat like O'Connor, Kennedy appears to have grown marginally more liberal in recent years, arguably in a backlash reaction to the acerbic conservatism of Antonin Scalia. As Aaron Epstein explains in his chapter, Kennedy sought to impose a truce among the Justices in which they would agree to avoid personalized attacks on one another in opinions. He also surprised a number of Court watchers with liberal rulings favoring freedom of speech, the free exercise of religion, and abortion rights, rulings that significantly moderated the Court's march toward the right.

Rounding out the middle ranks was David Souter, perhaps the most liberal of center group, a thoughtful, scholarly, nuanced jurist who, like Kennedy and O'Connor, seemed quite willing to take on Antonin Scalia and the conservative wing. A defining moment in the judicial careers of Souter, Kennedy, and O'Connor came in 1992 in *Planned Parenthood of Southeastern Pennsylvania v. Casey,* the case in which the Court was invited to overrule *Roe v. Wade.* A joint opinion written by Souter, Kennedy, and O'Connor stated that the Court should adhere to the essential core of the *Roe* decision: the recognition of the right of the woman to choose to have an abortion before viability and to obtain it without undue interference from the state. Although the opinion of Souter, Kennedy, and O'Connor did permit somewhat greater regulation of abortion procedures, the basic right to choose prior to viability remained secure. Those three votes to sustain *Roe,* when added to the votes of Blackmun and Stevens, prevented *Roe* from being over-ruled—something that most Court watchers had thought was inevitable. Scalia, Rehnquist, White, and Thomas all voted to discard *Roe;* when White was replaced by Ruth Bader Ginsburg it appeared that after teetering for years on the brink of being discarded by the Court, the right to abortion was once again reasonably well guarded.

The joint opinion of Souter, Kennedy, and O'Connor rested partly on the doctrine of stare decisis—the notion that the Court should have respect for precedent and not lightly overrule past rulings—and partly on an emphatic endorsement of the philosophical view that individuals possess a constitutional right of privacy.

"Liberty finds no refuge in a jurisprudence of doubt," the joint opinion stated. "Our duty is to define the liberty of all, not to mandate our own moral code." In a passage of the opinion, the three Justices spoke passionately about the essential nature of the right of privacy:

> These matters, involving the most personal choices a person may make in a lifetime, choices central to personal dignity and autonomy, are central to the liberty protected by the Fourteenth Amendment. At the heart of liberty is the right to define one's own concept of existence, of meaning, of the universe, and of the mystery of human life. Beliefs about these matters could not define the attributes of personhood were they formed under compulsion of the state.

The opinion then expounded on the unique implications of the privacy right in the context of childbearing, in which the liberty of a woman is at stake "in a sense unique to the human condition and so unique to the law." The pain and anxiety endured by a woman is too intimate and personal, the opinion explained, for the state to insist upon its vision of the woman's role. "The destiny of the woman must be shaped to a large extent on her own conception of her spiritual imperatives and her place in society."

Thus the composition and disposition of the Justices as the Court entered its October 1992 term. It was a Court dominated by the moderate and conservative appointments of Ronald Reagan and George Bush, a Court with one of the most brilliant conservative minds in its history in Antonin Scalia and one of the most stalwart conservatives of modern times as its Chief in William Rehnquist, a Court now without the powerful liberal presence of William Brennan and Thurgood Marshall. But despite all that, its ideological compass had not swung wildly to the right. In many areas of constitutional law, the competing values and philosophies often seemed still in equipoise.

The Process

Is there a sense in which the process of *judicial* decision making is unique? Certainly many Americans regard a large part of the decisions of the Supreme Court as misguided. And many others perceive those decisions as driven by nothing more than the political preferences of a majority of the Justices.

Clearly, if there is something special about the Supreme Court, it cannot be that the Justices or the process are somehow "superior" in any absolute sense to everything else that happens in Washington, D.C., or the state capitals and city halls around the nation. The manner in which the Court influences American social policy is not purer, more rational, or more efficient than the manner in which Congress, the president, the administrative agencies, or the governments of the cities and states participate in that policy making. But for both better and worse, it clearly is *different.*

As Tony Mauro's concluding chapter suggests, a portrayal of the Court's business by those who observe it closely and regularly is relatively rare, because the Court has traditionally conducted its business through what he describes as a cult of secrecy. The Justices shun the spotlight, avoid celebrity, do not hold press conferences to explain their decisions, and indeed do not allow television cameras to observe oral arguments, the announcement of decisions, or even purely ceremonial exercises such as the swearing in of new members. The Court tends to react with animosity to the release of "inside" information about its deliberations—most recently the Thurgood Marshall papers—and reacted with chill hostility to the effort by Professor Peter Irons to make tape recordings of the oral arguments of a series of famous cases available to the general public.

Some may find irony in this compulsive reclusiveness, believing that the Supreme Court has little, if anything, to hide. To be sure, the decisions of the Court are often controversial and may, on any given day, be deemed wrong by a majority of Americans. And without question, the decisions of the Court are influenced by "politics," at least in the sense that the men and women who become Supreme Court Justices are generally people who have previously been active in the American arena, people with political contacts and loyalties, people with political ideologies, habits of mind, special biases, and special sensitivities.

Yet there is a difference in the manner in which politics and ideology influence the Supreme Court, where they are filtered through the process of litigation, and the manner in which politics and ideology influence the other institutions in our democracy.

This book helps to illuminate that difference, in a manner that will, hopefully, be accessible to readers who are not lawyers or experts in constitutional law and history.

In modern Washington the process of deciding public policy on issues of the moment, whatever they may be (health care reform, crime, the budget, military intervention in foreign lands) often becomes a political cauldron. Political action committees, special interest groups, and major corporations and institutions are among the players who bring enormous pressure to bear on the administrative and legislative process, lobbying the White House, the Congress, and the agencies and using the many tools of modern public relations to generate letters, faxes, and phone calls from the hustings. The president, the White House staff, and members of the Senate and House of Representatives often engage in cold, partisan, hard-nosed political calculations as they negotiate through the debates. The debating, lobbying, and political maneuvering are carried into mass culture by the modern media, on local radio talk and call-in shows across the country, on national broadcast and cable networks, on the opinion and editorial pages of newspapers, in magazines, fax reports, and on the computer networks.

This is the modern American democracy. It is, at times, disturbing to behold, for it seems raucous, shrill, mean-spirited, and out of control. It is, at times, frustrating. For all the debate and pressure, there is often little to show for the effort at the end. No law dealing with the health care system is passed, the budget deficit is not reduced. To those who want action, movement, resolution, this is perceived as paralysis and gridlock. Thus the appeal of Ross Perot's simplistic campaign insistence that there are plenty of plans lying around Washington, we simply need someone in charge who knows how to get things done and get some of them implemented.

There is also some comfort in this picture. As a nation we may not be resolving our disputes over such issues as health care or budget reform, but we are at least actively disputing them—it is a genuine contest, a true cacophony of voices. The voices may often be more shrill or more slick than many of us would like. They may often be the voices of professionals paid by political parties, political action committees, special interests, or industries—the sorts of interests that James Madison described as "factions" in his famous essays in *The Federalist Papers*. But they are, in a certain sense, authentically democratic.

One of the most interesting puzzles about American government is how the courts fit into this booming, buzzing, electronic confusion. The romantic version is that the courts—most specially, the Justices of the *Supreme Court*—are above it all.

If one accepts this image, the Justices will take on a demigod quality. They will be perceived as men and women who hear arguments about law, history, and public policy, who reflect and debate among themselves earnestly and soberly, and who render judgments with reasoned explanations, in writing, of what they have decided and why. Their decisions are removed from the political fray: final, binding, and if not always correct or persuasively reasoned, they are nonetheless at least always *reasoned*.

These are myths. The "myth of remove" is that the Court is somehow separate and removed from the political fray. The "myth of finality" is that the Court has the last word on the issues that come before it and that its rulings inevitably bind the political process. The "myth of reason" is that the Court's judgments are always, or at least usually, defensible under some "neutral" regime of logic, precedent, or principle.

Many decisions of the Court are surely political, as Justices react to what is in the air and on the air. The Justices, after all, live in the same political culture as the rest of us.

More importantly, it must be understood that the Supreme Court, as well as the lower federal courts and the courts of the fifty states, are merely *part of the mix,* players in the process of decision making in American public life.

Although this book provides only a quick snapshot of one moment in the life of the Court, that snapshot does yield some clues as to how the Supreme Court and the other federal and state courts are connected to the democratic process. Perhaps the most important thing to bear in mind is that the judiciary is never more than one institutional player. Even when the topic is something that might normally be thought quintessentially *constitutional,* and thus *judicial,* in nature, such as freedom of religion, say, or freedom of speech—it turns out that while the judiciary has a significant influence on public policy, *that influence is inevitably limited.* To a large degree, decisions about such issues as religion, speech, equality, or privacy remain primarily within the domains of the larger democracy—the presidents and governors, the legislators, the lobbyists, the talk show hosts.

In the area of freedom of religion, for example, the Supreme Court held in *Employment Division v. Smith* that the Free Exercise Clause of the First Amendment did not require states to provide a "sacramental use" exception to the ingestion of peyote by Native Americans. Members of the Native American church could be penalized for the use of peyote, even though they used the hallucinogen only in small amounts as part of a sacramental ritual. The Court reasoned that drug laws are laws of "general applicability" and that when such laws happen to impinge upon an individual's free exercise of religion, the government need not satisfy the so-called strict scrutiny test. This test requires that the government justify its actions by demonstrating both that the government's objectives in enforcing its law are "compelling" and that it has chosen a "narrowly tailored" means of achieving its objectives. When the "strict scrutiny" test is applied to legislation, the legislation is often struck down. In holding that such laws of general applicability need not pass the strict scrutiny test, the Court closed the door on many challenges to governmental programs or laws that, in their practical application, penalize the exercise of an individual's religious beliefs.

Now the ultimate question of whether the Supreme Court was "right" or "wrong" in *Employment Division v. Smith* is, from the perspective of constitutional law or public policy, by no means obvious. There is much to commend the logic of the Court. Laws must be passed for everyone. As long as a law is not passed for the purpose of discriminating against a particular religious sect, it arguably should be upheld even though members of that sect will be forced to sacrifice to comply with it. To use one of the examples cited by the Court, if the government decides that polygamy is illegal, the law should be enforced, and the First Amendment should not be understood as granting a constitutional exception to members of religions who practice polygamy out of religious conviction.

There is also, however, much to be said for the opposite view. If an individual's religious beliefs and practices can be easily and simply accommodated with no significant harm to the overall structure of the law, why shouldn't the government be forced to "give the individual a break" to accommodate the religious practice? Thus a college student's exam at a state university could be rescheduled so that it does not fall on a religious holiday, or an employee allowed to take off work to observe his or her sabbath on a day other than Sunday.

What is most interesting about *Employment Division v. Smith* for the purposes of this discussion is not whether the Court was wrong or right, but rather the observation that its decision was *not final*. First, the Court merely held that the First Amendment did not *require* the accommodation of religious beliefs and practices. It did not say that the government was *forbidden* to accommodate those beliefs. Indeed, as the chapter written in this book by Aaron Epstein reveals, the Supreme Court has, in recent years, become more willing to permit government to engage in activities that do accommodate religious observance.

Second, and more important, the United States Congress reacted to the Supreme Court's decision in *Smith* by passing legislation that purported to "overrule" it. Late in 1993, Congress passed the Religious Freedom Restoration Act. The law and the legislative record openly declared that the purpose of the act was to reverse the result of the Supreme Court's decision in the *Smith* case, by subjecting laws that substantially impinge upon an individual's free exercise of religion to the rigors of the strict scrutiny test. Thus Congress passed what is, in effect, a new civil rights act, "restoring" as a *statutory* right a principle of religious accommodation that the Supreme Court had refused to embrace under the First Amendment.

The passage of the Religious Freedom Restoration Act, however, did not by any means end the debate. Within the executive branch, members of the Clinton administration were divided over how broadly or narrowly the federal government should be construed. Scores of lower court cases immediately began wending their way up through the judicial process, testing the contours of the act. And it is quite likely that the Supreme Court will ultimately be forced to interpret the act, and in that process, also determine whether Congress had the power, under the Constitution, to pass it.

This is but one example of how the Court participates, in a revolving process, in the ongoing American dialogue over law and public policy. The same sort of interplay is constantly at work in other areas. Thus, the Supreme Court decided in a series of decisions in the 1960s and 1970s that the Federal Communications Commission had substantial latitude to regulate the content of speech over the airwaves. The FCC and Congress in turn struggled in the ensuing years over the extent to which the principles that the Supreme Court laid down for broadcasting should also apply to cable television, over whether to maintain the "fairness doctrine," which required broadcasters to present both sides of controversial issues, and whether to extend the ban on vulgar and indecent speech to limit, label, or prohibit violence on television. In the midst of this administrative and legislative debate (which was intensified by the pressures of public interest groups and competing economic interests—billions of dollars are at stake in the new alignments that are forming in the communications industry), the Supreme Court intervened again. In a 1994 case entitled *Turner Broadcasting, Inc. v. FCC,* it elaborated on the constitutional principles applicable to cable television and the debate returned once more to the legislative and administrative arena.

This cyclical dynamic is repeated constantly in debates over equality issues. Congress has, on many occasions, enacted federal legislation designed to create or bolster antidiscrimination rights that the Supreme Court has refused to recognize as grounded in the Constitution. The Supreme Court refused to treat age discrimination, for example, as a form of discrimination prohibited by the Equal Protection Clause of the Fourteenth Amendment. Congress, for its part, passed the Age Discrimination in Employment Act, forbidding certain arbitrary age discrimination practices by public and private employers. As the chapter in this book by Paul Barrett demonstrates, however, the task of interpreting that law and resolving the difficult public policy conflicts that arise under it still remained largely with the Court.

In the area of sex discrimination, Congress has attempted to augment the protection of the Constitution by using its spending power to attach strings to the receipt of federal aid to education. Title IX of the Education Amendments of 1972 prohibited sex discrimination in federally funded programs. As Stephen Wermiel explains in his chapter, however, Congress left it to the Supreme Court to determine whether the courts or administrative agencies were to be responsible for enforcing Title IX and whether a person discriminated against by a covered program could use the courts as a forum for a suit for money damages.

The interplay between the political and judicial branches in the civil

rights field is often particularly complex. In a series of decisions in
the late 1980s and early 1990s, the Supreme Court gave several federal
civil rights laws relatively restrictive interpretations, often by placing
imposing burdens of proof on persons seeking to establish civil rights
violations. After intense public debate over what critics tried to label a
"quota bill," Congress passed a new civil rights law in 1991 that reversed
most of those restrictive Supreme Court decisions.

This seemingly perpetual interplay has also been prominent in the
area of jurisprudence that has generated the most intense modern controversy over the work of the Court: abortion. In the area of abortion
and abortion protest, which is the focus of Lyle Denniston's chapter
in this book, the Supreme Court has, of course, been the catalyst, first
establishing in 1973 a limited constitutional right to abortion in *Roe v.
Wade*, and then in 1992, in *Planned Parenthood of Southeastern Pennsylvania v. Casey*, reaffirming what a plurality of Justices described as
the "core" of *Roe*. In a series of decisions described by Lyle Denniston,
the Court has also dealt with attempts by abortion clinics and providers and pro-choice groups to invoke various federal laws and the
judicial injunction power to restrain efforts by abortion protesters such
as Operation Rescue to engage in protest and civil disobedience tactics
aimed against abortion.

The political branches at the state and federal level, however, continue to play as important a role in the abortion controversy as the
judiciary. At the state and federal level, numerous laws and regulations
were passed restricting the use of public funds for abortions and even
restricting the use of funds for counseling patients about the abortion option. (Some of these regulations have been rescinded or relaxed
under the administration of President Clinton.) Many states reacted
to the Supreme Court's decisions by placing regulatory restrictions on
the abortion process, such as requirements of parental notification or
waiting periods.

On the abortion protest front, Congress and the Supreme Court have
continued to act simultaneously to influence the balance between the
rights of pro-life forces to engage in protest and civil disobedience tactics and the rights of abortion providers and women seeking abortions
to freely access and use abortion clinics. In 1994, the Supreme Court
in *Madsen v. Women's Health Center* attempted to delineate the extent
to which courts could use their power to grant injunctions to restrict
efforts by abortion protestors to picket at abortion clinics. The same
year, Congress passed new legislation on the same subject, making it a

federal crime in certain circumstances to interfere with access to abortion clinics. The constitutionality of the new abortion clinic access bill was instantly challenged in the courts by pro-life forces, and the issue appears destined again for the Supreme Court.

Such interplay is not limited to the branches of the federal government. State courts, state legislators, and state executives also interpret and respond to Supreme Court decisions, sometimes acting in harmony with the mandates of the Court, at other times attempting to either augment or restrict the Court's holding. As the chapter by Kay Kindred illustrates, for example, officials in the state of Mississippi for decades acted only most reluctantly to apply and enforce the historic 1954 desegregation decision in *Brown v. Board of Education,* achieving what many civil rights advocates regarded as virtually no integration of Mississippi's state university system. When the controversy over the desegregation of that system reached the Supreme Court in *United States v. Fordice,* decided in 1992, the Court in many respects seemed unable to rise to the task, rendering an opinion that was indecisive and ambiguous, and remanding the dispute back to Mississippi, where it was once again placed in that state's political arena. The litigants and officials in the Mississippi case have been divided over how to interpret and respond to *Fordice;* one strongly held view within the state is that the decision necessitates the shutting down of some or all of the state's historically African American colleges and universities. If that ensues, undoubtedly the Supreme Court will be invited once again to scrutinize the Mississippi university system, and perhaps clarify its *Fordice* ruling.

Conclusion

The cases discussed in this volume have nothing special in common other than having all been decided within roughly the same period of time. They represent but a handful of frames in a film that is always moving. In a conversation I once had with Justices John Paul Stevens and Byron White, Justice Stevens said that each time a Justice leaves the Court and a new Justice is appointed, "the entire institution changes." Justice White voiced full agreement; the dynamics of the Court change, he explained, each time a new Justice arrives. As this book was being written, two new Justices joined the Court and new cases were argued and decided.

As readers contemplate the mutability of the Court and the law and the process revealed in these chapters, they may be disturbed by the results or the reasoning of particular cases, or because they perceive the Court as distracted or bogged down in legal scholasticism and technicality, as too concerned with legal jargon, multifactor tests, or fine points of language or law that seem distanced from the heart of the conflict at issue.

Other readers may be disturbed less by what these chapters reveal of the Court than by what they reveal of the commentators who write about the Court. The journalists who cover the Court for major news organizations are citizens themselves, with their own passions and prejudices. If one age-old puzzle about the institution itself is "How political is the Court?," these essays reveal a corollary question: "How political is public critique of the Court?" The writers who have contributed to this book all struggle, as good writers do, to make their reporting as objective and neutral as they can. And like all serious writers, they sometimes succeed and sometimes fail in their effort.

The contributors to this book, however, were not asked to be mere reporters but to be commentators, also. Writers like Lyle Denniston clearly come to this task with fervent beliefs about civil rights and civil liberties. Denniston is an outspoken advocate for freedom of speech, often articulating an "absolutist" view of the First Amendment; he is also a staunch defender of the right to an abortion established by the Court in *Roe v. Wade*. Readers who follow Denniston's treatment of how the Court has dealt with the conflict between the free speech rights of protestors and the rights of women to obtain abortions under *Roe* will be attracted or put off by Denniston's characterizations and judgments in direct proportion to their own subjective biases. There will undoubtedly be similar reactions to other essays, in which the ideology of the commentator seeps visibly into the commentary.

Yet one can no more sanitize public discourse critiquing the Court than one can sanitize the work of the Court itself. The process is simply not objective or value-neutral at any stage. There is no neutral objectivity to the decisions of the Court, or, indeed, to the process of making law in any society, whether that process is undertaken by bureaucrats, by politicians, or by judges. And there is no perfect neutral objectivity possible in the journalistic reporting of the lawmaking process, certainly not in public debate and critique of the process. Thus, as readers use this book to understand and critique the Court, they are also invited to use it to understand and "critique the critiquers."

In the end, there is also much to admire in this process. For all the shortcomings of the Supreme Court, the *conscientious concentration* of these Justices—conservative, liberal, and centrist—and the integrity with which they pursue their labor are genuinely impressive. If readers find themselves reacting to these stories at times with skepticism and at times with esteem, that reaction is probably fair and true to the mark.

This book is not *The Brethren;* it is not the purpose of this book to give readers "the inside story" of the secret life of the Court, the negotiations and deliberations of the Justices. Nor is it a treatise on constitutional law or the Supreme Court as an institution that explains all there is to know about constitutional adjudication in one easy volume. It is, rather, a book about process—the process of constitutional debate and resolution, a process uniquely American. It explains, through the insights of Supreme Court experts, how the disputes of real people, the strategies and tactics of lawyers, the personalities and values of Supreme Court Justices, the weight of generations of accumulated constitutional history, tradition, and legal practice, all combine, in a uniquely American alchemy, to influence the decisions in cases that ultimately will touch the lives of all citizens.

Our hope is that this account will assist readers, particularly those who do not make their lives as lawyers or commentators on the Constitution and federal law, to achieve a fuller sense of the role the Supreme Court in the perpetual interplay between politics and principle that defines our constitutional system.

CHAPTER TWO

Age discrimination has a unique chemistry: we all grow older. The elderly are the one minority group that everyone has the capacity to join, and fate willing, eventually will. Most of those who live out a normal life span will experience the discomfitures of age and be threatened by unfair treatment.

Firing or forced retirement at a premature age can have devastating economic and psychological effects. An elderly worker may often be a superior worker, with judgment, stability, or experience that younger workers cannot match. Age discrimination is an insult to a person's dignity, and it crosses lines of class, gender, and color.

Discrimination against older workers is a ubiquitous problem. As changes in the world economy cause companies to undergo many volatile and dislocating transformations, pressures are placed on jobs. Firms have a natural temptation to lay off senior workers, who may cost the company more than younger workers. A company may also be tempted to fire a worker before expensive pension benefits have accrued.

In 1967 Congress passed the Age Discrimination in Employment Act, which forbids arbitrary discrimination against public and private employees on account of age. To give the law bite, double damages are exacted for "willful" violations. From the perspective of American business, the age discrimination law can be extraordinarily intimidating. At a time in which companies are restructuring and laying off workers, any termination of more senior employees might trigger an age discrimination suit. If judges and juries routinely award punitive damages in such cases, companies will be loath to target older workers, even when the layoffs are economically sound and have nothing in fact to do with age discrimination.

Older workers, however, may be quite content with the chilling effect that potential double damages awards have on decisions to fire senior people, precisely because they are suspicious that companies often terminate older workers out of bias and crass economic calculations that have nothing to do with the skill and efficiency of the worker and that violate the letter and spirit of the age discrimination law.

In his account of the Supreme Court's latest interpretation of the age discrimination law, Paul Barrett describes a typical employer-employee dispute that through happenstance worked itself up to the Supreme Court. The case turns on a technical legal question with enormous, practical, day-to-day ramifications. Barrett shows us the world from both the perspectives of the older worker and the owners of the business who fired him, in a story in which there are no obvious villains or heroes, and demonstrates how a seemingly routine employment dispute may, when decided by the Supreme Court, end up having far-reaching consequences for all American workplaces.

—Editor

A Case of Old Age

PAUL BARRETT

It is the very essence of age discrimination for an older employee to be fired because the employer believes that productivity and competence decline with old age. . . . Congress' promulgation of the [age discrimination statute] was prompted by its concern that older workers were being deprived of employment on the basis of inaccurage and stigmatizing stereotypes.

. . . [A]lthough some language in our prior decisions might be read to mean that an employer violates the [age discrimination law] whenever its reason for firing an employee is improper *in any respect,* . . . this reading is obviously incorrect. For example, it cannot be true that an employer who fires an older black worker because the worker is black thereby violates the [age discrimination law].—Justice Sandra Day O'Connor, for the Court in *Hazen Paper Co. v. Biggins*

Walter Biggins is still surprised that his demand for a pay increase ever ended up before the Supreme Court. All he wanted, he says, "was the damn raise."

Thomas and Robert Hazen, cousins who employed Mr. Biggins at their family-owned paper company in Holyoke, Massachusetts, were equally surprised to find themselves embroiled in such a high-stakes battle. The Hazens take pride in their concern for workers, whom they call the "Hazen team." They were insulted when Mr. Biggins claimed Hazen Paper Company had been getting his services on the cheap. His request for a hefty increase—to $100,000 a year from $44,000—left the Hazens asking, Just who does Walter Biggins think he is?

Polite discussion gave way to charges of mistreatment and counter-charges of disloyalty. Mr. Biggins says he was strung along with promises of company stock. The Hazens reply that he not only exaggerated his contribution to the company's bottom line, he also was moonlighting for their competitors. There were ultimatums, but no raise. The Hazens fired Mr. Biggins shortly before he qualified for his pension.

Mr. Biggins, however, who in World War II braved German artillery fire and won a Bronze Star, "doesn't back down from a fight," says his son, Timothy. So the elder Biggins filed a suit alleging that he had been the victim of age discrimination. The story of *Hazen Paper Co. v. Biggins* shows how this sort of dispute can rise from obscurity to gain the attention of the highest court in the land.

Some suits are specifically crafted by lawyers from the outset as test cases, meant to set legal precedent. Other suits reach the Supreme Court because they involve hot constitutional issues such as abortion rights, race relations, or freedom of religion. Yet a surprising number of high court cases start with mundane disagreements that wend their way through the system, sometimes to the frustration of both sides, for a variety of seemingly unrelated reasons. Factors in the *Biggins* case included the plaintiff's stubborn personality, the creativity of his lawyers, the resistance of the defendants, and the raising of a legal question on which lower courts had issued enough conflicting rulings to arouse the interest of the Justices.

The Supreme Court is asked to hear more than 5,000 cases a year—so many that only one Justice, John Paul Stevens, still scans the requests himself. The other eight members lend their law clerks to a rotating pool that reviews the briefs and makes recommendations to the Justices, who decided only 107 cases in the 1992–93 term. With a one-in-sixty chance of getting heard, petitioning the high court for review is always a long-shot business.

The *Biggins* case also serves as a reminder that a big portion of the Supreme Court's business is business. The court referees arguments between business and individuals, between competing companies, and among hostile industries. Many of these cases involve the countless laws and regulations enacted by Congress and the states to control commerce. While the issues in business cases may sound technical, at stake are the fortunes of ordinary workers, consumers, and stockholders. What the Justices say in business decisions may affect thousands of people and companies.

Once the *Biggins* case got to the Supreme Court, lawyers watched it closely, because it had the potential to clarify the terms of engagement between workers and employers for the 1990s and beyond. These are edgy, uncertain times in the workplace. The fragile United States economy has crimped wages and benefits for many employees, including older people who had assumed they were headed for a comfortable retirement. Senior workers are also being laid off as companies try to cut costs. The Justices agreed to use the *Biggins* suit to decide two questions of keen interest to older employees and their employers. The first was what standard should be employed to determine when older workers should be eligible for large double damages awards in age discrimination cases involving "willful" violations of the law, a question that required the Court to interpret the term "willful." The second was whether plaintiffs could build such cases on evidence that employers interfered with their pension rights. The Supreme Court's answers demonstrated that even though the predominantly conservative Justices are skeptical of discrimination claims, they aren't necessarily friends of corporate America.

Walter Biggins joined Hazen Paper in 1977, having spent a quarter century working as a chemist in the paper industry. A stout, gregarious man and the grandson of Irish immigrants, he had shifted jobs a number of times. "Office politics," he admits, played a role in some of the moves.

He graduated from public high school in his home town of Worcester, Massachusetts, in 1943, and at age eighteen joined the army. He served in the infantry in northern Italy, drawing a perilous assignment: running messages between forward platoons and a command post far behind the lines. He is happy to speak at length about his heroics. One of only two decorations on the wall of his current office is a carving of the Virgin Mary he brought home from Italy in 1945. Like many veterans, he took advantage of the G.I. Bill to attend college and get started in life. After earning bachelor's and master's degrees in chemistry from Worcester's College of the Holy Cross, he easily found work in the paper business.

For generations, paper plants had been a mainstay of the economy of western Massachusetts. Papermakers had tamed and redirected the Connecticut River and its tributaries to turn the wheels that provided power for hundreds of factories in the area. The paper business also had shaped the region's social relations. Scrappy entrepreneurs transformed themselves into patrician employers of waves of immigrants—Irish in the nineteenth century, Hispanics more recently. In Holyoke, where the Hazen family went into business, the making of paper literally sculpted society. Factory owners took advantage of the hilly terrain, digging a series of canals that moved water from the high ground to the low, powering paper mills along the way. The owners built themselves fine houses above the canal network. From there, they could look down on their workers, who lived in shabbier quarters near the lower canals.

Mr. Biggins's first job was with a company that had helped develop the paper towel. Later, he worked at a firm that had advanced the quality of permeable paper used in tea bags. "I had seen the business from all sides," he says. After moving around for twenty-five years, he hoped that he had found a place to finish out his career when the Hazens hired him at age fifty-two to be their technical director.

Hazen Paper was founded by Thomas and Robert Hazen's fathers in 1925. Descendants of New Hampshire and Vermont farmers of English and German stock, the Hazens specialized in "converting," which means applying coatings to paper for such things as gift wrapping and book covers. It's a meticulous business, almost entirely based on customized orders. Quality, not quantity, is the key. When many businesses slumped or folded in the Great Depression, tiny Hazen Paper kept the converting machines rolling. As bulk paper producers began moving south in the 1960s to take advantage of lower wage scales and easier access to lumber, Hazen Paper was one of a handful of specialty companies that stayed in western Massachusetts and continued to prosper.

Tom and Bob Hazen grew up in the business, labeling rolls in the factory and taking orders over the phone. Tom, fifty-eight at the time of this writing, and his cousin Bob, sixty-one, signed on full time around 1960, after they had finished college and Tom had graduated from business school at Columbia University. Hazen Paper had only thirty employees then. Although the new executives lacked formal technical training, the company expanded steadily under their cautious leadership.

Slight, bespectacled men, they look like prep-school English teachers in their sweaters, Oxford button-down shirts and striped rep ties. They boast that they have never had to joust with unions because they give their workers a fair deal. A 1992 Christmastime edition of the company newsletter reflects the Hazens' enthusiasm for thrift. "Reduce the number of gifts you will buy," workers were told in a section on holiday tips. "Suggest drawing names for gifts instead of buying for all."

Tom, the more genial Hazen, seems comfortable mingling with workers on the remarkably clean and orderly floor of the company's redbrick factory. He greets employees—there are 180 today—by first name, and they do the same with him. The cheerful familiarity appears to be only slightly exaggerated for the benefit of a visitor. The Hazens live comfortable but unglamorous lives in a town near Holyoke. And in years past, they weren't even all that comfortable, at least not in warm weather. Mr. Biggins remembers that when he joined the company in the late 1970s, neither Hazen had air conditioning in his car. Mr. Biggins drove a power-everything Cadillac, and still does.

Mr. Biggins thought he could make a mark at Hazen Paper because, in his opinion, the company wasn't technically sophisticated and had been generating too few new products. The Hazens disagree but can't fault Walter Biggins for lack of energy. They acknowledge that he was industrious and inventive, if somewhat egotistical. He took his work home, fiddling with solvent formulas at the kitchen sink. His concoctions allowed the company to reduce releases of hazardous fumes in the paper-coating process and to increase sales. He developed a water-based coating, known around the factory as "Biggins Acrylic," which became popular with Hazen customers for its gloss and durability.

The Hazens regularly praised their technical director and over the course of 1983 and 1984 raised his pay from $30,000 to $44,000. But he wanted more—$100,000 a year, to be precise. "I had seen the sales numbers," he says. "I knew I was bringing in money, and I wanted my share." The Hazens balked. Sure, Mr. Biggins had helped improve revenues, but that was his job. The Hazens told him that no one at the company, themselves included, got paid $100,000 a year. They proposed giving him company stock instead. But time passed, and the shares didn't materialize. Legal and accounting problems stalled the stock plan, according to the Hazens. In December 1985, when Tom Hazen congratulated Mr. Biggins on his latest innovation, the employee responded, "Thank you much for the compliment. Where's my stock? I'm getting impatient."

Relations deteriorated. Bob Hazen took Mr. Biggins with him on a sales trip to Georgia, but they sat in different parts of the airplane, not exchanging a word on the flight down or on the way back. In May 1986, the Hazens accused Mr. Biggins of moonlighting as a consultant on waste disposal for competing paper companies. He claimed he was only setting up a business for his son Timothy. But the consulting firm was (and is today) called W. F. Biggins Associates. In any event, Walter Biggins said he had gotten the Hazens' permission for the sideline. The

Hazens demanded that he sign an agreement not to compete against Hazen Paper and not to disclose confidential company information. Mr. Biggins said he would sign the agreement only if he got the raise to $100,000 or the stock. No deals, responded the Hazens. No agreement, then, said Mr. Biggins. In June, Mr. Biggins, then sixty-two years old, was dismissed.

"It wasn't a surprise, really, because I had become a pain," he recalls. "But I didn't know how to get my day in court."

That might have been the end of the story. Mr. Biggins wanted to sue, but for months he couldn't find a lawyer to take the case. The first three he approached dawdled or weren't interested. A fourth saw only a Massachusetts state-law pension claim. Mr. Biggins had been fired only six months before his tenth anniversary at Hazen Paper, when he would have qualified for a total of $93,000 in retirement money. Indeed, Mr. Biggins interpreted the pension plan as making him eligible to begin drawing his money as early as June 14, 1986. It was no coincidence, he thought, that he had been fired on June 13.

Frustrated by his failure to find an enterprising lawyer, Mr. Biggins almost gave up. Then his wife, Anne-Marie, suggested he call John Egan, the son of an acquaintance from church. Mr. Egan, a prominent trial lawyer in Springfield, quickly discerned that the evidence of discrimination was less than overwhelming. "This wasn't the cut-and-dried age case," he recalls, "where the boss says 'Let's get rid of the old guy.'" Nevertheless, the lawyer thought he would be able to portray Mr. Biggins as a diligent middle-class toiler with whom a jury would sympathize—especially when the opponent was a company that in 1986 had $29 million in sales (a figure that would rise to $41 million by 1989). Mr. Egan agreed to file suit in return for one-third of any money awarded to Mr. Biggins, which is a typical "contingent fee" arrangement.

Forced to be creative, the Springfield attorney devised an aggressive set of federal claims. As he saw it, the Hazens had violated the federal pension-protection statute by dismissing Mr. Biggins specifically to deny him the retirement money. Such an action, in turn, indicated age discrimination. Mr. Biggins had, after all, been replaced by a thirty-five-year-old man who was given better terms on severance and noncompetition agreements. The *Biggins* suit was filed under both the pension protection law and the Age Discrimination in Employment Act of 1967. The act prohibits employers from discriminating on the basis of age against employees who are between forty and seventy. (There is an exception for jobs in which age genuinely precludes adequate job performance, such as firefighting or playing professional sports.) If a plaintiff proves bias, money damages are based on lost wages and benefits. But if an employer is found to have violated the law "willfully," the judge may order a doubling of the award.

Filed in 1988, the *Biggins* suit got bogged down in two years of pretrial skirmishing. While lawyers for each side probed for weaknesses, Mr. Biggins says he ran low on patience but not confidence. "As Jack Egan put the thing together, I thought a jury would buy it—but the question was, Would it happen in my lifetime?"

Bias against older workers has become a big problem in the increasingly unstable American workplace. Federal and state officials received 31,000 age-related grievances in 1992, a 30 percent increase from 1990. These sorts of cases are dominating the growth in the docket at the federal Equal Employment Opportunity Commission, says James Smith, a senior economist with the agency. But after some preliminary maneuvering, such claims typically end with out-of-court settlements. Neither side wants to risk the whims of a jury. Corporate defendants find it cheaper to pay off plaintiffs at a discount, rather than letting the lawyers' meter continue to run. The *Biggins* case was an exception. One reason was Mr. Biggins himself.

Mr. Egan was willing to gamble at trial because he believed his client would do especially well as a witness. "Walter is never at a loss for words, and he comes across as very sincere," says the lawyer. On the other side, Bob Hazen concedes, "Probably, we took the suit more personally than we should have." His cousin had recalled in trial testimony that he was "dumbfounded" and "very upset" by Mr. Biggins's outside work. "I felt I had been deceived by Walter, and I had been betrayed by him," Tom Hazen testified. Lawyers point out that when the owners of a company fire someone themselves, emotions tend to run higher and compromise comes harder. Insistent that Mr. Biggins's moonlighting justified dismissal, the Hazens made only faint noises about settlement.

When the case was heard in July 1990 in federal court in Springfield, the Hazen lawyers made disloyalty the centerpiece of the defense. Attorney Patrick McGinley sounded the theme in his opening argument. "Was Walter Biggins a traitor?" he asked the jury. "Was he really Benedict Arnold Biggins?"

Mr. Biggins testified as his own first witness, and the lead-off questions were about his impressive World War II record. "Anyone refer to you as a Benedict Arnold then?" asked Jack Egan's law partner, Maurice Cahillane. "No, they didn't," Mr. Biggins replied. The betrayal defense never got back on track.

The Biggins lawyers presented evidence that the outside consulting issue was merely a pretext for getting rid of a talented employee when he became a problem. Mr. Biggins testified that both Hazens had made critical comments about his age. On one occasion, Bob Hazen took out memberships for company employees in a local handball court. He told Mr. Biggins that it would not do him much good because he was "so old." On another occasion, Tom Hazen needled Mr. Biggins that it was costing the company a lot more for his life insurance policy—again, because he was "so old."

Despite defense evidence to the contrary, the jury, after a week of testimony, took fewer than four hours to rule for Mr. Biggins. "But for his age," the jurors found, "he would not have been fired." They awarded him $1.8 million. Of this, $100,000 was for violating the federal pension-protection statute, and a little over $1.1 million was a double-damage award for age discrimination. (The rest related to state-law claims; the jury found that the Hazens had broken their promise to pay Mr. Biggins with company stock and that this amounted to fraud.) For the victor, "it was a huge relief."

But a bitter Bob Hazen believes the jury instinctively favored the "little guy" over his wealthy employer. "The [jury] system is a little unfair that way," he complains. "While we can perhaps understand why a jury might choose to believe Mr. Biggins rather than officials of the company," adds Tom Hazen, "that doesn't change our position or the earnestness with which we feel an injustice [was] done."

Whatever the jury's biases might have been, the battle wasn't over. In a posttrial ruling, U.S. District Judge Frank Freedman called Mr. Biggins's case "circumstantial" and "a bit thin." He expressed doubt about whether a pension law violation necessarily implies age discrimination—especially when eligibility for benefits is triggered not by age but by a certain amount of time on the job. Finally, saying Mr. Biggins hadn't proved "willful" wrongdoing, the judge cut the age bias damages to $560,000 by eliminating the doubling of the award. Judge Freedman thus excised the heart of Mr. Egan's original conception of the case. Still, Mr. Biggins and his lawyers would have happily foregone an appeal on the willfulness issue, divided up the remaining $1.2 million, and gone home. "Hey, I'm not greedy," says the plaintiff.

The Hazens decided to appeal on other issues, however. Their concern wasn't so much legal principle as the financial hit they now faced. In addition to the modified jury award, the company had already invested hundreds of thousands of dollars in legal costs. By this point, says Mr. Biggins, "I was definitely starting to wonder whether I would live to see the thing end." Since the case was being appealed anyway, his side had nothing to lose by resuscitating the willfulness issue.

The appeals process took nearly eighteen months. And, again, the Hazens, overall, came up losers. In a decision issued in January 1992, the United States Court of Appeals for the First Circuit in Boston reversed Judge Freedman's finding that there hadn't been willful wrongdoing. Relying heavily on the evidence that the Hazens had fired Mr. Biggins to deny him his retirement pay, the First Circuit reinstated most of what Judge Freedman had cut from the initial award. As the appeals court understood the pension plan, Mr. Biggins would have become eligible had he worked only "a few more weeks" after being fired. Writing for a unanimous three-member panel of the appeals court, Judge Hugh Bownes also noted the derogatory comments about Mr. Biggins's age, as well as an offer the Hazens had made at one point to retain him as a "consultant" if he would surrender his pension rights. Summing up, Judge Bownes wrote that the jury could "have reasonably found that age was inextricably intertwined with the decision to fire Biggins. If it were not for Biggins's age, sixty-two, his pension rights would not have been within a hairbreadth of vesting."

Jack Egan couldn't have put it better himself: the Hazens didn't want to pay a troublesome employee the raise and pension he had earned, so they fired him. Since older workers are more likely to be eligible for retirement pay, it added up to willful, as opposed to inadvertent, age discrimination.

Judges on the highly regarded First Circuit—or on any lower court, for that matter—don't like the Supreme Court to second-guess their decisions. It's embarrassing to get overturned, especially when your colleagues across the country get to read about it in the newspaper. Accordingly, most judicial opinions sound as if they flow inexorably from statutes, precedents, and logic. Occasionally, however, a branch of law gets so tangled that judges send a distress signal to Washington. That's what Judge Bownes did in the *Biggins* case.

The judge methodically catalogued the conflicting definitions other federal courts had applied to willfulness in age discrimination cases. Some courts had required evidence only that the employer "either knew or showed reckless disregard" about whether the company's conduct was prohibited. This standard doesn't demand proof that the defendant was malicious. Instead, the plaintiff must show only that the employer understood or should have known that its actions were illegal. The Supreme Court had used this analysis in a 1985 decision involving Trans World Airlines. The airline had adopted a policy that forced some pilots to retire at age sixty, while younger pilots were able to transfer to the position of flight engineer and keep working past sixty. The high court ruled unanimously that the TWA policy was "discriminatory on its face." But the Court said that the airline reasonably thought it was acting legally, and thus double damages weren't due.

Despite the *TWA* decision, some federal appeals courts had resisted the knowledge-or-reckless-disregard standard. These courts said that in cases (like the *Biggins* suit) involving allegations of individual mistreatment, rather than the type of company-wide policy at issue in the *TWA* decision, the Supreme Court's standard was too tough on employers. To prove that individual mistreatment was based on age, according to this view, a plaintiff almost always has to show that the action was "intentional." A jury is likely to equate "intentional" with "willful," this argument goes, making double damages practically automatic. Concerned about unfairness to employers, some courts had required proof of "egregious" or "outrageous" company behavior. The lower courts justified this seeming disobedience of the Supreme Court's *TWA* ruling by insisting that the Justices had never commented on the meaning of willfulness in an age discrimination suit based on individual mistreatment.

The First Circuit, however, followed the knowledge-or-reckless-disregard standard used in the *TWA* case, and concluded that Mr. Biggins had met it. "Thomas Hazen testified that he was 'absolutely' aware that age discrimination was illegal," Judge Bownes wrote. "This is as strong evidence of a knowing violation of [the age discrimination act] as a plaintiff could wish." The judge acknowledged that employers would suffer under this approach. "But that is the nature of the beast," he asserted, "at least until the Congress or the Supreme Court changes the definition of willfulness."

The Hazens had switched lawyers after they lost at trial. Their new attorneys, John Harrington and Robert Gordon of the elite Boston firm of Ropes & Gray, recommended an appeal to the Supreme Court, pointing out that the First Circuit's plea would help them get the attention of the Justices.

A surprising number of lawyers mistakenly try to get their cases heard at the high court by pontificating about injustices visited upon their clients. This might have been a smart approach in some cases in the 1960s, when a liberal Court majority assumed a leading role in social reform. But a Court dominated by conservative Justices, who have a more limited view of their role, is less likely to take a case simply to right an earlier wrong. A better strategy in petitioning for review is to decry conflicting rulings among the lower courts. Most of the current Justices rely heavily on their young law clerks in deciding which cases to hear; lower-court conflicts are relatively easy for the clerks to identify. Moreover, most of the Justices are sympathetic to the argument that the law shouldn't differ on a significant point, depending on what federal jurisdiction you're in. Under the high court's unwritten "Rule of Four," it takes only four votes to put a case on the docket.

The conflict flagged by Judge Bownes was ideal. It involved a widely used federal statute that was likely to spur continuing litigation. The Justices, who prefer to consider issues after they have "percolated" for a while in the lower courts, had already turned down a few chances to address the willfulness question. The Ropes & Gray lawyers asserted that debate had reached a boiling point.

In June 1992, the Supreme Court said, yes, it would use the case to clarify the law governing age bias. The Hazens, who had already paid over $600,000 in damages related to claims they hadn't appealed to the Supreme Court, and roughly $500,000 more in legal fees, anticipated the Justices' ruling with a weary fatalism. "This has been a big part of my life for ten years," Tom Hazen said at the time. "It's been very emotionally upsetting."

Though annoyed at the prospect of further delay, Mr. Biggins couldn't hide his enjoyment of the spotlight. Reporters started calling him at the waste-disposal consulting firm he runs with his sons in a suburb of Springfield. On his office wall, a framed copy of the Supreme Court brief filed on his behalf by Egan and Cahillane joined the Virgin Mary carving. Apart from the temporary fame, though, Mr. Biggins seemed indifferent to the larger issues in the case. His wish: "We win, I get the money, the whole thing is finally over."

It wouldn't be that easy, or that simple.

Each term, lawyers, and lobbyists representing business, workers, and other interests scan the Supreme Court's docket for cases that could broadly affect their constituents. The Justices allow outside groups to file "friend-of-the-court," or amicus, briefs that identify the larger issues surrounding particular disputes. By shading these issues of public policy and law, the interest groups try to influence the Justices' ultimate decision. In the 1992–93 term, Hazen Paper's appeal was one of the most closely watched cases on the Court's dollars-and-cents docket.

In September of 1992, at its lavish annual breakfast reception for Supreme Court reporters, the United States Chamber of Commerce warned that if Mr. Biggins prevailed, employers would be buried beneath an avalanche of suits brought by older workers. Stephen Bokat, the group's top in-house lawyer, explained that there was "an absolutely huge amount of money at stake."

The argument went something like this: In a period when United States companies are trying to slim down to compete more effectively, every firing, layoff, or demotion that raises questions about an employee's pension rights or age would result in an expensive age discrimination suit. Making matters worse, under the First Circuit's approach to willfulness, the doubling of jury awards would become almost reflexive. All a plaintiff in an individual mistreatment case would have to show is that a company official knew that age discrimination is illegal and then went ahead with the firing or demotion.

The National Association of Manufacturers complained in its friend-of-the-court brief that a Biggins victory would amount to a "perversion of the valid ends of employment discrimination law," showering wealth onto plaintiffs and their lawyers. "Such wealth may come in the first instance from employers, but ultimately it is taken from the businesses they operate and from the economy as a whole," the association complained. "The double 'willfulness' damages awarded to a successful plaintiff represents funds that will not be available for the employer to use to increase the wages of current employees, to purchase new equipment or to return to stockholders."

Naturally, there were other points of view. The National Employment Lawyers Association, whose members represent workers, assured the Supreme Court that there really wasn't anything to get alarmed about. By endorsing the First Circuit's approach, the high court would leave plenty of room for juries and judges to distinguish between willful discrimination and circumstances in which an employer acted in "good faith," but nevertheless broke the law. "An employer's unconscious stereotyping, reliance on cost cutting motives, or negligent review of lower-level [supervisors'] biased recommendations may cause illegal discrimination, but may not necessarily involve a willful violation," the plaintiffs' advocacy group argued in its brief. Christopher Cameron, a professor at Southwestern University School of Law in Los Angeles, added in a separate analysis of the case that "double damages are a powerful deterrent to . . . workplace injustice, especially as our workforce grows older and the Baby Boom generation ages."

The United States Justice Department and Equal Employment Opportunity Commission also sided for the most part with Mr. Biggins. The agencies, whose views are taken very seriously by the Justices, acknowledged in a joint brief that in cases of individual age discrimination, a winning plaintiff often will be able to prove willfulness and get double damages. That is the system that Congress set up, the agencies observed. On the other hand, lower courts could follow the *TWA* ruling, as the First Circuit had, without necessarily concluding that there had been willful violations. A small, unsophisticated company could succeed in contending that it was merely negligent in thinking that the federal age discrimination law didn't protect people under fifty, for example.

The briefs of the parties themselves, as is customary, stuck more closely to the details of the unpleasantness at Hazen Paper. The Biggins legal team recounted their client's tale and ably defended the First Circuit's decision. Although the Ropes & Gray attorneys had persuaded the Justices to consider the Hazen appeal based primarily on the lower court's confusion over the meaning of "willfulness," in their final brief, the company's lawyers attempted a subtle but potentially important switch of emphasis. Rather than stress abstract legal standards, the Hazen brief attacked Jack Egan's original foundation for the suit: that the interference with Mr. Biggins's pension rights strongly implied that there had been age discrimination. This was a risky approach for Hazen to take. The high court frequently reprimands parties for trying to "reargue the facts." The Justices aren't trial judges, after all. They usually accept the case record as it is framed by the lower courts. Now the Hazen lawyers were asking, in effect, that the high court start from scratch, assuming that age had nothing to do with what happened in Holyoke.

Between the lines of the bold Hazen brief was a message aimed at the more conservative Justices, William Rehnquist, Antonin Scalia, Clarence Thomas, Sandra Day O'Connor, and Anthony Kennedy. There may have been some problem or misunderstanding involving Mr. Biggins, the brief hinted, but there wasn't discrimination. And it's discrimination, and only discrimination, that is banned by the Age Discrimination in Employment Act. This pitch would almost certainly get a sympathetic hearing.

The Rehnquist Court had in past years at times appeared to go out of its way to limit the reach of federal laws against race bias and sex bias. The Court, for example, limited the effectiveness of the anti-sex-discrimination provisions of Title IX of the Education Amendments of 1972, an important federal law that prohibits sex discrimination by educational institutions receiving federal funds, by limiting the reach of the law to cover only the actual department or division within an institution that engaged in discrimination. The Court had similarly limited the reach of the Civil Rights Act of 1964's prohibitions on employment discrimination on the basis of race, sex, and religion through a series of holdings on technical issues concerning the application of the civil rights act—issues that had a substantial practical impact on the utility of the law as a remedy for victims of discrimination. The Court thus established more onerous burdens of proof for plaintiffs in such cases and adopted a pro-employer interpretation of when the statute of limitations (the time limit within which a suit must be filed) for violations began to run. The Ropes & Gray lawyers were inviting the conservative Justices to use the Hazen appeal to make an analogous push to narrow the scope of the age discrimination statute.

Savvy as this approach was, it overlooked another theme popular with some members of the Rehnquist Court: the need for simple, clear legal rules. Advocated most forcefully by Justice Scalia, such "bright-line" rules, in theory, limit judges' ability to blur legal standards so they can reach the results they want. Simple rules also make it easier for ordinary citizens to understand the law. Skeptics worry that bright lines lead to arbitrary decisions because they ignore the nuances of particular cases. But whatever their wisdom, bright-line rules don't necessarily favor business. On the question of willfulness, for example, simplicity was on Walter Biggins's side. The pro-employee standard applied by the First Circuit suggests a relatively straightforward inquiry: Did the plaintiff prove that the defendant knew or should have known that it had violated the age discrimination law? A statement like Tom Hazen's, that he knew about the law, is sufficient proof, the First Circuit had observed. In contrast, the pro-employer standard applied by some other lower courts, and favored by the Hazens, required a more subjective inquiry into whether the defendant's conduct was egregious. Judges would inevitably define "egregiousness" in different ways. Perhaps the high court for that reason would reject the pro-employer version of willfulness.

The first opportunity to get a sense of the Justices' leanings on a case is at oral argument, the Supreme Court's most extensive public activity. In the case now known as *Hazen Paper Co. v. Biggins,* the argument was set for the morning of January 13, 1993—five and a half years after Mr. Biggins was dismissed. Neither of the two lawyers who would argue, Maurice Cahillane for Mr. Biggins and Robert Gordon for Hazen Paper, had ever appeared before the Supreme Court, but each had prepared extensively for his rookie performance. Mr. Gordon drew on the vast resources of Ropes & Gray, testing his arguments with lawyers who had served as clerks at the high court and others who collectively had appeared many times before the Justices.

Mr. Cahillane's much smaller firm had sent a lawyer to the high court only once before; that had been Mr. Egan's father, who argued a case in the 1940s. But Mr. Cahillane got plenty of coaching from experienced Supreme Court litigators with the Justice Department and liberal public-interest organizations in Washington. He also attended a seminar for first-timers offered by the chief administrator of the Supreme Court. There, he got key tips on protocol, such as, Don't stammer if you forget a Justice's name; just call everyone "Your Honor." And when someone on the bench asks for a "yes" or "no" answer, give one; you lose points for filibustering.

As the lawyer for the appealing party, Mr. Gordon stood up first to argue. A slim man in his mid-thirties, he smoothly explained to the Justices why they should set the willfulness issue to one side and focus on the overall weakness of the original *Biggins* suit. Sitting in the first row of spectators in the court's ornate chamber, Walter Biggins reacted with a bulldog's grumpy frown. Four places to his right sat an equally grim Bob Hazen.

This suit, Mr. Gordon said, contained no evidence at all of "bias or prejudice against Mr. Biggins relating to his age." The lawyer's rather extreme assertion quickly provoked a series of sharp questions from the bench—a brusque reminder to Mr. Gordon that oral arguments at the high court aren't an opportunity to make long speeches. The Justices are there to explore specific concerns they have about cases or to debate each other indirectly by means of their questions.

Justice David Souter pressed Mr. Gordon on whether the pension interference evidence was relevant in any way to age discrimination. Not at all, the attorney responded, refusing to give an inch. He said that employers are perfectly free to use "proxies" for age—such as pension eligibility—as the basis for decisions, as long as age itself doesn't come into play.

Justice John Paul Stevens asked hypothetically whether a company could hire young people to replace all veteran employees as a way to save money. Yes, said Mr. Gordon, so long as the goal was saving money, not getting rid of people strictly because they were old.

Chief Justice Rehnquist expressed skepticism over the contention that pension interference was all the case was about. There were also the negative comments about Mr. Biggins's age, for example. Mr. Gordon replied that the "two isolated remarks" had been "completely innocuous."

That remark got Justice Scalia's attention—he was, after all, fifty-seven, an enthusiastic squash player, and a quick wit who enjoys playing to the crowd. With mock innocence, he asked Mr. Gordon, Just what were those remarks, again? Answering his own question, the Justice continued, "Something like, 'An old duffer like you wouldn't need the handball court?'" Mr. Gordon appeared to blush slightly, as spectators and several Justices laughed loudly.

Trying to regain his balance, Mr. Gordon pointed out that the other remark, on insurance premiums, was "simply a true statement of what, in fact, every businessman in America knows to be the fact—that it does cost more to insure older people."

Could a company fire all older people for whom insurance premiums were higher? asked Justice Stevens. When Mr. Gordon said, no, not if workers were targeted based on their age, Justice Stevens added, "Well, then, this remark goes right to the heart of the [age discrimination] statute."

Mr. Gordon had failed to sell his notion that the plaintiff's case was entirely groundless. But he had succeeded in shifting the Court's attention to the quality and relevance of the evidence, as opposed to the willfulness question.

When he finally did address the matter of the standard for double damages, Mr. Gordon suggested that the Court should announce a new rule that favored employers. He praised lower courts that had departed from the standard the Justices used in the 1985 *TWA* case. Double damages should be allowed only "if the employer's age discrimination is especially reprehensible," the lawyer urged.

But the statute says "willful," not "especially reprehensible," Justice Scalia observed.

"We submit that 'willful' is a term of some elasticity," the lawyer responded—an answer that didn't appear to satisfy Justice Scalia, or several of his benchmates.

When his turn came, Maurice Cahillane, a slightly paunchy man of thirty-eight, tried to keep the discussion fixed on willfulness. He stressed that the definition proposed by his opponent was "extremely subjective" and designed only to protect employers against lawsuits. But the members of the Court seemed more interested in the evidence of discrimination than in the measure of damages.

Chief Justice Rehnquist said that the plaintiff's evidence was "extraordinarily weak"—an ominous sign for the Biggins side. Justice Scalia, despite his earlier teasing of Mr. Gordon, likewise indicated that he thought the plaintiff's case was wobbly.

Mr. Cahillane protested that the Supreme Court should take the jury verdict at face value, but he astutely sat down when skeptical questions from the bench persisted.

Justice Sandra Day O'Connor typically is a well-prepared questioner during oral argument, but she appeared somewhat distracted while Cahillane and Gordon had their say, remaining silent. Her thoughts returned to the case when John Dunne, the Bush administration's assistant attorney general for civil rights, stepped to the lectern to add a few words in support of Mr. Biggins.

If the high court were to find that the only reason Mr. Biggins had been fired was to deny him his pension, Justice O'Connor asked the government's lawyer, that couldn't be enough to sustain the jury's age discrimination verdict, could it?

Wary of rhetorical traps, Mr. Dunne conceded only that the First Circuit may have given too much weight to the pension issue. Since there was other evidence unrelated to the pension, he suggested, it might be best for the Supreme Court to send the case back to the appeals court for reconsideration. Although it wasn't possible to tell at the time, this exchange neatly foreshadowed the high court's ultimate decision.

When the Justices met later in their private conference room to discuss the *Biggins* case, the tentative vote was unanimous. The Chief Justice assigned the writing of the opinion to Justice O'Connor, making it very likely that the ruling would be cautiously worded and moderate in tone.

Sandra Day O'Connor is a historic figure: the first woman ever to serve on the nation's top court and a symbol of the movement toward the full inclusion of women in American public life. But as a jurist, she is anything but dramatic. Her approach is to take cases one at a time, generally avoiding broad philosophical statements. Critics point out that she doesn't possess the sparkling intellect of a Justice Scalia or Stevens, that she appears to lack a coherent vision of her role as Justice. O'Connor fans, however, praise her common sense and her independence from other, more consistently conservative, Republican appointees.

Born in 1930, Sandra Day was raised on an isolated cattle ranch, the Lazy B, on the Arizona–New Mexico border. By the time she was a teenager, she could ride horses, fix fences, shoot rifles, and brand steer. Sandra wasn't "the rugged type," a ranch hand later recalled, "but she held her own."

Her father, Harry Day, was a conservative Republican; he and his wife, Ada Mae, kept up with affairs far beyond their ranch. After attending school in El Paso, Sandra Day went to Stanford University; by the time she received her undergraduate degree in 1950, she had already finished her first year at Stanford's law school. In an era when few women attended professional graduate schools, she served on the prestigious *Stanford Law Review* and ranked near the top of her law school class. Just ahead of her in class rank was William Rehnquist, whom she would join three decades later on the Supreme Court.

Despite her sterling record, when she applied for jobs with major California firms, Sandra Day's only offer was a secretary's post. She chose instead to work as a law clerk for San Mateo County, where she quickly earned a promotion to deputy county attorney. Despite her many later successes, the experience of initially being rejected by her profession left a deep impression.

With her husband, John O'Connor, whom she had met in the Stanford Law School library, Sandra moved to Phoenix, where she initially concentrated on raising her three boys. She became active in Arizona Republican politics, working in 1964 on the unsuccessful presidential campaign of Barry Goldwater. Sandra Day O'Connor went back to full-time lawyering in 1965, when she became an assistant state attorney general. Three years later, she was elected to the state senate, where she rose to the post of majority leader—the first woman in the nation to hold such a job. In 1975, she was appointed to the Maricopa County trial court, where she was known for strictness with lawyers and toughness on convicted criminals. In 1979, Democratic governor Bruce Babbitt elevated Judge O'Connor to the state's intermediate appeals court, making her one of the most visible conservative women jurists in the country.

In his 1980 campaign, Ronald Reagan promised to appoint the first woman Justice to the Supreme Court. When Justice Potter Stewart announced his intention to retire in 1981, Judge O'Connor of Arizona was at the top of the list of women candidates that Reagan aides presented to the president. After interviewing her, Mr. Reagan told his staff to end the search. He had found his nominee.

Somewhat to the surprise of the Reagan White House, the selection enraged the Republican right wing, which wanted someone committed to overturning *Roe v. Wade,* the landmark 1973 abortion rights decision. Although she personally opposed abortion, Judge O'Connor refused during the confirmation process to declare her views on the constitutionality of government restrictions on the procedure. The nomination easily survived that gust of controversy, though, and O'Connor was confirmed by a unanimous Senate.

She became an immediate celebrity, heralded as a role model for all women, and women lawyers in particular. Yet she refused to portray herself in grandiose terms, saying in a rare television interview: "I wouldn't be here if it weren't for what . . . other women had done. It's not my accomplishments, but theirs that made it possible." She couldn't resist poking fun, however, at President Reagan's first attorney general, William French Smith, whose Los Angeles firm was the one that had offered her the secretary's job in the 1950s. When Mr. Smith called her in 1981 on the president's behalf, she recounted in an after-dinner speech some years later, she assumed it was for another secretarial job—perhaps Secretary of Labor or Commerce. But, she added, "he had something else in mind."

While she clearly has a sense of humor, Justice O'Connor tends to be formal, even somewhat nervous, with people she doesn't know well. She has grown self-conscious about health problems; in 1988 she had a mastectomy for breast cancer, and since then, there have been periodic rumors that she is about to retire. These difficulties don't prevent her from forming close relationships with her law clerks, especially the women. She expects her clerks to work late and over weekends, but occasionally surprises them by whipping up a Saturday Tex-Mex lunch served in her chambers.

Justice O'Connor has resisted some of the revisionist ambitions of the Justices to her right—Scalia, Rehnquist, and more recently, Thomas. Her main role has been to fashion middle positions on a conservative Court. The most notable example came in the controversial June 1992 abortion decision. Justice O'Connor contributed to a joint opinion with Justices Souter and Kennedy. Speaking for the Court, they narrowed the constitutional right to abortion but rebuffed the Bush administration's push to overrule *Roe v. Wade*. The joint opinion asserted that to achieve economic and social equality, women need some degree of reproductive freedom. This view was consistent with Justice O'Connor's empathy for women who have been the victims of sex discrimination.

But as Professor Stephen Wermiel of Georgia State University has pointed out, her views on discrimination depend heavily on the context. While women's equality has been a central concern of hers, she hasn't shown a comparable desire to extend protections for blacks and other minorities. She rarely has voted in favor of affirmative action based on racial classifications. In 1989, she wrote the Court's opinion in a ruling that struck down a minority "set-aside" program for government contracts in Richmond, Virginia. (A "set-aside" program is a quota that reserves a specified percentage of contracts for minority-owned enterprises.) In the same year, she joined the majority in a series of rulings making it tougher for minorities to win job discrimination suits. Before the *Biggins* case, Justice O'Connor's views on age discrimination weren't as distinct, although she did join the unanimous ruling in the 1985 *TWA* case.

The unanimous decision in *Hazen Paper Co. v. Biggins* was announced on April 20, 1993. Justice O'Connor divided her written opinion into two parts. The first addressed the relevance of pension disputes to age discrimination; the second, the proper standard for double damages. As a preliminary matter, then, the Ropes & Gray tactic had worked. The high court appeared to have taken the case primarily to clarify the rule on damages, but the company's lawyers persuaded the Court to look first at whether there had been any age discrimination at all.

The Justices were of one mind on the essential points. When pension rights are based on years of service, older workers must show more than interference with those rights to use the federal age discrimination law as a courtroom weapon. That was a clear win for business. But the victory was tempered by the second portion of the ruling, which said that older plaintiffs who do win their suits don't have to prove that the employer acted egregiously in order to claim double damages.

Underpinning the particulars of the ruling was the message that antidiscrimination laws ought to be interpreted as barring only some specific form of bias—not all bad behavior on the defendant's part. "It is the very essence of age discrimination for an older employee to be fired because the employer believes that productivity and competence decline with old age," Justice O'Connor said. The evil that Congress sought to prohibit was mistreatment "on the basis of inaccurate and stigmatizing stereotypes." Conversely, when an employer's action is "wholly motivated by factors other than age," she reasoned, the problem of inaccurate and stigmatizing stereotypes disappears. "This is true," she continued, "even if the motivating factor is correlated with age, as pension status typically is." At Hazen Paper, employees became eligible for pension money after ten years on the job. Older employees, on average, may have had more years of service, but that wasn't always the case. Someone who joined Hazen at twenty-five would hit the ten-year mark at thirty-five, while someone like Mr. Biggins, hired in his fifties, wouldn't become eligible until he was past sixty.

The *Biggins* case was somewhat unusual in that the sole criterion for pension eligibility was years of employment. Justice O'Connor didn't address the more typical and complicated situation, in which both years of service and age are factors in determining how much retirement money a worker will collect and when it will become available. She also didn't discuss special arrangements in which age alone is the basis of an employee's pension rights.

The ruling didn't sweep away all that Mr. Biggins had won at trial. "We do not mean to suggest," Justice O'Connor said, "that an employer lawfully could fire an employee in order to prevent his pension benefits from vesting." Such conduct clearly violates the federal pension-protection law, and the First Circuit properly affirmed the jury's award of $100,000 for that infraction by the Hazens, she added.

Moreover, an employer conceivably might fire a worker based on both his age and pension status. Mr. Biggins had presented additional evidence of bias, including the critical comments about his age, the offer of a consulting position without benefits, and his replacement by a younger man who was given more favorable terms of employment. The Supreme Court sent the case back to the First Circuit to consider whether the other evidence, separate from the pension dispute, was sufficient to support the verdict that the Hazens had committed age discrimination. The struggle between the Hazens and Mr. Biggins would continue.

The First Circuit wouldn't have to rethink the double-damages issue, though. In the second part of her opinion, Justice O'Connor expressed surprise and some irritation that after the *TWA* decision there was still confusion over the meaning of the term "willful." She scolded lower courts that had declined to apply the knowledge-or-reckless-disregard standard to cases of individual age discrimination. The Age Discrimination in Employment Act doesn't tell courts to give employers more leeway in cases of individual mistreatment, she said. The law says "willful," and there isn't any reason to complicate the high court's earlier definition with qualifications that depend on the details of each lawsuit.

Justice O'Connor didn't even discuss the warnings from business groups about the practical implications of this approach. Simplicity and clarity triumphed over employers' concerns. Double damages would be available to plaintiffs who could show that employers are aware of the law and its application to their actions. "Once a 'willful' violation has been shown, the employee need not additionally demonstrate that the employer's conduct was outrageous . . . or prove that age was the predominant rather than a determinative factor in the employment decision," Justice O'Connor said.

On the same day that the *Biggins* decision was issued, the high court heard arguments in a separate case, *St. Mary's Honor Center v. Hicks*, which also presented questions about the requirements for proving discrimination. It's worth pausing briefly to consider the two cases as a pair, because together they help illuminate the Supreme Court's thinking in this area.

Melvin Hicks, a black guard at a Missouri halfway house (the so-called honor center), sued his employer for demoting and eventually firing him. Corrections officials said that Mr. Hicks had violated a number of prison system rules. Mr. Hicks, who was replaced by a white man, said the reason was his race. He sued for damages under a federal civil rights law known as Title VII. A federal trial judge ruled that the corrections officials hadn't told the truth about why they fired Mr. Hicks. But the judge said the mistreatment stemmed from personal animosity toward the plaintiff, not from racial prejudice. A federal appeals court in St. Louis reversed that ruling; it said a plaintiff in such a case should automatically win once he has shown that the employer's purported motivation for its actions was "pretextual," or false.

But the Supreme Court, in a five-to-four ruling announced June 25, 1993, said the St. Louis appeals court was wrong. Even if an employer conceals its true motives, the high court said, that alone doesn't entitle a plaintiff to victory. An employer may be mistaken or dishonest without necessarily having discriminated, Justice Scalia wrote for the majority. Suspicion that an employer had lied is relevant, but it must be combined with other evidence of discrimination in order for a plaintiff to win. Justice O'Connor, along with the Chief Justice and Justices Kennedy and Thomas, joined the majority. In dissent, Justice Souter said that the decision was "unfair to plaintiffs, unworkable in practice and inexplicable in forgiving employers who present false evidence in court." Justice Scalia responded to the dissent by stressing that antibias laws ban bias, not lying.

In the two very different settings of the *Hicks* and *Biggins* cases, the high court emphasized that discrimination laws should be read narrowly to ban a specific type of bias and nothing more. Justice O'Connor acknowledged in her *Biggins* opinion that the Supreme Court hadn't always taken this stringent view. She cited an important 1973 decision in which a unanimous court had said that an employer accused of discrimination must produce a "legitimate, nondiscriminatory reason" for the action taken against the plaintiff. "This reading is obviously incorrect," she asserted, unceremoniously junking the expansive approach of an earlier era. "For example," she continued, "it cannot be true that an employer who fires an older black worker because the worker is black thereby violates" the age discrimination law. "The employee's race is an improper reason, but it is improper under Title VII," not the age discrimination statute. Plaintiffs, whether in race or age cases, would have to do more than show that employers acted in an unsavory way.

The *Biggins* ruling will favor employers in some disputes and older workers in others. The refusal to recognize a violation of pension rights as sufficient evidence of age discrimination "will have a major effect because so many of these age discrimination cases involve pension claims," predicts Stephen Bokat, the Chamber of Commerce lawyer.

Pension violations won't become totally irrelevant to all age bias suits, however. The Supreme Court didn't hand down an absolute rule prohibiting consideration of retirement benefits in age cases. As a practical matter, many lawsuits will continue to be filed under both the pension and age laws. Juries that hear evidence of interference with pension benefits are likely to sympathize with employees who claim that there was age discrimination as well.

The high court's ruling could hurt older workers more severely in cases involving other bases for firings, such as high salaries or seniority. It will now be difficult for plaintiffs to argue that mass layoffs violate the age discrimination law if they are based solely on pay level. Since younger workers may also take home big pay checks, older people will have to provide some kind of evidence other than salary to prove that age was the reason they were let go. In the usual situation, however, direct evidence of age bias isn't handy. Just as racist and sexist comments are disappearing from performance reviews, bosses are growing more careful about writing memos that refer to getting rid of the old folks so they can bring in low-wage replacements. That's why proxies for age like pension rights, salaries, and seniority have been critical to plaintiffs' cases.

The discouraging news for business—and the silver lining for workers—is that the *Biggins* decision will make it easier for employees who do have persuasive evidence to win double damages. That threat gives older workers an advantage in pretrial settlement talks, where most of these disputes get resolved.

Where will the Supreme Court go next in the field of age discrimination? Justice O'Connor may have provided a hint of battles to come. Early in her opinion, she observed that Mr. Biggins had presented a claim of individual discrimination—what lawyers call "disparate treatment." His was not a case alleging that a seemingly neutral practice actually harmed a legally protected group—older people—more than it did others. Employees alleging this type of discrimination, known as "disparate impact," generally don't have to prove that an employer had a discriminatory motive. In cases involving race and sex bias, disparate impact can be proven by statistics showing that an employment practice falls disproportionately on one group and cannot be justified as necessary to the business in question. Disparate impact has been the basis for the suits that employers fear the most: "class actions" brought on behalf of large groups of workers seeking millions of dollars. To business, these large suits are especially worrying because statistics can be malleable in the hands of skilled lawyers.

It was significant, therefore, that Justice O'Connor went out of her way in the *Biggins* ruling to note that the high court has "never decided whether a disparate impact theory of liability is available under [the Age Discrimination in Employment Act], and we need not do so here." This aside may have been a characteristic O'Connor effort to narrow the ruling and leave other problems for later cases. But most lower courts and lawyers had assumed that disparate impact class actions were allowed under the age discrimination act, as they are for race and sex discrimination suits filed under Title VII. In light of this assumption, Justice O'Connor's comment appears to be an invitation to business to argue in the future that the disparate impact theory shouldn't be allowed in age cases. Indeed business defense lawyers for major companies facing age discrimination lawsuits are already citing the O'Connor remark in efforts to get class action suits thrown out of court.

By declaring what her opinion did *not* say, Justice O'Connor raised new questions about the reach of federal age discrimination law. What might have motivated her comment? A strong possibility is that she wanted to mollify the Chief Justice and Justices Kennedy and Thomas.

In a brief concurring opinion in the *Biggins* case, that threesome emphasized that "there are substantial arguments that it is improper to carry over disparate impact analysis from Title VII" to the Age Discrimination in Employment Act. As authority for this assertion, Justice Kennedy, who wrote the opinion, cited a 1981 dissenting opinion by William Rehnquist in *Markham v. Geller.* Rehnquist had objected to the high court's refusal to hear a dispute over teacher hiring in Connecticut. That case had asked whether a school board could enact a fiscal belt-tightening policy that favored the hiring of less-experienced teachers if that policy disproportionately harmed older teachers. Rehnquist argued—unsuccessfully at the time—that Congress hadn't intended to allow the use of such statistically based claims to attack a policy that makes no explicit reference to age.

A future round of high court age discrimination litigation may well address whether the Rehnquist view, now endorsed by Justices Kennedy and Thomas, can garner the votes of Justice O'Connor and at least

one other member to form a majority. That development would protect employers against class actions and cripple plaintiffs in a far more
dramatic fashion than did the *Biggins* decision.

Meanwhile, there was one more round in the struggle between the
combatants from Holyoke. Their case went back to the First Circuit,
which asked for additional briefs on the question of whether there
was enough evidence of age discrimination—apart from the pension
dispute—to sustain a Biggins victory. The Hazen legal team, encouraged by comments made by some of the Supreme Court members,
argued that without the pension evidence, Mr. Biggins had no case.
The Hazens and their insurance company, however, didn't want to risk
another defeat before the First Circuit, especially since there would be
double damages if Mr. Biggins prevailed. The Hazens offered Mr. Biggins roughly $450,000 to settle the case and abandon still-pending
claims worth $1.2 million, plus interest.

"It was tempting," says Mr. Biggins, "but I decided to go to the wall."
He refused the truce offering.

It turned out to be a lucky gamble. On October 18, 1993, the First
Circuit announced that it was sticking to its guns: Mr. Biggins would
get the $1.2 million. As soon as he heard about the sweeping victory,
a jubilant Jack Egan telephoned his client. "Walter, it's a good thing
you didn't sell out!" the lawyer said. "Dumb Irish luck," Mr. Biggins
responded. "It's a good thing I'm stubborn."

Once again writing for a three-man panel of the appeals court, Judge
Bownes said that even if the pension dispute were ignored, the Springfield jury had had sufficient grounds to rule for Mr. Biggins. The appeals
court stressed that the jurors hadn't believed the Hazens' contention
that Mr. Biggins was fired for disloyalty. Instead, the jury found that
the Hazens replaced an older worker with a younger one, gave the
new man better severance and noncompetition terms, and deprived
Mr. Biggins of company stock that he had been promised.

Judge Bownes plucked a telling passage from the *Hicks* decision,
which said that a jury's conclusion that an employer has been dishonest may, together with other evidence, suffice to show intentional
discrimination. In the Biggins case, Judge Bownes continued, "There
can be no doubt" that Mr. Biggins established some plausible evidence
of age bias "and that the jury disbelieved the reasons put forward by the

defendants." The First Circuit thus demonstrated how *Hicks*—widely interpreted as a pro-employer ruling—could be used to vindicate a worker.

When this book went to print, the Hazens were considering asking the First Circuit to reconsider its decision—a fairly typical request in such cases, but one that rarely succeeds. "Obviously, we're very disappointed," says Tom Hazen. The three-judge panel's ruling "reinstates everything." Looking for something cheerful to add, Tom observes that at least "the saga that never ends," as he refers to the *Biggins* lawsuit, "looks like it's coming down to the wire, one way or the other."

Not surprisingly, the mood is brighter at W. F. Biggins Associates. The consulting firm has grown—from two men to three—since Walter Biggins brought aboard his other son, Peter, to join Tim and himself. "We're struggling," Walter admits, adding with a chuckle, "But things are improving."

CHAPTER THREE

In 1973 in *Roe v. Wade* the Supreme Court held that a woman has a constitutional right to obtain an abortion prior to the point in pregnancy at which a fetus becomes viable, and is able to survive outside the womb. Viability in most pregnancies comes at around the end of the second trimester.

The Court in *Roe* reasoned that a woman's decision over whether to carry a child to term implicated a fundamental privacy right, and therefore could be abridged by the state only if the state can demonstrate that it has a "compelling" interest to justify the regulation. The "potential human life" of a fetus prior to viability was not, the Court held, "compelling," and thus could not justify state prohibitions on abortion in the first two trimesters of pregnancy, before the fetus became viable. Once the fetus matured to viability, however, the state's interest was no longer that of preserving "potential" human life, but could be deemed tantamount to human life itself.

Roe held, specifically, that because abortion in the first trimester was actually safer for the woman than carrying the child to term, the state could regulate the procedure only through such minimal requirements as demanding that the operation be performed by a licensed physician. In the second trimester, abortions become more medically risky for the woman, and the state may regulate the procedure so as to promote safe abortions—but it may not ban them outright. Only in the third trimester did *Roe* permit abortions to be outlawed.

Roe proved to be one of the most controversial decisions of this century. Pro-life anti-abortion forces have employed a wide variety of strategies to attempt to secure the reversal of *Roe,* including a determined effort to influence President Reagan and President Bush to appoint Supreme Court Justices committed to overruling the case.

It never happened. To the surprise of most who followed the Court,

Justices David Souter, Anthony Kennedy, and Sandra Day O'Connor in 1992 joined Justice Harry Blackmun, the original author of *Roe,* and Justice John Paul Stevens to vote in *Planned Parenthood of Southeastern Pennsylvania v. Casey,* to sustain the "core" of *Roe,* the right of a woman to obtain an abortion prior to viability. While the joint opinion written by Souter, Kennedy, and O'Connor did permit somewhat greater regulation of abortion procedures, the basic right of a woman to choose prior to viability remained secure. When retired Justice Byron White— who joined Rehnquist, Scalia, and Thomas in *Casey* to oppose *Roe*— was replaced by Ruth Bader Ginsburg in 1993, it appeared that after years of doubt, the right to abortion was once again entrenched in the Constitution. The joint opinion of Souter, Kennedy, and O'Connor declared, "Liberty finds no refuge in a jurisprudence of doubt" and "Our duty is to define the liberty of all, not to mandate our own moral code."

To many who opposed *Roe,* the decision in *Casey* was a bitter disappointment. Justices Souter, Kennedy, and O'Connor had claimed that they had no right to mandate their own moral code. But to many in the pro-life movement those Justices had it all wrong—the moral code at issue was not that of any Supreme Court Justice, but of the Supreme Being. Abortion, to many, is murder in the eyes of God, a constitutional abomination more evil than slavery. For many of them, when faced with a law so clearly immoral, only one moral course remained: civil disobedience.

Pro-life groups such as Operation Rescue began to use tactics like abortion clinic blockades as part of a civil disobedience campaign. Indeed, "civil disobedience" is exactly the term leaders of Operation Rescue like to use to describe what they do. The leaders of Operation Rescue often invoke the example of Martin Luther King and the civil rights movement and tweak liberal abortion rights groups for hypocrisy, claiming that the protest tactics of Operation Rescue are indistinguishable from those of Dr. King.

To many women's groups and abortion rights advocates, however, the actions of Operation Rescue have often crossed the line separating peaceful protest or passive resistance and violent lawlessness. Martin Luther King, they point out, preached nonviolence; Operation Rescue, they claim, has gone beyond that.

Pro-life groups clearly do not violate the law when they merely engage in massive marches, peaceful picketing, and virulent rhetoric protesting abortion. Such activity is not only legal, but protected by the First Amendment's guarantee of freedom of speech. But the First Amendment does not protect bombing, murder, trespass, assault, battery, physical threats, or intimidation. Do the tactics of Operation Rescue consistently remain on the peaceful "Martin Luther King" side of civil disobedience, or do they go beyond nonviolence and into the realm of violent crime, violating the civil rights of patients and providers at abortion clinics? What legal actions are available to abortion clinics and women's groups to counter the efforts of aggressive pro-life groups?

In many respects, the civil disobedience tactics of contemporary pro-life protesters are not significantly different from the tactics of the civil rights era. It must be remembered that there were many different factions and strategies among civil rights groups in the 1950s and 1960s, just as there are differences among pro-life groups today. Some civil rights activists were openly militant, and even violent. Some were prosecuted for the violence and sent to prison.

More fundamentally, there is, on one level, a strong parallel between the two movements. In the civil rights campaign of the 1960s the protesters firmly believed, as a matter of deep moral conviction—as the anti-abortion protesters of the 1980s and 1990s do now—that the law had gone fundamentally wrong. The Constitution originally embraced slavery, but that did not make slavery morally defensible. When slavery was abolished, the Constitution was interpreted for nearly a century to sanction the regime of "separate but equal" races. Yet that did not make "separate but equal" morally defensible. To civil rights activists, civil disobedience designed to appeal to the conscience of the nation was morally justified, as the laws of Jim Crow were violated in order to stir the national conscience to adopt a law of higher principle.

The motivations of abortion protesters appear precisely the same. By taking their moral outrage to the streets, they hope to appeal to the conscience of the nation to reverse a regime that they perceive as nothing less than mass murder.

Indeed, it may well be that the principal difference between the civil rights movement and the pro-life movement is that the civil rights movement "won," while to date, the pro-life movement has largely lost. The Supreme Court allied itself with the civil rights movement. The Court declared the doctrine of separate but equal unconstitutional and, in a long series of decisions stretching across three decades, steadfastly reinforced the anti-discrimination principle. Similarly, the civil rights movement was largely victorious in the legislative arena, managing to secure the passage of major civil rights legislation prohibiting discrimination in employment, housing, education, transportation, and most other public and private institutions.

The Supreme Court supplied no similar victory to the pro-life forces, and has limited the ability of those forces to secure victories through the political process, because laws passed to prohibit abortion will be struck down. Civil disobedience is thus largely all the pro-life forces have. They have, for the time being, exhausted the remedies provided by the system and come up wanting. And for the pro-life forces, this is not the type of battle that one politely and civilly concedes once it is over. This is not an issue over which one argues with one's opponent and then shakes hands and accepts defeat graciously when defeat comes. For pro-life forces, the moral principle is too stark, the evil too immense.

Lyle Denniston's elegant account of the recent Supreme Court rulings on these issues explores the dynamics of the ongoing debate over the moral and legal dimensions of abortion. The reader should know that Lyle Denniston is one of the nation's foremost advocates for freedom of speech, often espousing an "absolutist" view of freedom of expression. Abortion protesters clearly are involved in freedom of expression, and yet, as the reader will discern, Denniston's judgment is that the rights of abortion protesters should, on balance, be forced to give way to the rights of abortion clinics and women seeking abortion, because the protesters have crossed the line from legitimate protest to what Denniston describes as "almost unrelieved violence."

In assessing where the line should be drawn for abortion protesters as this conflict works its way yet again through the courts, to what extent should rights of the protesters be given some solicitude because they have few other effective means of pressing the cause? To those on the pro-choice side of the dispute, the answer would be "none at all." They would, first, take issue with the assumption that pro-life forces have "lost" the abortion debate, arguing that while *Roe v. Wade* has not been overruled, there are now major regulatory, economic, and cultural obstacles that intimidate many women from exercising the rights emanating from *Roe*. The pro-life forces will maintain in response that such "victories" are hollow as long as abortions continue at all.

As readers assess for themselves what the appropriate balancing of the competing interests in such cases ought to be, they should bear in mind that the resolution of the conflicts is far from complete. As this book was being prepared for printing, the Supreme Court in *Madsen v. Women's Health Center,* decided in the summer of 1994, attempted to delineate the extent to which courts could use their power to grant injunctions to restrict efforts by abortion protesters to picket at abortion clinics. The *Madsen* decision upheld the power of courts to issue injunctions protecting clinics from protesters, but placed limits on the breadth of those injunctions. The summer of 1994 also witnessed the passage by Congress of new legislation on the same subject, making it a federal crime in certain circumstances to interfere with access to abortion clinics. The new law appeared, in certain respects, to go beyond the limits permitted by *Madsen.* The constitutionality of the new abortion clinic access bill was instantly challenged in the courts by pro-life forces, and the issue appears destined again for the Supreme Court.

—Editor

The Defining Moments of
Jayne Bray . . . and Justice Blackmun

LYLE DENNISTON

This is a simple case; it's a simple case because a group of people who believe very firmly in one point of view violate the rights of others, the well-established rights of others, in order to express that view. And that, the society cannot tolerate.—U.S. District Judge Thomas Selby Ellis III, at the close of the trial of the case that was later to be decided by the Supreme Court in *Bray v. Alexandria Women's Health Clinic*

Liberty finds no refuge in a jurisprudence of doubt. Yet 19 years after our holding that the Constitution protects a woman's right to terminate her pregnancy in its early stages, . . . that definition of liberty is still questioned.—U.S. Supreme Court, *Planned Parenthood of Southeastern Pennsylvania, v. Casey,* partly reaffirming *Roe v. Wade*

As the days left for Michael Dukakis to win the presidency dwindled down to a precious few in late October 1988, the abortion issue was, as usual, on America's mind. Like the nation, the two presidential candidates were split deeply on the issue, and they had talked often during the campaign about their opposing views: Dukakis strongly favored a right to abortion, and George Bush was firmly against it. On the final weekend of that October, Dukakis was making his stand on abortion a part of his closing theme, "I'm on your side." The Democratic candidate's political handlers thought that newly crafted slogan would help him surge back into the contest, and might help close the gap behind the GOP nominee, Vice President Bush, just in time.

As Dukakis sharpened his closing message for a final sweep across the vital state of California, the morning headlines on Saturday, October 29, made abortion prominent news in another way. New Yorkers read a page-one story in the *Times* telling of the French government's command to a French pharmaceutical company, Roussel-Uclaf, to make its "abortion pill," RU-486, available for wide use; the pill, French health minister Claude Evin said, is "the moral property of women, not just the property of the drug company."

RU-486 clearly is a miracle of science, with possible applications in medicine other than abortion procedure, but it is also potentially the most controversial pharmaceutical concoction in history. It could revolutionize medical abortions—and, as a result, fundamentally alter the politics of abortion in America, and change irrevocably the way Americans fight over that issue.

Very simply, the abortion pill makes abortion a matter of total privacy between a woman and her doctor. Thus, it could move many, perhaps most, abortions out of the clinics, where pregnant women routinely have been exposed to blockaders determined to stop abortion. Instead, pregnancies would be ended more often in the protected privacy of any doctor's office. To stop abortion by RU-486, anti-abortion forces would have to use political means to ban its importation or close down virtually every gynecologist's office in the nation, with no way of knowing which were doing abortions.

The RU-486 pill was originally banned by the Bush administration, but then approved by the Clinton administration and used on a trial basis nationwide. Its potential availability, and the likelihood that it will become more available over time, could offer women "the means, inexpensively, to control their own reproduction." As Supreme Court Justice Ruth Bader Ginsburg commented years later, just before she began serving as the second woman on the Court: "More and more, science will make this [abortion controversy] much less of a problem than it is today."

Within the ranks of anti-abortion forces in 1988, however, the prospect that science someday might make their goals even harder to achieve added new urgency to their efforts. The legal climate seemed to remain as threatening to them and to their cause as it had been through most of the years since 1973, when abortion was recognized as a fundamental constitutional right in the Supreme Court's decision in *Roe v. Wade*.

The Supreme Court had refused, despite repeated urgings by the government of President Ronald Reagan, to overturn *Roe v. Wade*. Although abortion rights remained fully protected by the Constitution only by the slender voting margin of five to four in the Supreme Court (the margin was narrowed to that in the 1986 decision in *Thornburgh v.*

American College of Obstetricians and Gynecologists), they did continue to hold in 1988 as they had for fifteen years, and clinic blockades looked like the only realistic way to put abortion out of reach as a practical matter.

Women who wanted or needed to end their pregnancies still were going primarily to abortion clinics, so the sidewalk around such facilities remained a convenient, and often effective, arena in which the opposition could make its stand. Randall Terry's Operation Rescue, or a myriad of local branches of that organization, began to be the symbolic and real "anti" presence outside clinic after clinic, across the country.

A loose-knit collection of militants, Operation Rescue had been unified and energized by a religious theme. The Book of Proverbs, chapter 24, provided Randall Terry and his followers a text: "If you faint in the day of adversity, your strength is small. Rescue those who are being taken away to death; hold back those who are stumbling to the slaughter." To Operation Rescue, an abortion clinic is a chamber dedicated to death, where "babies" are "slaughtered." The organization's literature describes its work in "rescues" as "heroic attempts by God-fearing people to save babies and mothers from abortion on a particular day by peacefully, but physically, blockading abortion mills with their bodies to intervene between abortionists and innocent victims."

Operation Rescue has insisted vigorously for years that it is a peaceful civil rights organization, exercising only its First Amendment rights of free speech and free protest, much in the way that Rev. Martin Luther King and other black preachers had inspiringly led the movement for racial equality. Because Operation Rescue had so often moved onto private property to jam clinic entrances or parking lots, so that no pregnant woman and no medical staff could enter, the organization's leaders and committed volunteers had been arrested over and over again for trespassing; the organization had begun paying soaring court-imposed fines, sometimes based upon convictions for contempt of court for violating orders against the blockades.

The clinics themselves, of course, have always seen a monumental difference between civil rights protests and antiabortion "rescues." The National Abortion Federation, the organization of clinics, views blockades as part of a "nationwide pattern of acts of violence and intimidation." Since 1977, NAF has kept a log of incidents of violence and disruption against abortion clinics or their staff members. (Over those sixteen years up through the summer of 1993, it had counted 1,380 acts of violence, 5,926 incidents of disruption, and 581 clinic blockades.) It considers Operation Rescue a principal actor in that catalog of sidewalk combat.

Likening Operation Rescue to the Ku Klux Klan of the nineteenth century, the federation finds "mob violence" to be a common characteristic: Operation Rescue, it says, engages in conduct that "is part of a campaign of violence and harassment intended, just as in the post–Civil War era, to instill fear, interfere with travel and prevent the exercise of constitutional rights."

In 1988, clinic disruption and potential violence were on people's minds in Falls Church, a bedroom suburb of Washington, D.C. Lt. Gregory D. King of the City of Falls Church police was fretting over what he had come to know about the tactics of Operation Rescue. He and the twenty-one officers of his uniform patrol expected a busy day on Broad Street, where the Commonwealth Women's Clinic stood: the leaders of Operation Rescue had declared October 29 a "Day of Rescue"—a day to prevent abortions in clinics in many communities, including Falls Church, Virginia.

The Commonwealth Clinic at 916 West Broad Street had been targeted repeatedly over the years, week after week, by anti-abortion vigilantes. It was, of course, hit again on October 29, and Lt. King and his troops arrested 240 people that day; the charges were trespass and unlawful assembly.

One of those 240 was Jayne Bray, a Bowie, Maryland, homemaker and mother, a part-time Mary Kay cosmetics saleswoman, wife of a minister—and anti-abortion activist since the early summer of 1980. Jayne Bray, who was acquitted of the charges in Falls Church, was no celebrity at the time of her arrest on Broad Street, but in time she would become a new heroine of the clinic blockaders: she would be named in a Supreme Court decision that would be an historic judicial victory for abortion foes—and would signal very clearly what George Bush's election as president in 1988 was to mean for the abortion controversy.

As the Falls Church police cleared up the paperwork for the unusually large number of arrests that day, presidential candidate Michael Dukakis was working his way westward across the country. He told a farm rally in Sioux Falls, South Dakota, "We're closing the gap!" He then flew to California, to whistlestop and hopscotch across that state, proudly and openly, for the first time in the campaign, acknowledging that he was a "liberal." "I'm on your side" was his repeated refrain.

When he reached Norwalk, California, a suburb about twenty miles out of downtown Los Angeles, on Monday, October 31, he was greeted by an enthusiastic throng—mostly students—in the outdoor Quad of Cerritos Junior College. There, Dukakis accused George Bush of being "on the wrong side of every issue of special importance to American women." And, of course, he said that Vice President Bush was on the wrong side on the abortion question.

"I believe," said Dukakis, "that a choice that personal must be made by the woman in the exercise of her own conscience and religious beliefs. And that's one of the reasons why we don't want George Bush and Dan Quayle appointing new Justices of the Supreme Court of the United States."

George Bush, of course, did win the election and, with it, the authority to name Supreme Court Justices. One of his nominees, Clarence Thomas, would cast what was probably the decisive vote in a ruling that vindicated abortion protesters in the sidewalk wars outside clinics and gave Jayne Bray a permanent place in Supreme Court history, just like Linda Brown, who is remembered for the 1954 school desegregation case, *Brown v. Board of Education.*

Jayne Bray was only seventeen years old when abortion sprang to the top of America's political, legal, and moral agenda with the Supreme Court's decision in *Roe v. Wade.* "I wasn't aware of it in 1973; it just came and went," she says. Later in that decade, she and her husband, Michael Bray, a clergyman in the deeply conservative Reformation Lutheran faith, began providing counseling support for pregnant women, but still they had no involvement in the organized challenge to abortion rights. But, she says, "we have always been against abortion."

In June 1980, the Brays moved to Bowie, a residential community of modest homes, some twenty miles north of Washington. The abortion issue, Mrs. Bray began to notice, "was in all the papers; they're talking about it." She and her husband decided: "We've got to look at this." After reflection, they began to develop "more fervently the feeling that something has to be done," and soon, they were "teaching, educating" against abortion in the Bowie area.

In early 1981 (January, as Jayne Bray remembers it), the couple got involved for the first time outside Bowie, joining in a protest in Washington. That year, Jayne also began volunteering in a pregnancy counseling center in Bowie—a center that encourages women not to have abortions but to continue their pregnancies to childbirth.

Michael Bray began to confront abortion clinics aggressively. He was convicted of conspiracy for a role in the bombings of ten abortion clinics in Maryland, Virginia, Delaware, and Washington, D.C., and served four years in prison.

When Jayne Bray joined in the Day of Rescue in Falls Church in late October 1988, it was the first time she had ventured into Virginia to participate in a clinic blockade.

A year later, in late October 1989, another Day of Rescue was declared by Operation Rescue; this one targeted clinics throughout the Washington, D.C., metropolitan area. Pregnant, expecting her fourth child, Jayne Bray decided not to engage this time in blocking any clinic doors, but, she says, "I had been involved in helping to make the 'D.C. Project' happen."

Leaders of Operation Rescue held a press conference at the National Press Building in downtown Washington; the leaders had called it to denounce public criticism of the Day of Rescue by the National Organization for Women and other feminist groups, and Jayne Bray was among the speakers. Among those in the audience was Kirsten Johnson, a staff member of the National Organization for Women, who had come to monitor what was said. Later, in court, Ms. Johnson testified about what she heard Mrs. Bray say: "She basically described who she was, as a homemaker, a wife and a mother, and someone who participated in rescues at the clinics. . . . [S]he was stating that it was a very peaceful protest, the rescues themselves."

The National Organization for Women and Washington area clinics promptly sued Operation Rescue, its national leaders and local figures of the specific D.C. Project. Lawsuits were filed in federal courts in all three jurisdictions in the metropolitan area, Virginia, Maryland, and the District of Columbia, seeking court orders to prevent the planned clinic blockades.

In the Virginia lawsuit, filed November 8, Operation Rescue and its allies were blamed for "a track record of unlawful activity" during "rescues," sure to be repeated at Washington area clinics on November 11, 17, and 18, "with the intended result that many women will have to delay their scheduled services," and face added health risks. Mrs. Bray was named in the Virginia lawsuit, the only woman among the defendants.

That case, by its very title, symbolized the nationwide clash that clinic blockades had become, pitting against each other not only ordi-

nary citizens like Jayne Bray and Commonwealth Women's Clinic administrator Nancy Dickinson-Collins but also well-organized national
groups waging the cultural battle over abortion. It was the case of
National Organization for Women v. Operation Rescue.

Along with Mrs. Bray, those sued included her husband, Operation
Rescue itself, its national director Randall Terry (then in jail in Atlanta
for violating clinic protection court orders there), Operation Rescue
consultant Patrick Mahoney, and Washington area rescue organizers,
Clifford Gannett and Michael McMonagle. Joining NOW in suing were
Washington area chapters of NOW and of Planned Parenthood, and
nine Washington area clinics, including six in Virginia (among them
the Commonwealth Women's Clinic in Falls Church and Alexandria
Women's Health Center, whose slightly modified name appears in the
Supreme Court's final ruling, along with Jayne Bray's).

The Virginia case was presided over by Judge T. S. Ellis III, a Reagan
appointee who had been on the bench since August 1987.

For Jayne Bray's part in the case, the key witness was Lt. King of the
Falls Church Police. His recollection of her as one who a year earlier
had gone limp on the sidewalk, helping prevent for a time the opening
of the Falls Church clinic during the 1988 Day of Rescue, would be
crucial testimony for Judge Ellis. At the 1988 blockade, King said, it
took police two and a half hours "or so" to get all of the clinic entrances
open. "Rescuers" gone limp would be arrested and moved, only to be
replaced by new ones.

King explained why his department was anticipating trouble that
weekend: "Information that we have now . . . indicates that the Operation Rescue will be performing rescue missions somewhere in the
Washington metropolitan area to include at least two to three clinics.
We just don't know which clinics those are. So, at this point I have
already put my people on standby and notified the State that we might
need assistance from them."

A moment or two later, he was asked: "Do you have any reason to
believe, Lieutenant, that after this weekend there will never again be
any more problems with Operation Rescue-type of operations?"

"No," he answered, "I have no belief like that at all."

In two days of proceedings, on November 16 and 20, Judge Ellis
ran a tight trial, frequently taking over the questioning to clarify the
evidence when the lead lawyer for NOW and the clinics fumbled or
wandered. The lawyers defending the other side chose to put on no

evidence at all and engaged in only half-hearted cross-examination of a few of their adversaries' witnesses.

From the perspective of NOW and clinic access advocates, the most chilling evidence describing what actually happened at a clinic "rescue" was not a tale of a peaceful civil rights "sit-in." Barbara Lofton, administrator for the Hillview Women's Surgical Center in another suburb, Forestville, Maryland, told of the events of the preceding Saturday, October 18, at the Hillview facility. It was a scene of almost unrelieved violence, keeping the clinic closed for thirteen hours—all day, and into the evening.

Ms. Lofton described patients bleeding in the preliminary medical stages of abortions as they waited for hours in cars surrounded by jostling, shouting, or praying "rescuers," recalled an auto chase through the Maryland suburbs seeking to evade pursuing "rescuers" in order to find a place to get some lunch for patients, and described the disdain of a Prince George's County police captain as he dismissed the court injunction Ms. Lofton held in her hand as not "worth the paper it's printed on. We're outnumbered. There's nothing we can do," he said. She also testified that the captain had told her "you have to close [the clinic] because there's nothing we can do, and it's not going to disband." She also described how she had timed the arrests the police made—"about once an hour they made an arrest."

The trial before Judge Ellis came to an end a little after 4 P.M. on the afternoon of November 20. At 4:30, after a recess that followed closing arguments by the lead lawyers, John H. Schafer for NOW and the clinics, Douglas W. Davis for the Brays and their side, the judge made an oral decision to convert his preliminary injunction against blockades of the clinics into a permanent order. Nothing in his decision, Judge Ellis stressed at the beginning, "is intended to or should be taken as intimating any view that this Court might have with respect to the legality or morality of abortion or otherwise."

He ticked off the list of opposing parties, mentioning testimony that Jayne Bray had been involved "in rescues or blockades in this metropolitan area." (His later, written findings would mention specifically her arrest by Lt. King at the clinic "rescue" in Falls Church in 1988.)

Then, the judge turned to the legal issues. In doing so, Judge Ellis was confronting the reality that, in the nationwide legal combat over abortion, the rules of law that would govern what abortion opponents could or could not do were as hotly disputed as the rules that governed when women could have abortions. In fact, when Judge Ellis ruled in the fall of 1989, less had been settled by the Supreme Court on the legality under federal law of opposition tactics than had been decided on the scope of the right to abortion itself.

Judge Ellis, of course, was aware of the Court's July 3, 1989, ruling in the celebrated Missouri abortion rights case, *Webster v. Reproductive Health Services*. There, the Court had held the line once more against overturning *Roe v. Wade*—even if *Roe* and the right to abortion it created seemed as a result to be more threatened than at any time since 1973. The administration of George Bush, like the Ronald Reagan administration before it, had urged the Court to overturn *Roe,* and the preliminary public speculation was that the votes might be there to do so: Chief Justice William H. Rehnquist and Justice Byron R. White, the original *Roe* dissenters, plus Justice Antonin Scalia, assumed to be an ardent foe of *Roe,* and Justices Anthony M. Kennedy and Sandra Day O'Connor, believed to be ready to cast it aside if a strong enough argument were made to justify that. President Bush had not yet been given an opportunity to name new Justices, but, so far as *Roe* was concerned, he might not need them—or so it seemed.

The private papers of the late Justice Thurgood Marshall reveal that Chief Justice Rehnquist had been determined, from at least the first private discussion of the *Webster* case on April 28, 1989, not to lead the Court to overrule *Roe* outright at that time, but in fact to cut it down very significantly, leaving little remaining to the right to abortion. The bold sweep of his first draft, circulated on May 25, was such that Justice Harry A. Blackmun—the author of *Roe*—angrily complained in the first draft of his planned dissent, on June 21, "The simple truth is that *Roe* no longer survives, and that the majority provides no substitute for its protective umbrella." In the following twelve days, the rapid evolution of the final ruling, and the slackening embrace of Justice O'Connor for the Rehnquist effort, made clear that *Roe* had survived, at least temporarily. Justice Blackmun dropped out of his draft dissenting opinion the phrase suggesting that "*Roe* no longer survives," but wrote in: "I fear for the future."

There was, in other words, still a constitutional right to abortion, even if it now was somewhat short of being truly "fundamental." In the Virginia clinics case, Judge Ellis acknowledged that it was "a hotly disputed constitutional issue after *Webster*" as to "what precisely remains of *Roe against Wade* and . . . where the right to privacy comes from and, hence, where the right to an abortion comes from." But, the judge stressed, he simply did not need to face those questions, and he did not.

In the case that *was* before him, though, Judge Ellis did have to decide another much disputed question, one involving the limits, if any, that federal civil rights law might impose upon abortion clinic blockaders.

In facing that, the judge was dealing with a key part of the strategy that clinics and their lawyers had been honing in recent years. Frustrated by what they regarded as the ineffectiveness of police protection under local laws against trespass, and fearful that local judges might be less than sympathetic to clinics' demand for protection, clinic attorneys had been developing ways to employ two federal laws against Operation Rescue: one was an 1871 federal civil rights law, a part of the Ku Klux Klan Act, that permits lawsuits against conspiracies to deprive "any person or class of persons" of their civil rights under the law. (This provision is usually referred to by lawyers and courts under its technical title, "section 1985 [3].") The other federal law was the 1970 Racketeer Influenced and Corrupt Organizations Act (often called RICO), which had become a nearly open-ended law, widely used in all kinds of business cases.

The 1871 civil rights law was potentially very useful, because it allowed for lawsuits challenging anti-civil-rights conspiracies among private individuals, acting independently of any government officials (a breadth the 1871 law had been given by the Supreme Court in the 1971 decision of *Griffin v. Breckenridge*). It also seemed to allow pregnant women to sue blockaders even if abortion clinics themselves did not.

The 1970 RICO antirackets law allowed for tripled damages for a pattern of repeated violations of state laws—such as laws against property damage or criminal trespass.

Both laws had been working quite well in the legal defense of clinics.

The United States Circuit Court of Appeals for the Second Circuit in New York City in September 1989, less than two months before Judge Ellis's ruling in the Alexandria, Virginia case, had decided that the 1871 civil rights act provided protection for women seeking abortions and that a blockade of abortion clinics by Operation Rescue was a plot to deprive women of their rights—precisely the issues before Judge Ellis in the Alexandria clinics case.

Moreover, in 1988, the United States Circuit Court of Appeals for the Third Circuit in Philadelphia had ruled that the 1970 RICO law could be used against attempts to shut down abortion clinics. The Third Circuit's decision in the *Northeast Women's Center* case was part of the deepening legal woe for Operation Rescue. Just as its organizers were making their final plans for the "National Day of Rescue" in the fall of 1989, the Supreme Court had refused to review the Third Circuit ruling. In the Justices' closed-door conference, only Justice White voted to hear the case. The other eight voted explicitly to turn aside the appeal, according to Justice Marshall's tally sheet. Justice White made public a brief dissent from the denial of review, saying the Circuit Courts were split on the scope of RICO, and the Supreme Court should resolve the issue.

While that defeat surely raised the level of anxiety for Operation Rescue, RICO itself was not at issue in the lawsuit Judge Ellis was facing that fall; as matters turned out in his court, the clinics did not need that law.

The judge concluded that the efforts of Operation Rescue in its blockades of suburban Virginia clinics constituted, in fact, a conspiracy in violation of the 1871 law. The aim of that plot, he went on to rule, was to deprive "a class of persons—namely, women seeking the services of these abortion clinics"—of a protected constitutional right. But the specific right that had been violated, according to Judge Ellis, was "the right to travel" across state lines to get to Virginia clinics; he declined to rule on whether the right to abortion itself had been violated.

The blockades, the judge concluded, had succeeded in obstructing and closing down clinics. "While the clinics are closed, patients are unable to receive any medical treatment or service," he said, and "some medical emergency could certainly arise." Blocking of clinics, he said, "can lead to serious harm to women seeking the services of those clinics."

Relying primarily upon the Second Circuit's decision the preceding September in the *New York State NOW* case, Judge Ellis said "it's untenable to believe that Congress would provide a statutory remedy against private conspiracies, the purpose of which is to deny rights common to every citizen, and exclude women as a class from the shelter of its protection." In short, he said, the right of women to travel to obtain abortions was protected under the 1871 law, whatever the status in the law of their separate right to an abortion.

The case, Judge Ellis opined, did not require him to settle "a clash of rights." He said, "This is simply a case where the defendants for their own reasons, deeply felt moral reasons, feel compelled to demonstrate in a way that violates the law. The law doesn't permit that, and, therefore, this Court will enjoin that activity permanently." He limited his ban on Operation Rescue blockades to localities in Virginia, refusing to extend the reach of his ban across the Potomac River to Washington or to Maryland; other federal judges, however, had banned the blockades in those jurisdictions.

As he finished, Judge Ellis chose to indulge himself in a bit of lecturing on good manners and general civility. "One of the things we must do—and I suppose there aren't many issues in this country's history that are as deeply divisive, perhaps, as this—but we must, after all, always remember that we cannot resolve these disputes without being civil toward one another and without respecting one another's views. And after all, it has to be resolved one way or another—not all the way one way or all the way the other way necessarily. But it would appear that the road upon which we're now embarked is to do so through the state legislature through legislation.

"What is required, if we're to continue this society . . . is to maintain reasonable, mutually respectful attitudes toward one another so that we can negotiate difficult issues like this and understand the views of each other. . . . The matter is ultimately going to have to be negotiated by our society in a political fashion. Litigation like this is terribly wasteful of the parties' resources, and it's not the forum in which the issue should be resolved. . . .

"This is a simple case; it's a simple case because a group of people who believe very firmly in one point of view violate the rights of others, the well-established rights of others, in order to express that view. And that, the society cannot tolerate."

Sixteen days later, when Judge Ellis issued his final, written decision, it contained not a word of his lecture. His legal conclusions remained the same, and he stated more precisely the factual basis for his conclusions that the blockades were illegal and violated the 1871 law, as well as Virginia law.

The case then moved on to Richmond, and the United States Circuit Court of Appeals for the Fourth Circuit. Both sides, dissatisfied with the scope of Judge Ellis's ruling, had appealed. The case was heard by three judges named by President Reagan: United States circuit judges

Robert F. Chapman of Columbia, South Carolina, a former federal district judge in South Carolina for ten years; J. Harvie Wilkinson III, a Virginian from Charlottesville, a former law professor and Justice Department official who had been a law clerk to Justice Lewis F. Powell Jr. during the term *Roe* was decided; and U.S. district judge Joseph F. Anderson Jr. of Greenville, South Carolina, formerly a private attorney.

The clinics case did not long detain the Circuit Court. Two months after hearing oral argument in July 1990, the court in September issued a brief unanimous and unsigned opinion, more than two-thirds taken up by a recital of the facts and of Judge Ellis's decision. It simply concluded that the judge had been correct in deciding that the blockaders "had crossed the line from persuasion into coercion and operated to deny the exercise of rights protected by law. . . . The legal premises under which the district court operated are also consistent with the law of the circuits." It cited, primarily, the Second Circuit decision in the *New York State NOW* case. Like Judge Ellis, it refused to face the question of whether any right to abortion had been violated by the efforts of "Operation Rescue."

By the time the Fourth Circuit decided the *Alexandria* case, the Supreme Court had refused to review the *New York State NOW* ruling, turning down Randall Terry's appeal on May 21, 1990. As usual, the justices gave no explanation. According to an internal memo in Justice Marshall's private papers, some at the Court did not view it as a proper test case on the use of the 1871 civil rights law as a shield for abortion clinics hit by blockades. Marshall's law clerk, Jordan M. Steiker, said in that memo to his boss that "this case would not be a good vehicle for addressing the issue" because the clinics actually had won an injunction against Operation Rescue under state law in New York, so the Second Circuit's comments on the 1871 civil rights law had not been legally necessary to the outcome.

The denial of review, whatever its actual meaning as a legal gesture, did amount to a new loss for Operation Rescue. Again, it had failed to get the Court to pay close attention to its complaints of being handled roughly and unfairly by the lower courts in reaction to its "rescue" efforts.

Within two months after the Court had voted not to hear the Second Circuit case, Justice William J. Brennan Jr. was forced to retire—a new sign of the narrowing of the liberal bloc, and thus a sign of the possibly waning fortunes of abortion rights. *Roe* seemed to be in greater jeopardy now, with the anti-abortion President Bush in a position to name a Justice who could help form a new five to four vote against abortion rights.

The eighty-four-year-old Brennan had suffered one or more small strokes on a trip abroad with his wife, and his doctor advised him, as a matter of survival, to give up his work on the Court. Mr. Bush thus had his first opportunity to name a member of the Court. Apparently, the president's choice came down to three federal circuit judges: David H. Souter, on the First Circuit; Edith Jones, on the Fifth Circuit, and Laurence H. Silberman, on the District of Columbia Circuit. The president reportedly vetoed Silberman because of an old personal grievance and was persuaded that the nomination of Jones would mean trouble in the Senate because of her aggressively expressed conservative views; she reportedly had enemies even among her Fifth Circuit colleagues. So Mr. Bush settled for Judge Souter.

As with all recent nominees, Judge Souter was quizzed extensively in Senate Judiciary Committee hearings about his views on abortion and the right to privacy; he would say nothing about *Roe v. Wade,* and would say only, as to privacy, that he did favor a right to *marital* privacy. When the Alexandria clinics case reached the Court on December 18, 1990, after the new term had begun, it appeared that the case would be Mr. Souter's first test on any issue relating to abortion rights. It shaped up as a more clearcut test than the *New York State NOW* case had been of the reach of the 1871 civil rights law.

By then, the *Alexandria* case was moving forward under a new name, given to it by lawyers for Operation Rescue (lawyers, in preparing appeals to the Supreme Court, have some discretion in the way they list the parties on the formal case papers). The case was now *Bray v. Alexandria Women's Health Clinic.* Jayne Bray says that the rearrangement was done only to put the names on each side of the case in alphabetical order; one of the effects, though, was to place the case before the Court as a symbolic contest between a woman and an abortion clinic, not between the contending giants of the national abortion controversy, NOW and Operation Rescue.

The remaining liberal members of the Court, and their clerks, apparently were troubled about risking review of the case. With the case scheduled for an initial vote for or against review on February 15, 1991, one of Justice Marshall's law clerks, Scott Brewer, wrote a memo to him on February 2: "For defensive reasons, I strongly urge that you vote to deny. There is a substantial possibility that, were this Court to treat this case under plenary review, it could do serious damage to the civil rights laws . . . *and,* perhaps, even to the right of abortion." The memo was a silent concession that the legal question was being put before the Court clearly and directly, and a concession that the liberals could not protect the clinics from a potential loss of the case, and thus the loss of federal civil rights protection against attempts to shut them down. In short, such a loss could be averted only by keeping the case out of the Court's hands. In the upper right hand corner of the Brewer memo, Mr. Marshall blue-penciled in a large *D*—deny review.

The Court, however, granted review, issuing its order on February 25 after discussing in a private conference the Fourth Circuit's decision in favor of the clinics. Voting to hear it, according to Marshall's tally sheet of the Justices' conference, were Chief Justice Rehnquist and Justices Kennedy, Scalia, and White. Although the Court has nine Justices, a majority of five is not necessary to grant review; long tradition permits review with only four votes in favor. (Originally, Marshall's tally sheet showed Kennedy as voting to deny, but that was crudely erased and a darker check was made for Kennedy, under the "grant" column; there was no explanation.) Voting to deny were Justices Marshall, Blackmun, O'Connor, John Paul Stevens, and Mr. Bush's first nominee, Souter.

Although there was no certainty that the Court would divide the same way once it reached a final decision on the case, that initial vote was a sign of potentially serious trouble for abortion clinics. All the clinics and their lawyers knew at the time was that there were four votes to hear the Alexandria dispute; they did not know which four, since the Court does not reveal publicly how its members vote when a case is put on the docket for review and a full-dress decision. But if the four who did vote to hear the case did stick together on a final decision against the clinics, all they would need was to recruit one more vote to prevail.

Randall Terry, obviously, was elated. "If we win, perhaps this will bring an end to the abuse of our civil rights through these unfounded and oppressive lawsuits," he said in a statement. Operation Rescue had gone mostly underground by then, closing its offices and laying off its employees to try to stop a legal pounding by repeated fines and damage awards against it. One of Terry's colleagues, Keith Tucci, saw the Court's agreement to hear the case as "a signal . . . that the pro-death industry is finally beginning to lose its grip on the minds of

America." The abortion rights community was deeply upset by the Court's gesture; it saw the same threat that Marshall's law clerk had. "This is alarming," Janet Benshoof, then with the American Civil Liberties Union (later head of the Center for Reproductive Law and Policy), told the *Baltimore Sun*. "It could lead the Court to really limit federal civil rights statutes [for use against clinic blockades]."

The case had been granted review too late in that term to be decided before the summer recess. The Court ordinarily reaches cases during a term only if it has agreed to hear them before the end of January; since all hearings are to be held before the end of April, the Court has to allow time after granting a case for lawyers to prepare written briefs and then make arguments at a public hearing.

So the Alexandria clinic case was put off to the Court's next term, starting in October. Soon, the prospects worsened noticeably, not only for abortion clinics but also for abortion rights advocates, and, indeed, for supporters of liberal causes in general. Justice Marshall, eighty-two years old, in failing health and missing the support of his longtime colleague, Justice Brennan, decided to retire. The last of the "true" liberals of the modern Court was departing. In fact, what remained of the liberal bloc were two Justices who, if the Court had not moved so far to the right in recent years, would more accurately be called "moderates" or even "centrists": Justices Blackmun and Stevens.

Mr. Stevens's liberal instincts, as a judge, were frequently on display, but seldom could be counted upon. He had earned, many times over, a reputation as a loner, a maverick, a judge always threatening to escape any pigeonhole, to stand apart from any "bloc." There was no doubt that he favored abortion rights; his angry internal memo in the 1989 *Webster* case deliberations, bitterly castigating Chief Justice Rehnquist's first draft for sweeping aside not only most of the remnants of a right to abortion, but also much of the foundation "right of privacy" upon which *Roe* had been built, was as impressive a credential of abortion rights liberalism as there could be. But no one in any sector of the liberal community felt comfortable having to rely upon Stevens's uncertain vote on an array of other issues.

The most predictable liberal remaining, then, was Justice Blackmun. He also did not vote a liberal "line" all of the time, wavering often toward conservatism when an issue of criminal law was before the Court. Deeply troubled in a moral sense about the death penalty, for example, he nevertheless had resisted the efforts of Brennan and Marshall to wipe out capital punishment as a constitutional matter, under the Eighth Amendment's "cruel and unusual punishment" clause.

But the Harry Blackmun of 1991 was profoundly different, as a Justice, from the Harry Blackmun who joined the Court in 1970 as President Richard M. Nixon's third choice for the seat left vacant by the forced retirement, amid heavy ethical scandal, of Justice Abe Fortas. (The Senate had not accepted Judges Clement F. Haynsworth Jr. or G. Harrold Carswell, Mr. Nixon's first and second choices to succeed Fortas: Haynsworth fell amid a dispute over what seemed like an inconsequential ethical lapse, and Carswell was unacceptable because of a widespread belief, founded upon considerable evidence, that he was a racist.)

On the Supreme Court, Mr. Blackmun in the beginning seemed to be indistinguishable from his longtime friend and fellow Minnesotan, Chief Justice Warren E. Burger. Reporters called them "the Minnesota twins," and there were enough statistics of parallel voting to justify the nickname, at least in the early years.

Blackmun, at the start, also was uncomfortable in the role of Justice; he complained early to Burger about having too heavy a load put upon him because his vote would be decisive in a host of cases left dangling by the delay in replacing Justice Fortas. He had trouble, too, making up his mind on big cases and acquired a reputation as a plodding, too-precise draftsman of dull opinions, who seemed to revel in the aching intricacies of tax law. Joining the Court at age sixty-one, Blackmun talked to his closest friends about the burdens of the work and suggested to some that he would not serve beyond his seventy-fifth birthday. That would have been in 1983.

In later years, as he grew more accepting of the role of a Justice, if not wholly comfortable with it, he and Burger broke with each other. In private gatherings, Blackmun's witty and vivacious wife, Dotty, would regale intimates with anti-Burger tales; there was no doubt that Harry knew full well what she was up to. He developed something of a caustic wit himself, and slowly he began acting out a self-appointed role as the Court's sensitive guardian of the rights of "little people." He won major press notice (and not a little press cynicism) for uttering in disgust, "Poor Joshua!" in the midst of an argument before the Court of a case involving depraved abuse of a child named Joshua by a vicious father. Mostly silent through many oral arguments, he would insert himself now and then to make a thoroughly irrelevant comment—once, he asked a government lawyer in a Haitian refugees case if she had read a Graham Greene novel, *The Comedians*, about Haiti's military repression. She had not. (After that, however, the Court's library had a lot of calls for the novel; it bought a copy.)

Single-handedly, Blackmun brought the elegant refinement of concert music to the Court. For several years, he hosted a "Music at the Court" event, illuminated by performers of the first rank. And the scholar that is certainly within him came out vividly for scores of summertime seminar participants when he taught annually about justice and society with Chicago law professor Norval Morris at the Aspen Institute in Colorado.

As Blackmun's years on the Court rolled on well past his seventy-fifth year, with no sign of his retiring, it became a convention to assume that he would never leave the Court voluntarily as long as a Republican president was in the White House. He had grown miles away from the conservative origins of his justiceship—and, apparently, all because of his defining moment in history, *Roe v. Wade*.

Harry Blackmun would forever be identified, for all intents and purposes, by his decision for the majority in *Roe* on January 22, 1973. His name became almost synonymous with *Roe* and, despite constant vilification from abortion foes, Blackmun became *Roe*'s stubborn protector, a determined adversary of Reagan and Bush administration lawyers seeking to scuttle what Blackmun came to regard as his signal contribution to American constitutional history. By 1986, he had taken *Roe* to its outermost logical possibility, so that almost any official restriction on abortion rights would fail to pass constitutional muster. He was not about to give up his seat, and his pro-*Roe* vote, to a nominee put on the Court by an anti-*Roe* president. When a pro-*Roe* president, Democrat Bill Clinton, took office, Harry Blackmun's now-short path to retirement appeared to be clearly laid out. The common expectation was that, after one more full term, with Clinton securely in the White House, Blackmun would take his leave—as his eighty-sixth birthday approached in 1994.

But, in 1991, the threat to *Roe* was still vivid indeed. After the ultimately threatening experience of the near-demise of abortion rights in the Missouri case in 1989, the Justice had every reason to be fretful about the colleague who would be picked by President Bush to succeed Marshall. When that nominee emerged, it was Clarence Thomas: a figure out of the Reagan government, who had honed his strongly conservative preferences during weekly "brown bag" luncheon gab sessions with some of the more committed Reagan ideologues at the Justice Department. The nation, and Justice Blackmun, assumed that the fifth vote to overturn *Roe* was on its way to the bench.

Justice O'Connor's vote, which was always uncertain, was no longer required to overrule *Roe;* neither was the vote of the enigmatic Justice Souter. Although Thomas had refused steadfastly to discuss his views on abortion with the Senate Judiciary Committee during nomination hearings (and had insisted that he had not even talked meaningfully about it as a law student), the supporters of his nomination who claimed to know his views gave private assurances that he would vote to overrule *Roe.* Thus, Chief Justice Rehnquist could presumably count on adding Justice Thomas to the expected lineup against *Roe* composed of the Chief and Justices Kennedy, Scalia, and White. That would make five.

The summer of Thomas's appointment hearings dragged on into fall, amid the scalding public fight over sexual harassment charges leveled at him by Oklahoma law professor Anita F. Hill. Nonetheless, it appeared that he would be confirmed and that, as a Justice, one of his earliest tests on the abortion question would be the Alexandria clinics case. No new test of abortion rights as such, or of *Roe,* was on the Court's agenda as the term opened.

The *Alexandria* case was scheduled for a hearing early in the term, on October 16. Thomas missed the hearing; the Senate had approved him only the day before, and he had not yet taken his oaths of office. The Court does not have to have all nine Justices on hand to hold a hearing, even though all nine do take part when they are all available; by law only a minimum of six is required. The Court, however, does not like to handle cases with only eight justices, because of the comparatively high risk of a split vote. When that occurs, the lower court decision being reviewed is simply upheld, and the Court issues no opinion, no account of how the Justices voted, nor any reasons for those votes.

The lawyers arguing the *Alexandria* case had faced off before the Fourth Circuit and had been opponents before Judge Ellis in the District Court. For Jayne Bray and her Operation Rescue colleagues, an experienced appellate lawyer was brought in to supplement the efforts of the lead trial lawyer, Douglas W. Davis. Jay Alan Sekulow, a fast-talking, quick-witted advocate who leads the law firm founded by Pat Robertson, known then as Christian Advocates Serving Evangelism and since renamed the American Center for Law and Justice, argued the case on appeal. For NOW and the clinics, the lawyer was John H. Schafer, a mild-mannered, slightly disorganized lawyer, acting pro bono, from Washington's prestigious firm of Covington & Burling.

Sekulow, arguing first, got predictable help from Justice Scalia and trouble, less predictably, from Justice O'Connor, when he attempted to portray Operation Rescue's efforts as a tactic aimed not at women seeking abortions, but at everyone taking part in the abortion process. When "rescues" do what they are intended to do, Sekulow argued, "no one is permitted to get in" to have or perform an abortion. "Well," said Justice O'Connor, "by that argument, just because a mob tries to prevent both blacks and whites from entering an integrated school, you would say the [1871] statute wouldn't cover it. That's a very strange argument. And I don't think it's consistent with this Court's precedents."

Operation Rescue, which had the Bush administration on its side during the summer as it waged a sidewalk war against two abortion clinics in Wichita, Kansas, got further help from the administration. The deputy solicitor general of that time, John G. Roberts Jr. eagerly echoed Sekulow's main point. The clinics and NOW, Roberts said, claim that "opposition to abortion is the same as discrimination on the basis of gender. That's wrong as a matter of law and logic." The blockaders, he argued, "do not seek to deny to some what they would permit to others. They seek to prohibit the practice of abortion all together."

Everyone observing the hearing knew, of course, that the case had to do only with the scope of the 1871 civil rights statute. But Justice Blackmun would not forgo an opportunity to castigate the government for its anti-*Roe* stance: "Mr. Roberts, in this case are you asking that *Roe v. Wade* be overruled?" Roberts replied: "No, Your Honor, the issue doesn't even come up." "Well," retorted the author of *Roe,* "that hasn't prevented the Solicitor General from taking that position in prior cases. Three or four of them in a row."

When Schafer's turn came, he tried immediately to turn the hearing away from a detached inquiry into legal meanings into a forum on Operation Rescue's "mob violence and mob action." When he got to the legal question, he relied upon a simple exercise in logic: the victims of "rescues," he argued, are not just women who are seeking abortions, but "all women." Since the abortion right that is the target of the blockades is a right that all women share, "the right of all women is lost" if Operation Rescue wins the case, Schafer contended. He urged the Court to rule explicitly, for the first time, that women are a group of the kind that the 1871 act was designed to protect against plots to destroy their civil rights. Scalia was Schafer's most difficult adversary.

Scalia began questioning the lawyer early in his argument, and continued throughout. Typical of their exchanges was this one, which came after Schafer had said that if the clinics lost the case "the losers are all women":

Scalia: Excuse me, but that's not true. The losers are not all women. Surely the doctors who want to make a living performing abortions are deprived of their right to engage in that specialty. They are kept out of the clinics, as well as the women, are they not?

Schafer: Yes.

Scalia: And does it not violate a right of theirs, or does it?

Schafer: In my judgment . . . they have their own independent cause of action. . . .

Scalia: I think that's right. So it is not directed just against the rights of women.

Schafer: Well, the purpose, though, the whole effort is to take away the right to choose. Not the right of physicians to practice medicine.

Scalia: The right of women to choose to have an abortion, but likewise the right of a physician to choose to give an abortion. I gather their animus against those who perform the abortion is the same as their animus against those who receive it.

Schafer: Well, yes, Your Honor, Justice Scalia, I'm not at all sure that the doctors have a constitutional right to practice medicine. I don't really know. But the right that these people are targeting is a woman's right.

As a case argued early in the term, *Bray v. Alexandria Women's Health Clinic* appeared to be a fairly good candidate for decision by early spring of 1992—that is, after five or six months of deliberation. But the case lingered, undecided, on into early June. Then, on June 8, the Court said it wanted to hear the case again, in the following term starting in October; as usual, it gave no explanation. Much speculation, of course, centered on the suggestion that the Court was split evenly, and wanted to examine the case with new Justice Thomas taking part, perhaps to break a tie. One consequence, whether intended or not: the case would not be decided until after George Bush had closed his campaign for re-election that fall. Kim Gandy, NOW executive vice president, was livid: "It's a political act by a political court. The delay was clearly intended to postpone a politically sensitive decision, and a possible political firestorm for George Bush, until after the election."

Not all of the politics over the abortion issue, however, in or out of court, was being waged in George Bush's favor. It had already become clear, months earlier, that abortion rights groups would make Bush's anti-abortion record in office a central issue in the 1992 campaign, and they had another Supreme Court case ready to launch in that effort. It was a new case from Pennsylvania, one of the next generation of cases developed to test what the Court would do with *Roe* after its rather in-conclusive—but threatening—1989 decision in *Webster,* the Missouri case.

The United States Court of Appeals for the Third Circuit in Phila-delphia had ruled in late October on anti-abortion laws enacted in that state in 1988 and 1989, upholding everything in those laws except a single section that required married women to tell their husbands be-fore obtaining an abortion. Obligingly, the Circuit Court decided the case in a way that made it a clearcut test of the Supreme Court's current interpretation of *Roe: Webster,* it said, had changed the constitutional rules on abortion. The part of *Roe* that had made abortion a "fundamen-tal" constitutional right, with all restrictions on abortion to be judged by the most rigorous judicial standard, was no longer the law of the land, the Circuit Court found. Instead, limits on abortion would now be allowed unless they imposed an "undue burden" on the right to abortion—a far more tolerant standard that had been espoused several times by Justice O'Connor as a possible alternative to *Roe.*

With that Circuit Court ruling coming down in plenty of time to get the case to the Supreme Court for the term prior to the presidential election, abortion rights groups saw a nearly perfect opportunity to push the Court as hard as they could to get a prompt ruling—privately expecting that the result would be a devastating blow to *Roe,* perhaps even its overruling, thus making the political stakes over abortion in the White House contest much higher. Just as Michael Dukakis four years earlier had run hard against George Bush's anti-abortion stance, the next Democratic nominee could do the same in 1992, as abortion rights strategists viewed the political situation.

So, in a bold gesture, clearly reflecting their political intent, they fashioned a momentous yet starkly simple question for the Court to answer in their appeal of the Pennsylvania case, *Planned Parenthood of Southeastern Pennsylvania v. Casey.* The question, unlike most put to the Court, skipped all references to the Pennsylvania laws' restrictions; it was phrased in this spare way: "Has the Supreme Court overruled *Roe v. Wade . . .* , holding that a woman's right to choose abortion is a fundamental right protected by the United States Constitution?"

It was a question that sounded more like one that a professor would put to a law school class than a petition for Supreme Court review. The lawyers for five Pennsylvania abortion clinics and a doctor, in fact, wanted the Court to interpret its own work, and to do so in a way that gave everybody unmistakable guidance on what, if anything, remained of abortion rights. "It is imperative," said the appeal, "that the Court end the current uncertainty in the law of abortion." (State officials filed their own, separate appeal, raising quite conventional questions.)

On January 21, with time still available for the Court to decide the case in that term, the Court agreed to rule on the Pennsylvania case, granting both appeals. It also took the somewhat unusual step of writing for itself the questions it would decide: all keyed directly and precisely to the specific clauses in the Pennsylvania laws. The revision looked like a rebuff to the grand gesture of the abortion rights lawyers. But, even with the rewritten version, the Court really was not in a position to avoid saying something significant about *Roe,* since the Circuit Court had based its decision on an interpretation that forced the Court's hand on the current state of abortion rights law.

The Court heard the Pennsylvania case April 22, and on June 29 produced the most important abortion ruling since *Roe,* partly reaffirming a constitutional right to abortion and adopting the O'Connor standard: abortion restrictions will be upheld unless they impose an "undue burden" on a woman's right to end a pregnancy, up to the point that the fetus she is carrying is capable of living outside the woman's body. Applying that standard, the Court struck down the husband-notice requirement, but upheld everything else in the Pennsylvania laws.

As fully reconstructed by David Savage in the *Los Angeles Times* later that year, the history of the *Casey* deliberations is basically a story about Justice Anthony Kennedy's agonizing reach for a way to preserve some abortion right, without saving all that *Roe* had established. (There is nothing, of course, in the Thurgood Marshall papers about *Casey;* the Court documents in those papers end with Marshall's retirement at the end of the 1990–91 term.) Originally, Kennedy was supporting a strong anti-*Roe* maneuver led by Chief Justice Rehnquist. But, according to Savage, Kennedy pulled away, choosing instead to write a joint opinion with Justices O'Connor and Souter that salvaged something of the abortion right. With Justices Blackmun and Stevens clearly in favor of keeping *Roe* intact, there now was a five-to-four majority that ended this campaign to overturn the 1973 decision outright.

Recalling his anxiety at the time of the *Webster* decision three years earlier, Justice Blackmun wrote, "But now, just when so many expected the darkness to fall, the flame has grown bright. . . . Make no mistake, the joint opinion of Justices O'Connor, Kennedy and Souter is an act of personal courage and constitutional principle." Still, he lamented that there now were four clear votes "to extinguish the light" lit by the new ruling: the anti-*Roe* votes of the Chief Justice and Justices Scalia, Thomas, and White. Justice Thomas had cast his first-ever judicial vote on abortion with the core of Justices who were committed against *Roe*.

As a political document for the abortion rights movement, however, the *Casey* decision was too opaque to have a profound influence on voters. It made abortion rights seem safe again, at least in some vague legal sense, and it was harder for abortion rights activists to maintain the tone of urgency they had expected to generate when they anticipated a major ruling against *Roe*. (Later, they would have trouble convincing Congress, as it pondered a sweeping new abortion rights law, that there still was a problem that needed a solution.)

One major effect of the *Casey* decision, however, was to put a strong new emphasis on the "other" major question still unresolved in abortion law: what limits existed in federal law to quell the sidewalk war still raging outside clinics?

The *Alexandria* case, set for its second-round hearing that fall, would supply a major part of the answer. The outlook was grim for the clinics: Operation Rescue had attracted four votes to grant review of that case, and the postponed argument with its hint of a four-four split suggested that those four Justices could be holding together to withdraw coverage of the 1871 civil rights law's protection for the clinics. Now, after *Casey,* it seemed quite apparent that, if they were in fact inclined to do that, they would have Justice Thomas with them.

Jayne Bray, who had visited the Court to hear the first argument, came back for the second, in the opening days of the new Court term. She was now close to her thirty-sixth birthday. Two weeks before the first argument, in 1991, she had borne a fifth child, a daughter she and Michael Bray had named Perseverance. At that time, she told the *Baltimore Sun*'s Ellen Uzelac, "I wished we lived in a different time—we don't. I can only hope that I can pass on to my children a society that doesn't kill babies anymore. Until then, we will persevere."

As the Court worked its way in private through the final decision-making process in the *Bray* case, Jayne Bray became pregnant again, with twins, whom she named Isaac—which she says means "laughter"—and Alethea, meaning "truth." "With seven kids, I'm a full-time wife and mother," she said after the twins were born.

Bray was still persevering when the case bearing her name returned again to the Court on the first Tuesday in October, 1992. Jayne Bray had not cooled in her personal war against abortion. This time, she and her lawyers had every reason to believe that Operation Rescue was on the verge of winning big, for the first time, in the Supreme Court.

The lawyer for her side was Jay Sekulow again. On the other side, Schafer had been replaced. In his place, the clinics and NOW had recruited Deborah A. Ellis of New York City, legal director of the NOW Legal Defense and Education Fund (and no relation to Judge Ellis of Alexandria).

Sekulow, up first, made exactly the same plea he had a year earlier: blockades are aimed at abortion, not women, so there is no "class" of people targeted as victims by Operation Rescue's efforts. The Justices left him almost entirely alone to make that plea during his allotted twenty minutes; only Justice Stevens asked him a few questions.

Again, John Roberts spoke for the government, in support of Operation Rescue. During his ten minutes at the podium, he was asked a single question by Justice Stevens and three by Justice Kennedy, who wanted to know whether local police in Falls Church had been "overwhelmed" by the clinic blockades. The city had filed a brief in the case, saying it did not have the forces to handle those incidents.

Ellis rose to argue, aware that she probably started with four votes leaning against her, and four leaning in her favor. Her task was either the long-shot one of winning over Justice Thomas, who had cast no votes in the case so far, or to get one of the Justices who voted to hear the Operation Rescue appeal to side with her. She described Operation Rescue as "a mob," one that did not engage in harmless violations of others' rights, but in acts that "are part of a nationwide, systematic conspiracy to use force to deny women in America the equal protection of the laws, to do precisely what Congress sought to prevent in enacting section 1985 (3) [of the 1871 civil rights law]."

Instantly challenged by Justice Scalia, she countered with a reference to the recent *Casey* decision, which, she noted, recognized that the right to abortion "is necessary for that class [women] to be equal citizens." She went on to note that the Court, in *Casey,* also had recognized that "womens' reproductive capacity has served as the benign rationale to deny women a host of equal opportunities." It seemed like an appeal directed largely at the troika of authors of the main opinion in *Casey:* Kennedy, O'Connor, and Souter. Their votes, together with those of Justices Blackmun and Stevens, would make a majority for Ellis's plea.

Soon, Justice Kennedy was testing Ellis with tough questions about her main legal point, identifying women as a targeted group of victims. He dismissed the point as "a legal fiction"—a strong hint of trouble. Thereafter, Scalia continued as her primary inquisitor.

A day later, the Court met in private, discussed the case and cast its first vote. That tally remains undisclosed. Justice Scalia would, in time, wind up with the assignment to draft the Court's decision—a task assigned by Chief Justice Rehnquist. At the time, however, no one outside the close circle of the Court would know that. Had it been known, of course, no one would have doubted that the clinics' side had lost, by at least a five to four vote: Scalia, as author of the *Bray* decision, would be against the use of the 1871 statute to protect clinics.

The Court decided in favor of *Bray* and Operation Rescue after deliberating for three months. On January 13, 1993, they issued ninety-six pages of printed opinions: Justice Scalia's twenty-two-page decision, speaking for a total of five Justices (himself, Rehnquist, Kennedy, Thomas, and White); two pages in a separate opinion by Justice Kennedy; twenty pages by Justice Souter partly supporting the result and partly dissenting; forty pages by Justice Stevens, representing his views, joined by Blackmun; and twelve pages by Justice O'Connor, also joined by Blackmun.

Thus, the four Justices who had voted in February 1991 to review the Fourth Circuit decision upholding Judge Ellis voted in the end nearly two years later to strike it down. Justice Thomas made up the majority for that outcome. The four who had opposed review (along with Thurgood Marshall) were in total or partial dissent. Marshall's retirement and Thomas's confirmation had made the difference.

The decision written by Scalia stated that abortion clinics were not entitled to most of the protection of the 1871 civil rights law, including the key clause that had been used successfully by clinics against Operation Rescue, which outlaws conspiracies to deprive a class of individuals their rights. Accepting entirely the legal thesis put forward by Operation Rescue, the majority ruled that blockades were not aimed at women but at abortion.

Justice Scalia's opinion, and the various other concurring and dissenting opinions that were filed with the decision, engaged in a debate over the history, intent, and meaning of the 1871 law. The law was originally part of a group of post–Civil War civil rights laws that had been enacted to guarantee civil rights to African Americans. As previously noted, in the 1971 decision *Griffin v. Breckenridge,* the Supreme Court held that the law reached not only conspiracies conducted "under color of state law," but also purely private conspiracies. The Court held, however, that there must be "invidious discriminatory motivation" in order for the law to be invoked. In a key sentence in *Griffin* the Court also held that the law's requirement that there be discriminatory intent meant "that there must be some racial, or perhaps otherwise class-based, discriminatory animus behind the conspirator's action."

Thus an important issue for the Court in *Bray*—an issue it had left unresolved since *Griffin,* was how broadly or narrowly to construe this concept of "otherwise class-based" discrimination. Many other Civil War–era civil rights laws—which were passed out of concern for the rights of African Americans—had not limited their application to claims of racial discrimination. Indeed, even the 1871 provision at issue in *Bray* had previously been extended outside of the context of race discrimination to include discrimination against the right to travel.

Justice Scalia's opinion for the Court did not attempt to resolve all aspects of this interpretative debate but rather concentrated on the question of whether Operation Rescue's anti-abortion efforts could be construed as a form of "class-based" discrimination.

Justice Scalia wrote: "Opposition to voluntary abortion cannot possibly be considered . . . an irrational surrogate for opposition to (or paternalism towards) women. Whatever one thinks of abortion, it cannot be denied that there are common and respectable reasons for opposing it, other than hatred of or condescension toward (or indeed any view at all concerning) women as a class—as is evident from the fact that men and women are on both sides of the issue, just as men and women are on both sides of [Operation Rescue's] unlawful demonstrations."

The majority also rejected the clinics' claim that their right to travel had been violated by the blockades. There was no proof in the case, Scalia said, that the blockaders intended to interfere with that right.

Then, going beyond what the Fourth Circuit and Judge Ellis had decided, the majority said that the 1871 law does not apply to private conspiracies to deprive women of the right to abortion. That is a right that is protected only against official actions of government, not private acts, Scalia declared.

Then, responding to remarks made in the dissenting opinions of Justices Souter and Stevens (joined by Blackmun), the majority suggested that it would be improper at this point to rule on the clinics' separate claim that Operation Rescue had violated the 1871 law because its mass blockades had overwhelmed local police efforts to protect the clinics (a claimed violation of a second clause of section 1985 [3] of the 1871 law). But, if that issue were before it, the majority said, it, too, would fail, because it also requires proof that targets of blockades are protected by the law, and the Court already had rejected that claim.

Justice Kennedy agreed with all aspects of the Scalia opinion, but wrote his brief separate statement to denounce "wholesale commission" of crimes under state law, saying they "are designed to inflame, not inform." In comments that reminded one of Judge Ellis's closing lecture in the Alexandria federal courtroom, Justice Kennedy said that such crimes "subvert the civility and mutual respect that are the essential preconditions for the orderly resolution of social conflict in a free society." He noted that there was a federal law allowing for "powerful federal assistance" if state and local authorities are threatened by "organized lawless conduct" and ask for federal help to deal with it.

Both sides greeted the decision with predictable responses, praising or denouncing the ruling. They agreed on one aspect, however: since the Court's ruling merely interpreted a federal law, and was not based on the Constitution, the legal battle around the clinics and the sidewalk combat would not end. Instead, the issue would shift to Congress to react, if it wished, to the ruling. Because it was a decision based solely on a federal statute, Congress was entirely free to rewrite the law.

Perhaps by coincidence, the ruling came just eight days before President Clinton's inauguration and nine days before the twentieth anniversary of *Roe v. Wade*. Both occasions brought out the anti-abortion protesters—victors in the *Bray* decision, at least partial victors in the *Casey* decision with its lowered constitutional standard for reviewing abortion restrictions, but perhaps also facing imminent defeat on a variety of issues because the White House now had a pro-*Roe* occupant. Clinton symbolically and practically signaled the new era two days after inauguration day, on *Roe*'s twentieth anniversary, by issuing five presidential memos to ease access to abortions in federal facilities and federally financed clinics, and beginning the process that led toward the relaxation of the Reagan and Bush administrations' ban on the import of the "abortion pill," RU-486.

Indeed, as this book was being prepared, events in 1994 and 1995 increased the intensity of the conflict between the tactics of abortion protesters and the rights of patients and providers at abortion clinics. On March 10, 1993, Dr. David Gunn was shot in the chest several times as he got out of his car at the abortion clinic he operated in Pensacola, Florida: Pensacola Women's Medical Services. He died two hours later at a hospital. Michael Frederick Griffin, a thirty-one-year-old anti-abortion activist allied with the group Rescue America, was arrested and charged with murder. For the first time, the National Abortion Federation's compilation of violent clinic incidents had an entry under the column for deaths. Griffin was convicted of first-degree murder.

On August 19, 1993, a physician in Wichita, Kansas, was shot outside a clinic, wounding him in both arms. His attacker, Rachell "Shelley" Shannon, was convicted of attempted murder. On July 29, 1994, John Britton and an unarmed escort, James Barett, were shot and killed outside a clinic in Pensacola, Florida. The assailant, Paul Hill, was convicted of the murders and sentenced to death. And on December 30, 1994, a gunman dressed in black opened fire on two abortion clinics in Brookline, Massachusetts, killing two staff workers and wounding five others. The next day another shooting occurred at a clinic in Norfolk, Virginia, resulting in the apprehension of a suspect who allegedly perpetrated the Massachusetts shootings, John C. Salvi III.

In the midst of this escalating violence, President Clinton signed the Freedom of Access to Clinic Entrances Act into law on May 26, 1994. The new law, popularly known by its acronym FACE, provides for a variety of criminal penalties and civil remedies designed to guarantee access to abortion clinics and places of religious worship. In the legislative hearings conducted while the legislation was moving through Congress, the Senate Labor and Human Resources Committee issued a report finding that from 1977 to April 1993, more than 1,000 acts of violence against abortion providers were reported in the United States. These acts included at least 36 bombings, 81 arsons, 131 death threats, 84 assaults, 2 kidnappings, 327 clinic invasions, and 1 murder. Over 6,000 clinic blockades and other disruptions were reported since 1977. According to a survey by the Washington-based group Feminist Majority Foundation, more than half the abortion clinics in the nation experienced one or more types of violence in the year 1994, the most common being threats to the staff.

In order to make the coverage of the act more evenhanded and to attempt to placate the complaints of many pro-life activists that the law unfairly and unconstitutionally singled out one religious and political point of view for prosecution, a "religious liberty amendment" was inserted in the final version of the new clinic access law. This amendment, proposed by Senator Orrin Hatch, resulted in the inclusion of religious places of worship as facilities protected by the legislation. The law prohibits the use of "force," "threat of force," and "physical obstruction" to block access to abortion clinics or places of worship. The term "physical obstruction" is defined in the law as "rendering impassable ingress to or egress from a facility that provides reproductive health services or to or from a place of religious worship, or rendering passage to or from such a facility or place of religious worship unreasonably difficult or hazardous." To fall within the prohibitions of the new law, the use of force, threats, or physical obstruction must be done intentionally to "injure," "intimidate," or "interfere with" access. The term "interfere with" is defined by the law as "to restrict a person's freedom of movement." The term "intimidate" is defined as "to place a person in reasonable apprehension of bodily harm to him- or herself or to another."

Obviously sensitive to the need to balance remedies against force and obstruction with the legitimate rights of free expression of abortion protesters, the new law states explicitly that nothing in the law shall be construed "to prohibit any expressive conduct (including peaceful picketing or other peaceful demonstration) protected from legal prohibition by the First Amendment to the Constitution." The law further provides that it shall not be construed to "create new remedies for interference with activities protected by the free speech or free exercise clauses of the First Amendment to the Constitution, occurring outside a facility, regardless of the point of view expressed, or to limit any existing legal remedies for such interference."

As the Congress was in the process of creating new legislation regarding clinic access and protest, the Supreme Court's own docket continued to fill with important abortion protest cases. The Court in early 1994 rendered a decision in *National Organization for Women, Inc. v. Scheidler,* holding that the federal RICO law could be used against allegedly violent abortion protest conspiracies. In *Scheidler* a RICO case was brought by the National Organization for Women against certain pro-life groups, alleging that those groups had engaged in such violations of federal law as "the obtaining of property from another, with his consent, induced by wrongful use of actual or threatened force, violence, or fear, or under color of right." The Supreme Court held that the RICO statute could be used to prosecute such allegations, even though abortion protesters were not traditional "racketeers" engaged in conspiracies for pecuniary gain.

In the summer of 1994 the Supreme Court rendered an important decision in *Madsen v. Women's Health Center, Inc.,* involving a state-court injunction in Florida limiting the rights of abortion protesters by placing restrictions on where and how they could picket an abortion clinic and the residences of abortion clinic staff members. The Court upheld some aspects of the injunction and struck down others. The guiding principle in the *Madsen* decision was a distinction between actual interference with access and mere psychological disturbance caused by the confrontation with the protesters' graphic messages. The Court thus sustained the injunction to the extent that it banned protesters from obstructing access to the abortion clinic or creating noise that penetrated the clinic's interior. But the Court struck down those aspects of the injunction that primarily shielded patients and staff from confrontation with disturbing messages of the protesters.

These decisions in 1994 turned out to be among the last in which Justice Harry Blackmun, the man who largely started it all with his historic opinion in *Roe v. Wade,* would participate. Justice Blackmun announced his retirement at the end of the 1993–94 term and has now been replaced by Justice Stephen Breyer. Blackmun's retirement came the year after the retirement of Byron White, replaced by Justice Ruth Bader Ginsburg.

And so the politics and the law of abortion continued to evolve. As Justice Ginsburg remarked in 1993 to reporters at the American Bar Association Convention: "I have seen a tremendous change in public attitudes on that question in my lifetime. I don't think we will ever return to the old ways."

CHAPTER FOUR

Violence and crime have emerged as front-burner issues in the public consciousness. Political leaders in both major parties position themselves to appear tougher on criminals than their counterparts; there is rejuvenated interest in abolishing parole, as well as longer prison sentences and more police.

There was a time when many in the public believed that courts, particularly the Supreme Court, were aiding and abetting criminal activity. The Warren Court was often perceived as coddling criminals, putting handcuffs on the cops instead of the crooks, letting the guilty go free on "technicalities."

The perception was probably always a caricature, but, whether deserved or not, the perception is no longer completely accurate. The Burger and Rehnquist Courts have generally not been willing to expand the rights of criminal defendants, and in many instances have restrictively interpreted rights first recognized in the Warren Court era.

The Fourth Amendment has been critical in this historical progression. It provides that the "right of the people to be secure in their persons, houses, papers, and effects, against unreasonable searches and seizures, shall not be violated, and no warrants shall issue, but upon probable cause, supported by oath or affirmation, and particularly prescribing the place to be searched, and the persons or things to be seized." What is the meaning of this amendment for life on the street? When may a police officer walk up to someone, or stop a vehicle, and detain people, question, pat them down, search, arrest them? In this chapter, Richard Carelli describes an effort by the Court to define the limits of police behavior on the street and the meaning of the Fourth Amendment.

Carelli's account reads like a crime and courtroom drama: he focuses, like a good crime reporter, on the actions of the accused, the police, the prosecutors and defense lawyers. One of the most disturbing aspects of this story is the contrast between the matter-of-fact realism of the arrest, search, and trial, and the highly abstract and scholastic distinctions utilized by the Supreme Court to determine whether the actions of the police were constitutional.

The rule adopted by the Court in the case described by Carelli is ultimately this: A police officer may, when he or she observes behavior that leads the officer to believe that criminal activity may be afoot, briefly stop the suspicious person to make "reasonable inquiries." When stopping an individual who has engaged in suspicious behavior, the officer may, for the officer's own safety, engage in a "patdown" to determine whether the person is carrying a weapon. Once an officer's patdown reveals that no weapons are present, the patdown must cease. If in the course of a patdown, however, the officer's sense of touch provides the officer with probable cause to believe that individual is carrying contraband—such as a package containing drugs—the officer may seize the contraband without a warrant. Thus, if an officer is satisfied that an object is not a weapon and that the suspect has no weapons but continues to search the suspect and finds drugs, the drugs have been illegally seized. But if an officer's fingers reveal all in one moment that an object is not a gun, but is contraband, the object may be seized.

This distinction is too subtle and too subject to abuse to provide meaningful and coherent guidance to police officers or trial courts. Yet, as Richard Carelli's account reveals, it is the type of legalism that sometimes results when crime and police detection as practiced on the streets pose issues that reach the Supreme Court.

—Editor

A Search on the Street

RICHARD CARELLI

In defining the reach of the Fourth Amendment, the court goes a long way toward defining the type of society we live in. The scope of the amendment determines whether society wants to govern our police instead of being governed by them, and greatly affects the amount of privacy and personal security we enjoy in our everyday lives.—Tracey Maclin, Professor of Law, Boston University

Because the strongest advocates of Fourth Amendment rights are frequently criminals, it is easy to forget that our interpretations of such rights apply to the innocent and guilty alike. . . . The Fourth Amendment protects innocent persons from being subjected to overbearing or harassing police conduct carried out solely on the basis of imprecise stereotypes of what criminals look like, or on the basis of irrelevant characteristics such as race.—Justice Thurgood Marshall

Tim Dickerson's lightweight nylon jacket provided enough warmth as he left the apartment building at 1030 Morgan Avenue North; it was unusually mild for early November in Minnesota. As things turned out, he didn't have far to walk.

As he descended the building's front steps shortly after eight o'clock, on November 9, 1989, Dickerson was being watched by two Minneapolis policemen in a marked squad car parked nearby. Officers Vernon Rose and Bruce Johnson didn't know Dickerson, but they were familiar with the three-story building he was leaving.

Rose, a fourteen-year veteran, later described the building as "a known crack house" where crack cocaine was sold in the hallway twenty-four hours a day. Rose had participated in several searches inside the twelve-unit building, raids that had netted drugs, guns, and knives.

Dickerson, who was twenty-three and had never before been in trouble with the law, had bought a tiny amount of crack cocaine while inside. He later said he had purchased it for a friend and was on his way to take it to him. He said he immediately walked around the side of the building to an alley because it was the fastest route, but Rose testified that Dickerson had started walking down the street toward the squad car before stopping, abruptly changing direction, and heading toward the alley after seeing the policemen.

Rose told Johnson to drive the squad car into the alley, and they were waiting there as Dickerson approached. What occurred next would, eventually, alter two centuries of law governing such common confrontations between police and people, guilty or innocent, who find themselves criminal suspects.

Rose stopped Dickerson and made him submit to a patdown search, so, Rose said, he could question Dickerson without worrying that he might be carrying a weapon. Rose also conceded, however, that he also thought he might find illegal drugs. Dickerson, soft-spoken and cooperative, offered no resistance. During the patdown, Rose felt a small lump in the nylon jacket's front pocket. He later testified: "I examined it with my fingers and it slid, and it felt to be a lump of crack cocaine in cellophane."

Until the early 1980s, cocaine was an elite, expensive drug almost always used in powdered form. But enterprising dealers discovered a lucrative recipe: they mixed powdered cocaine with water and other substances and boiled it. When cooled, the mixture formed a solid "rock." Dealers could break a rock into tiny pieces for smoking, pieces that could be sold at prices low enough to make crack—named for the crackling sound made when it's smoked—enormously popular among even the poorest of junkies.

Rose reached into Dickerson's pocket and removed a small, rock-like substance wrapped in cellophane. Later testing confirmed it was one-fifth of a gram of cocaine. The officer arrested Dickerson, who was charged with possession of a controlled substance.

Dickerson's subsequent journey through the state's criminal justice system, at least initially, proved routine: a January 4 "first appearance" in the Hennepin County District Court; another court date on February 1 after Judge Robert H. Lynn had been assigned the case; and a February 20 hearing on Dickerson's request that the crack cocaine seized by Rose not be used as evidence against him.

At that suppression-of-evidence hearing, Dickerson's public defender, Mary Moriarty, offered Judge Lynn two alternative reasons for ruling that Dickerson had been the target of unlawful police conduct. She said Rose had violated the Constitution's Fourth Amendment by stopping Dickerson, or, if he had not violated the amendment, his search was not as limited as the amendment required.

At bottom, the amendment is aimed at protecting ordinary citizens against overzealous police officers. It provides a fundamental rule in an open society's attempt to balance two important concerns, public safety and individual freedom. That rule: police normally need a court's permission before they may search someone.

Growing out of the English maxim "A man's house is his castle," the colonial ideal of being free from unreasonable governmental intrusion found voice in the Fourth Amendment. It states: "The right of the people to be secure in their persons, houses, papers, and effects, against unreasonable searches and seizures shall not be violated; and no warrants shall issue but upon probable cause, supported by oath or affirmation, and particularly describing the place to be searched, and the persons or things to be seized."

Early in this century, the Court ruled that evidence obtained through searches and seizures that violate the Fourth Amendment is not admissible at trial. But the amendment originally restricted the conduct only of the federal government and its agents, until a liberal Supreme Court led by Chief Justice Earl Warren applied the rule to state and local governments as well.

Numerous other Supreme Court rulings on the amendment's meaning and scope generally have classified as unreasonable, and therefore unlawful, those searches and seizures by police or their agents conducted, no matter where, without court warrants. There are exceptions, however.

In 1968, even the Warren Court recognized that sometimes a police officer's suspicions are aroused by someone's behavior when there's not enough "probable cause" to arrest that person. So in a decision called *Terry v. Ohio,* the court said police who have a "reasonable suspicion" do not violate someone's rights by detaining that person just long enough for the officer to find out whether a crime was, or is being, committed.

The *Terry* decision said police also are justified in patting down such suspects, moving their hands over a suspect's outer clothing to make sure they are unarmed.

"The purpose of this limited search is not to discover evidence of crime, but to allow the officer to pursue his investigation without fear of violence," is how the Court explained it, emphasizing that any such search must be "strictly limited . . . to that which is necessary for the discovery of weapons which might be used to harm the officer or others nearby."

In his *Terry* opinion for the court, Warren acknowledged that minority groups, "particularly Negroes," had complained of wholesale harassment by police. He cited, in a footnote, a presidential commission report indicating that a growing number of police departments were encouraging officers to "routinely stop and question persons on the street who are unknown to them, who are suspicious, or whose purpose for being abroad is not readily evident."

The report said the frequency with which "frisking" comprises a part of such field investigations varied greatly with the locale of such encounters.

In addition to the *Terry* exception, the warrant requirement was waived by the "plain view" doctrine created by the Court that allows police without warrants to seize obviously illegal objects on sight, as long as the officers are somewhere they have the lawful authority to be and the illegality is obvious.

These legal theorems were familiar but only in the abstract to Moriarty, Dickerson's lawyer. A public defender for all of one month, she was fresh from the University of Minnesota's law school when she drew his case as her first felony assignment. She later recalled feeling "very strongly" that Dickerson's rights had been violated.

Judge Lynn did not agree, and ruled that Rose's stop and search had been justified. The seized crack cocaine could be used as evidence against Dickerson, the judge said, because its seizure was based on a "plain feel" exception to the Fourth Amendment's warrant requirement, an exception comparable to that for weapons or illegal substances— contraband—found "in plain view."

The suppression-of-evidence fight over, a perfunctory stipulated-facts trial before Judge Lynn ended in Dickerson's conviction March 7. The following May, he was sentenced to two years probation. Under Minnesota law, the sentence, along with the underlying charge, was wiped out when Dickerson successfully completed his probationary period. But Moriarty did not wait that long.

As a newcomer to the county public defender's office, she had not yet inherited the heavy load of cases endured by her colleagues. "I had the time to put a lot of work in on Tim's case, write a lot of memos suggesting how we could follow up with an appeal," Moriarty said years later. "Here is a young black guy who lives in the neighborhood. Merely because he comes out of that building, he's suspicious. He might have been stopped if he had been white, but you don't find this kind of a drug stop in a white neighborhood. I think the racial aspect played a role. That's why I felt it was so important we challenge this stop and search."

Dickerson's appeal was handled by Peter W. Gorman, an appellate court specialist in the public defender's office, who in April 1991 won a reversal of the conviction. A state appeals court refused to adopt the plain feel exception, and concluded that Rose's search had gone beyond the limits defined in *Terry v. Ohio*.

State prosecutors appealed, but the Minnesota Supreme Court, without hearing arguments, upheld the appeals court's ruling in March 1992. "Because we do not believe the senses of sight and touch are equivalent, we decline to extend the plain view doctrine to the sense of touch," a four-to-three majority of the state's highest court ruled. "The sense of touch is inherently less immediate and less reliable than the sense of sight. . . . But even more important, the sense of touch is far more intrusive into the personal privacy that is at the core of the Fourth Amendment. . . . Observing something that is held out to plain view is not a search at all. Physically touching a person cannot be considered anything but a search."

Writing for herself and two other dissenters, Justice M. Jeanne Coyne noted that other courts, both state and federal, already had upheld plain feel seizures when the police officer had discovered criminal evidence while making a *Terry v. Ohio* patdown.

"It is well to remind ourselves occasionally that law enforcement is not a game in which liberty triumphs whenever the policeman is defeated," Justice Coyne wrote. "Certainly, evidence obtained as the result of any unreasonable search or seizure should be excluded. But a policeman should not be compelled to ignore what his senses—whether sight, sound, smell, taste or touch—tell him in clear and unmistakable language."

The close vote and the conflicting conclusions among state and federal courts convinced Hennepin county attorney Michael O. Freeman and his staff that Dickerson's case might be an attractive one for review by the nation's highest court.

Soon after the state Supreme Court ruling, Gorman began hearing rumors that county prosecutors were at work preparing an appeal to the United States Supreme Court. He later recalled being greatly relieved when the sixty-day deadline for filing such an appeal, officially called a petition for a writ of certiorari, had passed without incident. Then a colleague informed him the relevant deadline was not sixty, but ninety, days.

But even after learning that the county attorney's staff had, indeed, sought review from the nation's highest court in June 1992, Gorman remained confident his victory would be left intact. Dickerson had completed his probationary sentence a month before and the record of his conviction was to be expunged, so neither the state nor Dickerson still had any stake in the outcome of such an appeal, Gorman figured.

In the first fourteen pages of his response brief to the appeal in *State of Minnesota v. Dickerson,* Gorman urged the Supreme Court, which is confined to deciding "cases and controversies," to find that no lasting controversy remained. They were winning arguments, Gorman thought.

On October 5, 1992, the first day of the Supreme Court's 1992–93 term, Gorman received an unpleasant surprise. The Court had granted review to the appeal prepared for Freeman's office by Assistant County Attorney Beverly J. Wolfe. The question her petition presented was, even if wordy, straightforward: Does the Fourth Amendment to the United States Constitution permit a "plain feel" exception to the warrant requirement clause for seizures of objects where a police officer develops, through the sense of touch during a lawful pat down, probable cause to believe that the suspect possesses contraband or other evidence of a crime?

"This case extends *Terry* to the next logical step—that the Fourth Amendment permits police engaged in a lawful touching to rely upon their sense of touch to determine if an object is contraband or other evidence of a crime," Wolfe wrote. But her brief offered no view as to how long—a few seconds, a few minutes or longer—prosecutors believed a lawful touching could last.

Like most appellate lawyers, Gorman had always dreamed of arguing a case before the United States Supreme Court. But being the respondent—the winner of the lower court ruling being reviewed—in a Fourth Amendment case before a court widely viewed as increasingly hostile to protections asserted under the amendment was not his ideal scenario. He remembers his first reaction to hearing the news that he'd be traveling to Washington to defend his victories in the Dickerson case: "Aw shit, there goes two and a half years of work."

Meanwhile, Tim Dickerson was being kept up to date by his lawyer, Moriarty. "I wouldn't say he was really that interested in the case by then," she recalled. "He was kind of startled, though, when he saw his picture on the TV news. He's not the kind of person who likes to be singled out or in the limelight. He's somewhat shy."

Both Gorman and Freeman, who decided he would replace his assistant Wolfe and argue before the Supreme Court himself, devoted huge amounts of time to preparing a second round of briefs and getting ready for their one-hour, in-person appearance before the Court. Most of a lawyer's work in any appellate court is in preparing written briefs. But each of the 110 or so cases granted Supreme Court review each year also are argued before the nine Justices in the majestic courtroom that offers virtually the only public view of their cloistered professional lives.

Gorman and Freeman were told the Dickerson case would be the first argued March 3, 1993.

"We put three hundred hours into that case, in writing briefs and going through the mock arguments getting ready for the real thing. It was an incredible professional experience, one that challenged every fiber of my being," says Freeman.

Gorman, too, was tested by mock sessions in which law professors or public defender colleagues zipped questions at him and critiqued his responses. At each of four such sessions, Gorman was advised to spend no time during his oral argument making what he once considered his strongest point—the Court's lack of jurisdiction because the case became moot when Dickerson finished his probationary sentence and became eligible to have the conviction expunged.

Even if the conviction were reinstated, it now would no longer exist, the public defender had been prepared to argue. But he remembers being told, "They granted review so they obviously found your mootness argument defective." He decided not to mention mootness.

Neither of the adversaries ever had argued before the Supreme Court, but both made a point of attending argument sessions as spectators as part of their preparations. Nevertheless, both men remember being nervous on the morning of their argument.

Sitting at the lawyers' table just steps from the imposing mahogany bench, Freeman was joined by Richard Seamon, an assistant United States solicitor general representing the federal government. The Justice Department, as a friend of the Court, had submitted a written brief urging it to reinstate Dickerson's conviction, and had been given ten minutes of Minnesota's allotted half hour to make its pitch.

(In addition to the briefs filed by the actual parties to a lawsuit, the Supreme Court permits parties not directly connected to a case to file briefs as outside advisers to the Court. Such briefs are known as *amicus curiae* (for "friend of the Court") briefs. They are typically written by public interest groups, trade associations, governmental entities, corporations, and private persons whose interests will be affected by the outcome of the litigation. The Justice Department's Office of the Solicitor General frequently files such friend of the Court briefs on behalf of the United States Government.)

The case had attracted only three other friend-of-the-court briefs, far fewer than the average. Minnesota's appeal was supported by Americans for Effective Law Enforcement, joined by the International Association of Chiefs of Police and other law enforcement officials.

Supporting Dickerson were briefs submitted by the American Civil Liberties Union and the National Association of Criminal Defense Lawyers.

Freeman and his allies had to be buoyed by their prospects. The court under Chief Justice William H. Rehnquist had shown no great warmth in recent years to arguments aimed at corralling police powers. The Chief Justice was comfortable giving considerable discretion to officers in the field who acted reasonably, and Freeman believed strongly that Rose had acted reasonably in his confrontation with Dickerson. Freeman also knew that Rehnquist's views in criminal law cases most often were those of at least five of the nine Justices—all the votes he needed.

Gorman recognized he had an uphill struggle, but thought his arguments, too, might attract five votes. Justice Antonin Scalia, although considered the Court's leading conservative, had written for the Court five years before, when it refused to expand one avenue of police authority to search for evidence without court warrants.

In that case, police in Phoenix, Arizona, were searching an apartment from which a bullet had been fired through the floor into an apartment below, injuring a resident. They were looking for the assailant, the weapon, and possibly more injured people. They found three guns, a makeshift mask and some expensive stereo equipment.

One officer, thinking the equipment looked out of place in the low-rent, unkempt apartment, lifted some of the components to check their serial numbers to determine whether they might be stolen. They were.

Police left, obtained a court warrant and seized the equipment as contraband. State courts ruled that the seizure was unlawful because police had no court warrant when they entered the apartment the first time, and checking the serial numbers had nothing to do with making sure there was no gunman or injured person there. In the Supreme Court, Arizona prosecutors argued that the stereo equipment had been in plain view so no warrant was needed to check the serial numbers.

Scalia didn't buy that argument, writing that lifting the equipment to look at the numbers went beyond what the Court previously had allowed under its plain view doctrine. "A search is a search even if it happens to disclose nothing but the bottom of a turntable," he wrote in the case called *Arizona v. Hicks*. Scalia conceded that the ruling could help the guilty, but added, "There is nothing new in the realization that the Constitution sometimes insulates the criminality of a few in order to protect the privacy of us all."

Those words gave Gorman some hope that Scalia and Justice Byron R. White, who had joined Scalia's opinion in 1987, might see Rose's touchy-feely police work as carrying the *Terry* doctrine too far. Gorman thought he might get the votes of Justices Harry A. Blackmun and John Paul Stevens, the Court's two most liberal members but no pushovers for defendants' rights in criminal justice cases. The possibility also existed that he could get some help from the Court's centrist conservatives, Justices Sandra Day O'Connor, Anthony M. Kennedy, and David H. Souter.

He mentally had written off Rehnquist and, to a certain extent, the newest Justice, Clarence Thomas.

Freeman led off, his voice steady, but not quite sure what to do with his hands while he spoke. "This case has been called a plain touch, a plain feel or plain view case. But when all the labels are set aside, this Court must decide whether police officers in the field, under a variety of circumstances, may continue using all their experience, all of their knowledge and all of their senses in arriving at probable-cause determinations," he said.

Freeman managed to call Rose's search a "limited, careful and reasonable" one "well within the limits of the *Terry v. Ohio* doctrine" before the first interruption came. "He went a little bit further" is what the state court found, said Souter.

Yes, Freeman said, "but we believe the court erred."

The prosecutor knew to expect interruptions, but he was surprised how quickly he had been cut off. His friend and fellow Minnesota prosecutor Jack Tunheim, in the courtroom that day, had actually timed it, Freeman later recalled. "Forty-seven seconds into the thing and boom."

Freeman contended that Rose's realization that Dickerson was carrying crack cocaine occurred at the precise moment he knew there was no gun, prompting Kennedy to inquire just how willing Freeman was to let slightly slower-thinking police officers reach the same conclusion.

"Now, can he linger for three or four seconds to determine whether or not it might be contraband?" Kennedy asked. Freeman was ready with his most ambitious gambit. "Your honor, he could, under the concept of a continuing search based on reasonable suspicion. This court in the discussion beginning in *Terry* and extending to *Arizona v. Hicks* . . . suggested that if, in fact, a reasonable suspicion existed in the mind of the police officer that, in fact, a limited additional investigation might occur under four criteria."

Freeman took a slight breath and continued, "First, the officer . . ." He got no further before Kennedy interrupted.

"That would be an extension of our precedents, I take it?"

"That would be."

"Thank you."

There appeared to be no sentiment for making this case the vehicle for letting police use a stop justified by *Terry* as a launching pad for a full-blown search, and Freeman decided to move on.

The loquacious Scalia interrupted to suggest that the *Terry* decision might have created an arbitrarily drawn line for police conduct. "Why shouldn't we adopt another arbitrary rule?" he asked Freeman. "You get [to use as trial evidence] weapons, you don't get anything else. If you're lucky enough to find crack cocaine, well, it's tough luck. You shouldn't have been looking anyway."

Freeman tried replying but got out only a partial sentence before another line of questioning interrupted him. "But Your Honor," he began in response to Scalia, "the problem with crack cocaine and what it's causing in the streets and among the people . . ."

"If I had been able to finish that sentence," Freeman said months later, "I would have told the Court that we in law enforcement see the crime, the carnage and the lives ruined by crack. I think it's important the Court know what's out there."

Seamon rose to argue next, and quickly made clear that the Justice

Department also had no desire to tell police nationwide they could bootstrap *Terry* stops into searches for drugs. "Suppose the officer determines it is not a weapon, may he proceed further to determine whether it's contraband if there is just a few seconds involved and it is not intrusive into the interior of the garment?" Seamon was asked. "No, he may not," was his answer.

Seamon's argument was a narrow one: The seizure was lawful because Rose had probable cause to suspect the object he touched through Dickerson's jacket was crack cocaine just at the moment he concluded it was not a weapon.

Toward the end of Seamon's ten minutes, several Justices voiced curiosity about the size of the package taken from Dickerson's pocket. Neither the cellophane wrapping nor the crack cocaine had been introduced as evidence at Dickerson's stipulated-facts trial, and there had been no testimony about the contraband's size. "I never saw it," Moriarty recalled. "I should have gotten the size into the record but never did. That was my mistake."

At one point in the trial court proceedings, Moriarty referred to the seized contraband as perhaps being as big as a pea or a marble. The "marble" description found its way into the state supreme court's decision.

But Gorman had made a point of seeing it, and discovered it to be much smaller than a marble. "I took an up-close Polaroid of the crack. At its largest, its one-fourth or five-sixteenths of an inch, and perhaps as small as one-thirty-second of an inch. We're talking about a very, very minuscule thing."

During the oral argument, Seamon was asked if the seized drug was "the size of a piece of gum, you know a Chiclet or something." He said the package was certainly quite small. Scalia followed that up with conjecture about what might have passed through Rose's mind when he felt something that small.

"If he could have been in doubt that this was not a . . . you know, a sixgun, you're always going to allow the search and seizure of contraband is what it means," Scalia said. "And certainly, the policeman's not going to come in and say, 'Oh yeah, I knew right away it wasn't a gun but I felt around to make sure what it was, I was just curious.' He's going to say, 'You know, I wasn't sure what it was and by the time I found out what it was I said gee, not only isn't it a gun, it's crack cocaine.' What we will be authorizing, effectively, is search and seizure . . . stop, search and seizure for contraband. Realistically, that's what we're talking about here, isn't it?"

Seamon sought to assure Scalia, "That's not what we're talking about, in our view." But Gorman, the last of the three lawyers to address the court, thought Scalia had put it well. Allowing police to seize drugs in a limited search aimed at weapons "means that any time an officer is in the vicinity of a troubled part of town and sees someone, that he can search that person for drugs rather than for weapons."

Gorman asserted that such a ruling "would allow an enormous potential for pretextual abuse by police officers" and said later that he winced when the Chief Justice immediately asked, "What's the matter with that?"

Scalia evoked a gust of courtroom laughter when Gorman tried to distinguish between the senses of sight and touch. The public defender said he could see the smallish microphones on the bench in front of each Justice and recognize them for what they were, but might not be able to identify them while blindfolded and touching them.

"On the other hand, you might see a Hollywood set that looks like New York City, and then you go up and feel it, and by God . . ." Scalia suggested before his voice was drowned out by his audience's reaction.

Gorman had no comeback. "I remember thinking to myself that this guy thinks he's a real comedian," Gorman said later. "My next thought was what the hell do I say now." Had he thought of it at the time, Gorman said he would have told Scalia that on closer inspection of the movie set, it would have been his eyes, not his hands, disclosing his initial mistake.

Gorman's pre-argument handlers had been right about mootness being a lost cause. The issue evoked not one question from the bench.

But the public defender nevertheless thought the argument had gone well. "They beat Freeman up pretty good," he said with a chuckle.

Freeman, for his part, came away from the argument session full of confidence. "The P.D. was really sliced up," he remarked.

Although he agreed with Moriarty that Dickerson's case had a racial aspect, Gorman felt constrained about initiating any discussion of it before the Justices. The fact that Dickerson was a black man in a largely black neighborhood had not been made an issue in the state appellate courts. And besides, Gorman's research told him such a seed might not find any fertile ground.

That research had included numerous articles in newspapers and legal journals, contending that police officers treat black suspects more aggressively than white suspects because they consider them more dangerous. In one such article, Boston University law professor Tracey Maclin called the *Terry* decision "a significant setback in the fight against discriminatory police tactics."

"Because of the loophole created in *Terry* and a subsequent line of cases expanding the contours of the *Terry* exception," Maclin wrote in a 1991 article for the *Valparaiso University Law Review,* "police officers are now free to accost, detain and search individuals on criteria that have a chameleon-like way of adapting to any particular set of observations. While law enforcement officials deny it, in many places it appears that race still has much to do with who is chosen for investigatory detentions and searches."

Those "places" most often are inner cities marred by a seemingly endless cycle of poverty and crime, home to those minorities occupying the bottom rungs of the American socioeconomic ladder. Frictions between these residents and the police are old and numerous, a fact of life on the streets not only in the nation's largest cities but in suburban and rural towns as well. "A dangerous, humiliating, sometimes fatal encounter with the police is almost a rite of passage for a black man in the United States," a commentator observed in the *New York Times* editorial pages in 1989.

The war on drugs is part of that world and increasing attention is being paid to the statistical disparities between the number of whites and blacks arrested by police on drug charges.

A study by the newspaper *USA Today,* based on a computer analysis of 1991 drug arrest statistics for the FBI's Uniform Crime Report, showed blacks are four times as likely as whites nationwide to be arrested on drug charges. In Minneapolis, the study showed, blacks are twenty-two times as likely as whites to be arrested on drug charges.

Freeman, noting that Hennepin County accounts for 40 percent of all Minnesota's crimes, is familiar with the study's findings and doesn't think it indicates any racist attitude among police. It's pretty clear in Minneapolis and elsewhere, he said, that crack cocaine is used predominantly by blacks in poor neighborhoods. Critics such as Moriarty, however, contend the statistics reflect the reality of the streets: blacks are far more likely to be viewed with suspicion and stopped by police.

Given the facts of the matter, should the Supreme Court take into account a criminal suspect's race when judging the reasonableness of police conduct? Gorman's research showed that although Tracey Maclin believes the Court should, he did not think the Court would reach that conclusion. "Instead of acknowledging the reality that exists on the street, the court hides behind a legal fiction," Maclin wrote. "The court constructs Fourth Amendment principles assuming that there is an average, hypothetical person who interacts with the police officers. This notion is naive, it produces distorted Fourth Amendment rules and ignores the real world that police officers and black men live in."

Gorman also thought it would do no good to air the debate at the Supreme Court in Dickerson's case. "Had Thurgood Marshall still been on the Court, the stuff I was reading showed he might have raised the racial question. If he hadn't, I might have," he said later. But Marshall was gone, and who on the Court was going to pay attention? Perhaps Clarence Thomas, Marshall's successor and the only black Justice? Gorman said he never considered that a possibility.

Thomas, the first person born after World War II to be appointed to the Court, has roots in the poor, rural South. Born to a teenage mother in Pinpoint, Georgia, in 1948, Thomas was taken to Savannah at an early age to be raised by his maternal grandparents, devout Catholics. After attending a succession of parochial schools and, for a brief time, a seminary, he earned an undergraduate degree from Holy Cross College in Massachusetts and a law degree from Yale University.

He had grown up in a segregated South undergoing, with great reluctance, fundamental changes. Thomas remembered the wounds inflicted on his grandparents by racial bigots. He left the seminary, where he had been the only black student, because of the racial taunts he received. He later discovered that life for a young black man in the North was no better. "It was more difficult for me to live in Massachusetts than it was for me to live in Savannah," Thomas has said. "In Savannah, the rules were indeed clear."

Right out of Yale's law school, Thomas moved to Missouri and worked as an assistant state attorney general. Three years later, he left for a job as a lawyer for the Monsanto Company for a couple of years before moving to Washington to work for Senator John Danforth, a prominent Republican who considered Thomas his protégé. Thomas moved on to become an assistant secretary for civil rights in the Department of Education and then, in 1982, was appointed chairman of the Equal Employment Opportunity Commission.

In his years of government service, Thomas built a reputation as one of a new breed of politically active and outspoken black men, a social conservative noted for opposing conventional affirmative action and welfare programs. But his embrace of black self-help did not make him blind to the sometimes frightening realities of being black in a white-dominated society. Talking about his life in the nation's capital, Thomas once complained, "In my own neighborhood, I used to get stopped by the cops."

His conservative credentials attracted attention at the highest levels of government, and in 1990 President George Bush appointed him to the United States Court of Appeals for the District of Columbia Circuit. He easily won Senate confirmation.

Fifteen months later, Bush had bigger plans for Thomas. When Thurgood Marshall, civil rights icon and the Supreme Court's first black Justice, announced his retirement because of failing health, the president quickly chose Thomas to replace Marshall. His confirmation by the Senate this time was anything but easy. Thomas proved a reluctant witness before the Senate Judiciary Committee, which split seven to seven in recommending his confirmation by the full Senate.

Thomas had backed away from some of his more controversial writings, and in one of his more compelling responses, had assured the committee that he would bring a unique sensitivity to the court. He told the senators that his appellate court office overlooked a street where prisoners, many of them black men, were brought to a District of Columbia courthouse to face the criminal charges against them.

Thomas said his thought at those times was always "There but for the grace of God go I."

As agents for the president and Danforth were busy counting noses in advance of a vote by the full Senate, allegations of a University of Oklahoma law professor, Anita Hill, were made public. She said that Thomas, her superior at the Education Department and the EEOC, sexually harassed her by persistently asking for dates and making lewd comments.

Forced to reopen the confirmation hearings, the Senate committee delved into the allegations and Thomas's impassioned denials before a riveted national television audience. Never before had pubic hairs and a pornographic movie star named Long Dong Silver been part of a Supreme Court confirmation process. Vendors made a killing on "I Believe Her" and "I Believe Him" T-shirts.

In the end, Thomas won confirmation by a fifty-two-to-forty-eight vote. But at what cost? Legal scholars predicted he might never live down the ignominy of having to answer such allegations. Thomas, in his second round of appearances before the Senate committee, assessed the toll in terms that sounded as if he no longer cared about being confirmed:

"In my 43 years on this earth I have been able with the help of others and with the help of God to defy poverty, avoid prison, overcome segregation, bigotry, racism and obtain one of the finest educations available in this country, but I have not been able to overcome this process. This is worse than any obstacle or anything that I have ever faced.

"I am proud of my life, proud of what I have done and what I have accomplished, proud of my family. And this process, this process is trying to destroy it all. No job is worth what I have been through. No job. No horror in my life has been so debilitating. Confirm me if you want. Don't confirm me if you are so led, but let this process end. Let me and my family regain our lives."

Once confirmed, Thomas moved his family from their suburban Virginia home to one much further from Washington. They avoided public places. Friends described the new Justice as seeking refuge in his work, and that work provided few surprises as Thomas quickly joined the Court's most conservative wing.

Thomas's votes in two decisions particularly galled civil libertarians. In *Withrow v. Williams,* he joined Scalia in seeking to drastically curtail federal court access for state prison inmates who want to challenge their criminal convictions. Scalia, joined by Thomas, said the Court should not allow any such federal court appeal, no matter the claim raised, if an inmate had received a full and fair hearing on that claim in state appellate courts. No other Justice endorsed that view.

In *Hudson v. McMillian,* announced only four months after he joined the Court in October of 1991, Thomas dissented from the Court's ruling that unnecessary force by a prison guard violates the Eighth Amendment's ban on cruel and unusual punishment even if no serious injury results. Writing for himself and Scalia, Thomas accused the Court of trying to stretch constitutional protections too far.

"Abusive behavior by prison guards is deplorable conduct that properly evokes outrage and contempt," he wrote. "But that does not mean that it is invariably unconstitutional. The Eighth Amendment is not, and should not be turned into, a National Code of Prison Regulation."

Thomas likened inmate claims of excessive force to lawsuits over prison conditions, a comparison Justice O'Connor criticized. "To deny the difference between punching a prisoner in the face and serving him unappetizing food is to ignore the concepts of dignity, civilized standards, humanity and decency that animate the Eighth Amendment," she wrote.

Thomas's opinion, and O'Connor's reaction to it, established him as a law-and-order hard-liner. "Going in, we knew about Thomas what the world knew," Gorman recalled about arguing Tim Dickerson's case. "We pretty much had written him off."

When Dickerson's case was argued, Thomas sat passively and silently in his black leather chair. He asked no questions.

The gestation period of a Supreme Court decision varies. Some take only a month; most take several months at least. Almost all cases are decided during the same October-to-June Court term in which they are argued. In *Dickerson v. Minnesota,* the Court announced its decision on June 7, 1993, three months after it had been argued.

Justice White, who had written the opinion for the Court, told the courtroom audience that morning that the Minnesota supreme court decision had been affirmed but offered little else. When other members of the Court have written for the Court's majority, they offer brief summaries of the case, the legal issues involved, and the conclusions enunciated in the decision. White, whose abbreviated announcements customarily leave lawyers and tourists present in the dark, does not.

An affirmance of the state supreme court's ruling meant victory for Dickerson. More significantly, White's fourteen-page opinion also gave police nationwide a victory, one that could improve their odds big-time in the war on drugs.

"The question presented today is whether police officers may seize nonthreatening contraband detected during a protective patdown search of the sort permitted by *Terry,*" White wrote. "We think the answer is clearly that they may, so long as the officer's search stays within the bounds marked by *Terry.*"

White, in undramatic phrases, portrayed the Court's conclusion as the logical outgrowth of previous high court rulings. "We have already held that police officers, at least under certain circumstances, may seize contraband detected during the lawful execution of a *Terry* search," he wrote.

As an example, White cited a Michigan case decided in 1983 in which police approached a man who had driven his car into a ditch and who appeared to be drunk. Police noticed a knife on the floorboard of his car, so they patted him down and inspected the car's interior for other weapons. During that search, they found an open pouch with marijuana in it. The Supreme Court upheld that search and seizure, saying police are justified in such roadside encounters not only to pat down the suspect for weapons but to check out the passenger compartment of his car.

Writing for the Court in that 1983 decision in *Michigan v. Long,* Justice O'Connor had added: "If, while conducting a legitimate *Terry* search of the interior of an automobile, the officer should, as here, discover contraband other than weapons, he clearly cannot be required to ignore the contraband, and the Fourth Amendment does not require its suppression in such circumstances." O'Connor had written that such a conclusion was supported by the plain view doctrine.

Now, ten years later, White borrowed snippets from earlier opinions to define the doctrine anew: "If police are lawfully in a position from which they view an object, if its incriminating character is immediately apparent, and if the officers have a lawful right to access to the object, they may seize it without a warrant." White's opinion emphasized that seizures cannot be justified if the incriminating nature of what was seen was not immediately apparent.

White also cited the doctrine's "obvious application by analogy" to cases in which the sense of touch, not sight, is used. "The rationale of the plain view doctrine is that if contraband is left in open view and is observed by a police officer from a lawful vantage point, there has been no invasion of a legitimate expectation of privacy and thus no 'search' within the meaning of the Fourth Amendment—or at least no search independent of the initial intrusion that gave the police officers their vantage point," he wrote. "The same can be said of tactile discoveries of contraband. If a police officer lawfully pats down a suspect's outer clothing and feels an object whose contour or mass makes its identity immediately apparent, there has been no invasion of the suspect's privacy beyond that already authorized by the officer's search for weapons; if the object is contraband, its warrantless seizure would be justified by the same practical considerations that inhere in the plain view context."

Acknowledging the Minnesota supreme court's statement that touch is less reliable than sight and more intrusive into personal privacy,

White added a mildly worded rejection. "We have a somewhat different view," he wrote. The *Terry* decision already allowed police to seize guns and other weapons based on their sense of touch, he noted, and even if it were true that the sense of touch generally is less reliable than the sense of sight, "that only suggests that officers will less often be able to justify seizures of unseen contraband."

And the state court's concern about touch being more intrusive, White wrote, "is inapposite in light of the fact that the intrusion the Court fears has already been authorized by the lawful search for weapons. The seizure of an item whose identity is already known occasions no further invasion of privacy."

Lost somewhere, for it surely was nowhere to be found in White's opinion, was the warning voiced by Justice Scalia three months earlier during the oral argument session, that embracing a plain feel doctrine could allow police officers with an enhanced sense of touch or slightly faulty memories routinely to stop and search for drugs without first having probable cause.

No police officer, Scalia might say, henceforth could be expected to say anything but what the Court had required. The police officer's most likely testimony would be, "I was patting down the suspect and as my hand touched this object through his clothing it was immediately apparent to me not only that this wasn't a gun but that it was crack cocaine."

That's not what Rose had said of his encounter with Dickerson, however, and the Court had to apply its newly adopted doctrine to the particular set of facts before it. "The dispositive question before this Court is whether the officer who conducted the search was acting within the lawful bounds marked by *Terry* at the time he gained probable cause to believe that the lump in respondent's jacket was contraband," was how White framed the inquiry.

The abbreviated trial record had not established precisely just when it dawned on Rose the tiny object in Dickerson's pocket was not a gun but a piece of crack cocaine. But the state supreme court decided that Rose had identified it as crack only after "squeezing, sliding and otherwise manipulating the contents of the defendant's pocket," after realizing the pocket contained no weapon.

That was enough for White. "Under the state Supreme Court's interpretation of the record before it, it is clear that the Court was correct in holding that the police officer in this case overstepped the bounds of the "strictly circumscribed" search for weapons allowed under Terry. . . . Here, the officer's continued exploration of respondent's pocket after having concluded that it contained no weapon was unrelated to . . . the protection of the police officer and others nearby," he concluded.

White's fourteen-page opinion relegated Gorman's claim of mootness to one of four footnotes. Yes, the charges against Dickerson had been dismissed after his successful completion of probation. But Minnesota law says that a nonpublic record of those charges "shall be retained by the department of public safety for the purpose of use by the courts in determining the merits of subsequent proceedings" against Dickerson. The state supreme court had construed that law to allow "use of the record should a defendant have future difficulty with the law."

"Thus, we must conclude that reinstatement of the record of the charges against respondent would carry collateral legal consequences and that, therefore, a live controversy remains," White wrote.

The vote was nine to zero for adopting the plain feel doctrine, but three Justices objected to upholding the state court ruling that left Dickerson totally off the hook. Chief Justice Rehnquist, in a short opinion dissenting from that part of the Court's decision, noted that the state trial court record was "imprecise and not directed expressly to the question of the officer's probable cause to believe that the lump was contraband."

Rehnquist voted to send the case back to the state's highest court for further study of that point. The Chief Justice's opinion was joined by Justices Blackmun and Thomas.

Scalia, who signed on to White's opinion for the Court, felt compelled to speak for himself in a four-page concurring opinion. He began by asserting that "it is a fundamental principle of constitutional adjudication that the terms in the Constitution must be given the meaning ascribed to them at the time of their ratification." So an unreasonable search or seizure, Scalia wrote, is one that would have been deemed unreasonable when the Fourth Amendment was ratified in 1791.

Liberals scoff at the doctrine, preferring to believe that the Constitution and the individual rights it confers is a living document adaptable to changing times.

Scalia's first paragraph, therefore, must have had his many liberal critics shaking their heads and muttering about this great eighteenth-century jurist two hundred years behind his time. But he next launched into a truly remarkable discussion, showing the libertarian, get-government-off-the-people's-back strain that occasionally surfaces in the jurisprudence of the high court's most impetuous conservative.

"My problem in the present case is that I am not entirely sure that the physical search—the "frisk"—that produced the evidence at issue here complied with that [1791] constitutional standard," Scalia wrote. "The decision of ours that gave approval to such searches," he noted of the *Terry* ruling, "made no serious attempt to determine compliance within traditional standards, but rather, according to the style of this Court at the time, simply adjudged that such a search was 'reasonable' by current estimations."

Terry allows police to stop and frisk suspicious people, Scalia noted, but common law and colonial practices suggest that only the stop would have been deemed reasonable. "I am unaware . . . of any precedent for a physical search of a person thus temporarily detained for questioning," he wrote. "Sometimes, of course, the temporary detention of a suspicious character would be elevated to a full custodial arrest on probable cause—as, for instance, when a suspect was unable to provide a sufficient accounting of himself. At that point, it is clear that the common law would permit not just a protective "frisk" but a full physical search incident to the arrest."

But routine patdowns of someone stopped for questioning? "I frankly doubt . . . whether the fiercely proud men who adopted our Fourth Amendment would have allowed themselves to be subjected, on mere suspicion of being armed and dangerous, to such indignity." Maybe the Fourteenth Amendment, adopted in 1868 and the basis for applying the Fourth Amendment to the states, permits the frisk, Scalia speculated, or perhaps it was some more recent legal phenomenon.

If the Court were once again to scrutinize its *Terry* decision, he wrote, there might be good grounds for getting rid of it. But the constitutionality of a patdown search for weapons was not an issue presented in Dickerson's case, Scalia wrote, and he was assuming the patdown, or frisk, was valid. Therefore, any evidence incidentally discovered during it would be admissible.

It was early afternoon in Minneapolis and Mary Moriarty was in court when she learned from a friend about the Supreme Court decision. "She gave a thumbs-up sign and said they had ruled my way," Moriarty recalls. Dickerson's conviction was once again overturned.

Gorman and Freeman had learned of the decision earlier in the day and both lawyers found cause for celebration.

"They won the battle, but we won the war," was Freeman's assessment, one that long afterward still angered Gorman.

"No one won any war," the public defender said. "We each won a skirmish, and the legal fight will continue as lower courts try to apply what the Supreme Court said in this case.

Freeman, interviewed later in the summer after the high court's *Minnesota v. Dickerson* ruling, said courts in his state already had ruled against defendants in two *Dickerson*-type cases.

"In one, the big issue was whether the officer violated the suspect's rights when he 'scrunched' the clothing and discovered drugs. The state court said that was okay. The officer had testified that the content of the pocket was 'immediately apparent' and those were the magic words," Freeman said.

But Freeman agreed with Gorman that more court decisions, fleshing out the dos and don'ts of police conduct in such confrontations, were inevitable.

The legal battle—one seen by police as a struggle for control of the streets and viewed by civil libertarians as a preemptive strike against the onslaught of a police state—would continue.

CHAPTER FIVE

The story is told of two Puritans on a ship approaching the New World, one saying to the other, "Religious freedom is my immediate goal. . . . But my long-range objective is to go into real estate."

Since Puritan times the nation has incessantly wrestled with the interplay of the spiritual and the secular in public life. Some of those who forged this nation saw religion and government as natural partners. Roger Williams thought it appropriate for the state to "countenance, encourage, and supply" ministers. Others saw religion as a kind of public utility, like the gas or electric company, that should be supported by government because it in turn provided government with support—with the moral and spiritual content necessary to form a decent and just community.

Yet others saw danger in the collaboration. Thomas Jefferson advocated a "a wall of separation between Church and State." James Madison sought to keep the church and the government apart because of the "tendency to a usurpation on one side or the other, or to a corrupting coalition or alliance between them." These values were distilled in the language of the First Amendment, which emphatically prohibits laws "respecting an establishment of religion, or prohibiting the free exercise thereof." Yet another constitutional clause (Article VI) states that "no religious test shall be required as a qualification to any office or public trust under the United States."

In modern times the Supreme Court has toiled over what the concept of separation ought to mean. Much of the debate has centered on the connection between religion and the schools. For those Americans who resonate with Roger Williams and the importance of spirituality in the raising of children, the Court's pronouncements against prayer and other religious influences in schools has seemed godless and perverse. For separationists in the tradition of Jefferson and Madison, the

Court has often fallen short of imposing the fastidious neutrality they believe the First Amendment mandates.

On balance, the separationists have prevailed in recent decades. As the Supreme Court recently explained in a 1987 ruling in a case called *Edwards v. Aguillard,* in "no activity of the State is it more vital to keep out divisive forces than in its schools." And schools surely do have a powerful interest in rising above religious and political contests, an interest borne of the tension that exists between the pluralism of the student population and the inculcation inherent in the school's educational mission.

The Supreme Court has steadfastly required that the schoolchildren of America not be compelled, coerced, or subtly pressured to engage in activities whose predominant purpose or effect was to advance one set of religious beliefs over another, or to prefer a set of religious beliefs over no religion at all.

The Court has counseled against creating "a crucial symbolic link between government and religion, thereby enlisting—at least in the eyes of impressionable youngsters—the powers of government to the support of the religious denomination."

But how should we approach the issue of separation when a student attending a parochial school claims an entitlement to some form of state educational assistance that is routinely provided to students in public schools? On this issue the Court's jurisprudence has been hopelessly confused.

In an early case decided in 1947, *Everson v. Board of Education,* the Court held that parochial students could be provided with bus transportation to their schools, as part of a general program providing free bus transportation to all students, public and private. Providing this transportation did, in one sense, "aid" the parochial schools, because, in picking up the tab for bus transportation, the parochial schools and the parents of their students were relieved of an expense they would otherwise have been forced to subsume as part of the cost of the religious school enterprise. But the Court reasoned that religious institutions are entitled to the same public services that all citizens and institutions enjoy, such as police and fire protection, and that a general program of school bus transportation fitted that description. Since that decision, the Court has followed a tortuous path, approving of some types of aid, disapproving of others. These cases have forced many to wonder whether the ideal of public school "neutrality" regarding aid to religion is genuinely feasible.

Aaron Epstein's narrative describes one of recent episodes in this tale, a case involving the rights of a deaf student to public assistance for the services of an interpreter during that child's attendance at a Catholic high school.

—Editor

The Interpreter
and the Establishment Clause

AARON EPSTEIN

When . . . you ask a public employee to go to work and . . . convey to James
Zobrest that Jesus Christ was the son of God or that he died to save his sins, I
think that's active [government] involvement in a religious activity.—John C.
Richardson in oral argument of *Zobrest v. Catalina Foothills School District*

I can only stretch my imagination so far, but it goes to the breaking point when
I'm thinking of Jim's peers, these impressionable youngsters, saying something
like, awesome. Right here in chem lab, we're seeing a violation of the Establishment Clause of the First Amendment.—William B. Ball in oral argument
of *Zobrest v. Catalina Foothills School District*

First, let us be clear on one point. What lured Jim Zobrest to sign up
for four years at Salpointe Catholic High School wasn't Jesus Christ.
It was Michael Jordan. Or at least the spirit of Michael Jordan—which
arguably is a kind of religion among young Americans these days.

Most of all, Jim wanted to play basketball for Salpointe. "I thought it
was a better place to go," Jim said. "I liked the sports program there."
It was Jim's mother who thought he needed some religious training.

Had Jim registered at one of Tucson's public high schools instead
of Salpointe, there would have been no legal dispute, no five-to-four
decision of the Supreme Court in *Zobrest v. Catalina Foothills School
District*—and no story about a deaf boy and the constitutional principle
of separation of church and state.

Jim Zobrest has been severely deaf since infancy. A hearing aid helps,
but without a sign language interpreter it is virtually impossible for
him to learn and communicate. "I can hear music with heavy bass
sounds, but I can't hear the words," he explained in the slurred mono-
tone that is typical of those who have never heard the speech of others.
"I hear voices and sounds but not the words."

Jim's mother, Sandra, has fought for Jim's education all his life. When Jim was little, the Zobrests lived in Erie, Pennsylvania, where Jim got some early schooling at the Gertrude Barber Center for Exceptional Children. By a curious quirk of fate, his first speech therapist was Virginia Duncan, the daughter of lawyer William Bentley Ball of Harrisburg, Pennsylvania, a leading courtroom advocate of religious causes. Many years later, that connection led Ball to the highest court in the land to argue Jim's case.

Erie's education programs for the deaf didn't satisfy Mrs. Zobrest. She wanted her son to attend "mainstream" classes with kids who can hear. "They had a deaf classroom in the public school and they would put him in an art class and sit the deaf kids in the corner and that was their idea of mainstreaming," Mrs. Zobrest recalled scornfully. "There was nothing in Erie for him."

On a trip to Arizona to visit a relative, Mrs. Zobrest and her husband Larry, discovered the Arizona School for the Deaf and Blind, moved across the country and put Jim in the first grade. But Jim's five years at the segregated school for the handicapped left Mrs. Zobrest disappointed. "They didn't have history or social studies. He wanted to go to college. We had these goals for him and he wasn't going to be able to do that if he didn't get a better foundation. So we mainstreamed him in our school district and it was just wonderful. At first, the school district wasn't sure he was able to go into his grade level. And we fought for that."

"We knew that if the other kids are up here," she said, drawing her outstretched fingers across her forehead, "then Jim will work harder. He just didn't want to be different."

But Jim *is* different, and for him, as for many deaf people trying to live in two worlds, the dilemma is chronic and perpetually frustrating. He learned a form of sign language which tracks the grammar and word order of English sentences as spoken by the hearing. He shunned American Sign Language (ASL), a method of communication based primarily on visual concepts and extolled by a growing number of deaf separatists who consider it the wellspring of deaf culture, pride, and power.

"He is real isolated," Jim's mother explained. "He is not deaf 100 percent, he's not hearing 100 percent. He's been basically brought up with hearing people, but he doesn't quite fit in there because he's deaf. And because he's been brought up with hearing people and has their customs and their ways, he doesn't fit in with the deaf community either. He's in the middle."

One rain-drenching night in the winter of 1993, in the Zobrest family's sprawling home in an affluent suburb overlooking the flooded streets of Tucson, nineteen-year-old Jim poured out in sound and sign his feelings of social isolation: "I thought it was kind of impossible to communicate with some of the deaf people because they really don't know what's going on in the world. That's why I separated from deaf people. Now I realize they do understand. So I changed my old thoughts about deaf people. But I disagree with the ideas of the deaf community. They want to separate and do things their own way. I think they should learn to communicate correctly and shouldn't be separate."

In 1987 Jim and his parents ran headlong into a barrier of a different sort: the constitutional notion, based on centuries of European history, that if government and religion are not kept apart, each would suffer from interference by the other.

The legal dilemma arose when Jim's parents, who are Catholic, decided to send him to Salpointe, the highly regarded Catholic high school in Tucson. "I wanted him to go to a Catholic school," Jim's mother explained. "We tried religious education at the church. I interpreted, and the whole time at Mass, he'd say 'When is this going to be over? I'm hungry.' I really felt it had to be an everyday thing. I wasn't satisfied with what he was learning about his religion. It was a 'Do I have to go?' kind of thing. I went to a Catholic school and a Catholic college. I liked the atmosphere, the way religion is kind of included in the whole day. It's a real moral kind of atmosphere."

Terry Downey, an assistant superintendent at the Catalina Foothills public school district, was Jim's middle-school principal in 1988. "His mother came to me and asked, 'Will you pay for an interpreter for Jim as Salpointe?'" Downey recalled. "Now we're a public school system and we don't provide any services to parochial schools. It's not unconstitutional to bus students there but we just don't do it. For us, it's a pretty cut-and-dried thing. It's the law."

When consulted, Pima County deputy attorney JoAnn Sheperd thought so, too. She conceded that federal and state laws "require the provision of special education and certain related services to handicapped students attending non-public schools." But if a government-paid interpreter were to transmit religious views to a parochial school student, she said, "excessive entanglement of state and church may well result." The state attorney general agreed.

At Salpointe's cluster of well-tended buildings, Rev. Leo McCarthy, the school's genial principal, had a problem, too. The school had never had a deaf student before, lacked money for extra services, and didn't go out of its way to help the handicapped, Christian morality notwithstanding. "I guess the thinking is, this is the school that we have, and if you can fit into it, you're certainly welcome," Father Leo explained. "But if you need special services that we don't have, we're not necessarily going to provide them. There is a state school for the deaf and blind in town."

So, in 1988, Jim and his parents faced this dilemma: Send Jim to a public high school, where the taxpayers would absorb the $7,000 or $8,000 a year for a certified sign language interpreter, or enroll Jim at Salpointe and dip into the family savings. "I felt, why should he not be able to go to the school of his choice?" Mrs. Zobrest said. "We're being denied state services and funding because of his religious choice." The Zobrests sent Jim to Salpointe—and filed suit against the school district.

To Sandra and Larry Zobrest, the denial of an educational service so vital to her son's education was blatant religious discrimination. The Zobrests' suit asserted that the federal Individuals with Disabilities Education Act (IDEA), which requires public schools to provide special services to handicapped students, and the First Amendment guarantee of "the free exercise" of religion compelled Catalina Foothills to furnish an interpreter.

But a federal trial judge in Tucson ruled against them, declaring that church and state would become unconstitutionally entangled if a government-paid interpreter were to "act as a conduit for the religious inculcation of James." The Zobrests appealed to a three-judge panel of the United States Court of Appeals for the Ninth Circuit—and lost again in May 1992. Placing a public employee in a sectarian school would create a "symbolic union of government and religion," the appeals panel concluded.

The Zobrests headed for the Supreme Court, which agreed five months later to hear the case. It was one of three religious disputes on the Justices' 1992–93 calendar and aptly illustrated the persistent tension between the twin religious clauses written into the First Amendment.

One clause, the easier one to understand, bars laws "prohibiting the free exercise" of religion. Beginning in 1963, the Supreme Court construed that clause to forbid any law that discriminates against some or all religious beliefs, or limits religious conduct—unless the government proves that the law is "compelling" enough to be applied to religion. That analysis led the Court in the 1972 case of *Wisconsin v. Yoder* to bar a state from enforcing its public school attendance laws against the Amish for refusing to send their children to public high schools for religious reasons. Only government "interests of the highest order" could outweigh "legitimate claims to the free exercise of religion," the Court said then.

But in the 1990 case of *Employment Division v. Smith,* a Scalia-led majority sharply reduced the constitutional protection of religious freedom. This was the new rule: A generally applicable law that doesn't target a religion, such as a compulsory school attendance or drug statute, is valid—even if it outlaws or hampers a particular religious practice. Retreating from the liberal reasoning of *Wisconsin v. Yoder,* the Court declared that a general law could be upheld without proof that it meets a government need of the highest order. Thus, as the *Smith* case decided, state drug laws could bar Native Americans from using the drug peyote to communicate with "the Great Spirit," as they have for thousands of years.

A drumbeat of criticism swiftly followed. The *Smith* decision "reduces free exercise law to a shell of what it once was. It's devastating," said a lawyer for the American Jewish Congress, Amy Adelson. University of Chicago law professor Michael McConnell, a specialist in religion issues, complained that the Court had demonstrated both hostility toward religion and "an inordinate faith in government." Oliver S. Thomas, general counsel of the Baptist Joint Committee, traced increased public hostility toward religion to church financial scandals, a growing involvement of ministers in politics, sexual misconduct by clergymen, an increasing proportion of Americans without religious affiliations, and the proliferation of unpopular religious cults.

Certainly, no religious group could have been more unpopular than the South Florida followers of the Santería religion, whose tradition of animal sacrifice made them targets of Hialeah city ordinances prohibiting their ritual killing of ducks, chickens, guinea pigs, goats, and sheep. Santería combines the customs of the Yoruba people of West Africa and elements of Roman Catholicism. Spiritual power comes from a pantheon of as many as 1,700 orishas, or spirits, each blessed with a specialized link to God, each requiring the sacrifice of small animals for their survival. To believers in Santería, the blood of sacrifice is required to obtain divine releases of energy essential for gaining health, children, wisdom, and other benefits. The orisha called Ogun, a fierce warrior with bloodshot eyes, helps forge tools from materials of the earth and prefers red and white roosters. Oshun, the smiling maiden of rivers, swells the wombs of barren women with the joy of children and favors the sacrifice of white hens for best results.

Unpleasant as Santería's religious practices may be to modern sensibilities, its legal appeal was constitutionally irresistible. A week before deciding the *Zobrest* case, all nine Justices voted to strike down Hialeah's animal sacrifice laws. "Legislators may not devise mechanisms, overt or disguised, designed to persecute or oppress a religion or its practices," Justice Anthony M. Kennedy wrote for the Court. The case was notable, though, for Justice David H. Souter's call for a reexamination of the *Smith* decision. There is "a strong argument" that the Establishment Clause was intended to shield religious activities even from laws not aimed at religion, Souter observed.

The far more perplexing First Amendment provision bars laws "respecting an establishment of religion." After nearly a half century of Supreme Court interpretation, there remains profound disagreement about what the clause means—whether there is a Jeffersonian wall of separation between church and state, or a Rehnquistian volleyball net, or something in between. Some scholars argue that the Establishment Clause was written simply to prevent the national government from interfering with state-authorized religious practices existing when the First Amendment was proposed.

But in the seminal 1947 case of *Everson v. Board of Education,* Justice Hugo Black used the "wall of separation metaphor" and concluded that the Establishment Clause means that neither a state nor the federal government "can pass laws which aid one religion, aid all religions, or prefer one religion over another."

To navigate in such waters of neutrality, the Court developed a strict three-part test in the 1971 case of *Lemon v. Kurtzman.* The *Lemon* test, which its many critics believe to be aptly named, would strike down a law or government policy if it lacks a secular purpose, advances or inhibits religion, or fosters excessive government entanglement with religion.

For two decades, the Supreme Court has used the *Lemon* test to torpedo various efforts to provide government aid to parochial schools or reintroduce religious exercises into public schools. But four or five Justices appeared ready to scrap *Lemon* in 1993.

In school aid cases, Supreme Court rulings have been especially bewildering and controversial. A reader of these cases may understandably believe, as University of Virginia law professor A. E. Dick Howard remarked, "that he has stumbled into the forest of Hansel and Gretel, the birds having eaten all the crumbs that mark the way out." Supreme Court rulings have allowed states to reimburse parents for the cost of bus transportation to parochial schools but not for the cost of field trips to museums or state capitols. States may lend nonreligious textbooks to students in parochial schools but not maps, photographs, films or tape recorders. Students may obtain diagnostic health services from public employees in a mobile unit parked next to a parochial school, but not in the school itself.

William B. Ball, in his brief for the Zobrests, leaned heavily on two earlier Supreme Court decisions, *Mueller v. Allen* (1983) and *Witters v. Washington Department of Services for the Blind* (1986). The ruling in *Mueller* upheld a Minnesota law that allowed all taxpayers to deduct educational expenses—even though more than 90 percent of such deductions benefited parents whose children attended religious schools. *Witters* allowed a state vocational rehabilitation program to finance a blind man's study for the ministry at a private Christian college. Justice Lewis Powell explained that the rationale underlying both decisions was that "any aid to religion results from the private choices of individual beneficiaries." Similarly, Ball argued that the primary effect of providing a government-paid interpreter to Jim Zobrest would not be to benefit religion but to advance "the general education of a citizen."

For his part, John C. Richardson, the lawyer for Catalina Foothills, relied heavily on 1985 rulings in *Grand Rapids School District v. Ball* and *Aguilar v. Felton*. In those cases, the Court had struck down government programs in which public school teachers provided remedial courses to needy children in religious schools. "The danger of government-funded transmission of religious instruction was only speculative," Richardson argued, but in the *Zobrest* case "the publicly funded transmission of religious dogma is a factual certainty."

The *Zobrest* case provoked a parade of friend-of-the-court briefs from church groups, school leaders, constitutional scholars and organizations of the handicapped. The Bush administration supported the Zobrests. Eleven religious organizations rushed to the Zobrests' side, telling the Court that the *Lemon* test was "deeply flawed" because it "invites lower courts to discriminate against religion in the administration of public programs." Surprisingly, the case split the separationists.

Most backed the school district, but the American Jewish Congress and two allied organizations supported Jim Zobrest on grounds that he had been victimized by a good principle "carried too far." But they urged the Court to preserve *Lemon*.

Meanwhile, young Zobrest—tall, bright, good-looking, and well-liked—was attending a community college after compiling a B-average at Salpointe with the assistance of a sign-language interpreter and student note-takers. No one doubted the pervasiveness of religious training at Salpointe. Mass is celebrated each morning in a small chapel, though attendance is not mandatory. "Christian Morality" and "Jesus in the Gospels" are among several theology courses required of all 1,300 students, including the 20 percent who are not Catholic. Crosses hang on the classroom walls. The faculty handbook says, "A lively sense of God's presence and the struggle to experience that presence should permeate the atmosphere of our schools."

Every school day, an interpreter accompanied Jim through the halls, during liturgy, and sometimes at lunch. In classes, other students took notes for Jim while he watched the interpreter. Jim and his interpreter were together, too, at basketball practices and during games. At six-foot-four, Jim played low post but warmed the bench most of the time because, his coach said, it was hard for a deaf boy to keep pace with fast-changing offensive plays and defensive assignments. Jim did have one advantage. In enemy gyms, he was oblivious to the hooting and jeering from the stands, which probably helped him calmly sink six consecutive shots from the foul line in his freshman year. Whatever happened, Jim's interpreter was always there, on the bench and in huddles, even during the pregame Hail Mary or Our Father prayers. When the team won a city title, the interpreter got a trophy, too.

To a great extent, the outcome of the Zobrests' case depended on how the Justices perceived the interpreter's role in a religious school. Is an interpreter a mere transmission line conveying information from teacher to student, much as a hearing aid does? Or is an interpreter an active participant in religious education?

In the Supreme Court's packed courtroom on February 24, 1993, Ball told the Justices that Jim Zobrest's interpreter was much like a hearing aid, transmitting information but doing no teaching of religion or anything else. Moreover, the parochial school gained nothing merely "by taking on the burden of accommodating a certified sign-language interpreter for one boy," he said.

But, Justice David H. Souter gently inquired, isn't an interpreter "just as much an integral part of the conveyance of a religious message as some of the equipment . . . which was denied to schools under prior cases?"

"He will be conveying religion, no doubt about it," Ball replied. "But the fact that he does that does not create an image of authority . . . in any sense that a teacher does."

Still, wouldn't a publicly paid interpreter at a parochial school symbolize a union of church and state, just as the federal appeal court said?

"I can stretch my imagination so far," Ball replied, "but it goes to the breaking point when I'm thinking of Jim's peers, these impressionable youngsters, saying something like, 'Guys, you see that fellow who's making those signs? Well, it's like awesome. Right here in chem lab, we're seeking a violation of the Establishment Clause, of the First Amendment.'" Laughter rocked the courtroom out of its customary decorum.

In arguing for the school district, Richardson said that federal law (IDEA) authorized, but did not require, the school district to furnish an interpreter in any private school. The critical constitutional question, he said, was "whether the person in the classroom transmitting the religious information is or is not a public employee functioning at public expense."

What about a robot capable of acting as an interpreter? Justice White wanted to know. That's no different from a tape recorder, which the Court ruled out in a 1975 case, *Meek v. Pittenger,* replied Richardson.

How about allowing a religious ceremony in a public hall using loudspeakers rented from the government? That's passive government accommodation of religion and thus constitutional, Richardson said.

"But," he added, "when . . . you ask a public employee to . . . convey to James Zobrest that Jesus Christ was the son of God or that he died to save his [Zobrest's] sins, I think that's active involvement in a religious activity."

Scalia leaned forward. Was the public school being fair to Zobrest or neutral toward religion by telling him he could have an interpreter but not if he went to a parochial school? "We don't have to do anything but provide you a secular education," Richardson replied.

Privately, Richardson predicted his side would lose. He figured, correctly as it turned out, that Chief Justice William H. Rehnquist and Justices Byron R. White, Scalia, and Clarence Thomas would vote for Zobrest and against the church-state separationists. To win, the Zobrests needed only one more vote and, Richardson figured, the Justice most likely to cast it was Anthony Kennedy.

While growing up in small-town Sacramento, California, Anthony McLeod Kennedy had earned a reputation as bright, eager, religious, bookish, reserved, efficient, squeaky-clean, and straight-laced. As a Supreme Court Justice, that reputation remains intact.

From an early age, Kennedy balanced church and state in his personal life. He was a page in the state senate on weekdays and an altar boy at Holy Spirit Catholic Church on weekends. When young Tony's friends plotted some mischief, he begged off, saying he had something to do at home. When the other kids ventured downtown to see movies that dared to show the cleavage of a buxom actress or to allow the word "virgin" to be heard, prim Tony stayed away, just as the Catholic Legion of Decency had instructed. When his father packed a bottle of one-hundred-proof Yellowstone whisky in his luggage for a trip to Europe, Tony said it was strictly for medicinal purposes and proceeded to cope with a sore throat by gargling and then spitting it out.

"I think we all tried to coax Tony as often as possible into breaking any of his rules," one longtime friend confided. "I can't remember that we ever did." Other friends swear that, to this day, Kennedy refuses to jaywalk. Perhaps the worst thing he ever did was to drop a piece of chewing gum from the Washington Monument while on a school trip, according to his high-school classmates. As a law school teacher in Sacramento, Kennedy got rave reviews from students although, as the dean said, he was "not the kind of professor who's going to go to the pub for a few beers." As for girls, Kennedy started late and found one, Mary Davis. They have been married to each other for more than thirty years.

Kennedy scarcely seemed the son of Anthony J. "Bud" Kennedy, a politically powerful, cigar-chomping, hard-drinking, poker-playing lobbyist for liquor distillers, opticians, an oil company, a recording firm, and an outfit that wrapped sausages in animal intestines. But after the death of his father in 1963, young Tony, a star student barely out of Harvard Law School, became a twenty-seven-year-old lawyer-lobbyist. Never gregarious, he was uncomfortable in the lobbying role, but managed to push the legislative aims of both the liquor industry and the Catholic Church with money and intellect rather than glad-handing and a round of drinks.

Kennedy's roots in the comfortable suburbs of manicured lawns in the southern part of Sacramento isolated him from poverty and minorities and social injustice. But his sensitivity grew. In 1975, after President Ford made Kennedy, at thirty-eight, the youngest judge then on the federal appeals bench, the nominee regretfully confessed that at Harvard "we regularly excluded all women from our study group and thought nothing of it. We just weren't aware of the problem." He joined all-white private clubs, defending their right to discriminate without government interference, even though they owed their existence to government tax breaks and liquor licenses. When President Reagan named him to the Supreme Court after the failure of the Robert Bork nomination in 1987, Kennedy said he recognized that "real harm can result from membership exclusion regardless of its purported justification."

In personality, style, and approach to the law, Kennedy resembles Lewis Powell, the Justice he replaced. He is a restrained, pragmatic conservative lacking any overarching legal ideology or philosophy. But in his first years on the high court, Kennedy voted more conservatively than Powell, casting pivotal votes that gradually pushed the high court to the right. He scorned racial preferences, making possible five-to-four rulings that made it tougher for racial minorities and women to prove bias in the workplace, and opened affirmative action plans to new challenges from white workers. He wrote the majority opinion approving drug testing for Customs employees, provoking a scathing dissent from Antonin Scalia. But Kennedy surprised court observers by supplying the fifth vote needed to declare flag-desecration laws unconstitutional.

Increasingly, Kennedy came to resent Scalia's slashing style, both in internal memos, known as "Ninograms," and in published opinions. At one point, Kennedy vainly sought a civility agreement, calling for a moratorium on personal attacks in official rulings.

In 1992 Kennedy's basic concern for traditions of society, stability of the law and respect for the courts led him to switch sides and create extraordinary majorities that temporarily halted the Rehnquist Court's drive to the right. Most significantly, Kennedy joined Souter, O'Connor, and liberals Blackmun and Stevens to preserve abortion rights first announced in *Roe v. Wade* and bar school-sponsored prayers at high-school graduations. To strike down *Roe* would undermine "the people's acceptance of the judiciary as fit to determine what the nation's law means," Kennedy declared. Conservatives denounced Kennedy as a turncoat and a wimp. The press proclaimed the emergence of a new moderate bloc, prematurely as it turned out. The purported center did not hold beyond 1992.

For the lawyers in the *Zobrest* case, Kennedy's seemingly zigzag church-state rulings were particularly important. In a 1989 case, *Allegheny County v. Greater Pittsburgh ACLU,* he dissented sharply from the Court's decree that a city-sponsored nativity scene was unconstitutional. Joined by conservatives Rehnquist, White, and Scalia, he accused the majority of being hostile to religion, called for "substantial revision" of church-state doctrine and declared that government could assist religion so long as it does "not coerce anyone."

Kennedy alarmed the separationists. His views seemed to endorse school prayers and government aid to parochial schools. But three years later, in *Lee v. Weisman,* Kennedy stunned his conservative colleagues by leading a five-to-four majority to leave the *Lemon* test intact and declare that prayers have no place at public school graduations. Yet Kennedy consistently applied his view that coercion is a key to deciding church-state cases. "The Constitution forbids the state to exact religious conformity from a student as the price of attending her own high school graduation," Kennedy declared. An angry Scalia unleashed his most scathing essay yet, denouncing Kennedy's opinion as "incoherent" and "senseless," likening it to "psychology practiced by amateurs."

What would Kennedy do in the *Zobrest* case? He provided no clues when, on June 7, 1993, the Court announced a unanimous ruling in the only other church-state case of the term, *Lamb's Chapel v. Center Moriches Union Free School District.* It was a relatively easy case. A public school open to various after-school community uses had refused to allow a church to show a film on family issues. That was a violation of the Freedom of Speech Clause, White wrote for the Court. Applying the *Lemon* test, White found that there would have been no Establishment Clause violation had the school permitted the film to be shown.

Scalia excoriated the *Lemon* test in a concurring opinion: "Like some ghoul in a late-night horror movie that repeatedly sits up in its grave and shuffles abroad, after being repeatedly killed and buried, Lemon stalks our Establishment Clause jurisprudence once again, frightening little children and school attorneys. . . . Over the years . . . no fewer than five of the current sitting justices [naming Scalia, Kennedy, O'Connor, Rehnquist and White] have, in their opinions, personally driven pencils through the creature's heart, and a sixth [White] has joined an opinion doing so."

Retorted White: "While we are somewhat diverted by Justice Scalia's evening at the cinema, we return to the reality that there is a proper way to inter an established decision and *Lemon,* however frightening it might be to some, has not been overruled."

Eleven days later, Jim Zobrest won a five-to-four victory. Just as the school district's Richardson had feared, Kennedy's pivotal vote went against the government. He joined Rehnquist, White, Scalia, and Thomas in concluding that furnishing a government interpreter for Zobrest would be a neutral act that neither adds to nor subtracts from Salpointe's pervasively religious environment.

"If a handicapped child chooses to enroll in a sectarian school," Rehnquist wrote for the majority, "we hold that the Establishment Clause does not prevent the school district from furnishing him with a sign-language interpreter there in order to facilitate his education."

Rehnquist stressed the *Mueller* and *Witters* precedents. In those two cases, he said, the Court had approved government programs that neutrally provided benefits to a broad group of citizens without regard to their religion. Such programs did not violate the Establishment Clause just because some sectarian institutions benefit indirectly, he said.

The Chief Justice then applied that reasoning to the *Zobrest* case: The federal law on education of the handicapped (IDEA) benefits children rather than sectarian schools and gives parents freedom to select a school of their choice. That ensures "that a government-paid interpreter will be present in a sectarian school only as a result of the private decision of individual parents"—and not any decision of the government.

Moreover, Rehnquist said, the facts of the *Zobrest* case differed from the Court's rejection of government programs that provided teachers, teaching materials, and equipment to parochial schools. *Zobrest,* he said, involved no direct government subsidy to a religious institution and no government-paid teacher. "Nothing in this record suggests that a sign-language interpreter would do more than accurately interpret whatever material is presented to the class as a whole," Rehnquist wrote. He didn't rely directly on the *Lemon* test. But he didn't overturn it, either, suggesting that he lacked the votes to do so.

Four Justices—Blackmun, Souter, Stevens, and O'Connor—dissented. The Court, they said, should not have decided the constitutional question because it was still uncertain whether the IDEA compels public schools to provide interpreters in private schools.

Blackmun, joined by Souter, then presented the separationist view of the case, accusing the majority of straying from nearly five decades of Establishment Clause rulings. "Until now," Blackmun declared, "the Court never has authorized a public employee to participate directly in religious indoctrination. . . . In an environment so pervaded by discussions of the divine, the interpreter's every gesture would be infused with religious significance."

The programs approved in the *Mueller* and *Witters* precedents allowed government payment of a cash benefit or a tax deduction. "This case, on the other hand, involves ongoing, daily and intimate governmental participation in the teaching and propagation of religious doctrine," explained Blackmun.

In the three religion cases decided by the court in June, 1993, the score was church three, state zero. The driving principle in all three decisions was that, in religious matters, government must be neutral, and may not discriminate against a church, an individual's religious practice, or religion in general. But, as Souter observed in the Santería case, "neutrality is not self-revealing." The three decisions, which generated ten opinions, showed that the Justices are badly split over the meaning and application of neutrality doctrine, and that their rules for interpreting both the Free Exercise and Establishment clauses hang by a slender thread.

The Santería case, while leaving the law unchanged, demonstrated that the Court remained committed to protecting an unpopular religion from direct, deliberate suppression by government. More broadly, Souter's concurring opinion laid a foundation for a reexamination of the controversial *Smith* decision, unless Congress overturns it first. As many as four Justices—Souter, Blackmun, O'Connor, and probably Ruth Bader Ginsburg—appear willing to back stronger protections for unpopular religious practices. All they need is a fifth vote.

The *Lamb's Chapel* ruling, predictable though it was, seemed to have rescued the *Lemon* test, at least for a while. Rehnquist, Scalia, Thomas, and Kennedy still dislike it, but most Justices agreed that it remained the law.

In the *Zobrest* case, the Court, for the first time, authorized a public employee to participate in sectarian education on the premises of a parochial school. It was a new crack in the wall of separation, to be sure, but one unlikely to endanger the wall itself.

The larger question for the future was whether the rationale underlying the *Zobrest* decision gave a constitutional green light to parental vouchers, tuition tax credits, or other broad "educational choice" programs designed to benefit all private schools. Absolutely, exclaimed many advocates of aid to parochial schools, one of whom called the *Zobrest* ruling "truly a slam dunk" for his side.

Certainly Rehnquist's majority opinion contained language that helps the parochial campaign, especially his undisguised applause for the *Mueller* and *Witters* precedents. Those two cases had endorsed government programs which directly helped individuals. They allowed financial benefits to flow indirectly to parochial schools, if those benefits resulted from private choices of parents or students.

But future Supreme Court approval of parental voucher programs remained doubtful for three reasons. First, Rehnquist's opinion was narrow. It distinquished the task of a sign-language interpreter from that of a teacher or guidance counselor and continued to prohibit public employees from teaching or advising any students in religious schools. Second, the major purpose of voucher programs is to aid parochial schools, which would be more than mere "incidental beneficiaries." Third, the replacement of Justice White by Ginsburg is expected to shift the balance in church-state cases on the closely divided court. The evidence, though sparse, suggests she is a more consistent separationist than White.

As for the Zobrests, the ruling in their favor did not end their litigation. Richardson immediately prepared to argue in lower courts that, under federal law and the Arizona constitution, Catalina Foothills could not be forced to pay $28,000 plus interest for Jim Zobrest's interpreter during his four years at Salpointe.

Still, said Mrs. Zobrest of the family's Supreme Court triumph: "I'm elated. We worked so hard for this. I certainly think it's going to be easier now for handicapped students to have freedom of choice of schools and get the services they're entitled to."

CHAPTER SIX

Does it violate the Constitution to execute an innocent man? That question, it turns out, is more complicated than it seems. In *Herrera v. Collins* the Court faced this issue against the backdrop of decades of legal and policy debate over the death penalty and over the appropriate division of authority between state courts and federal courts in reviewing issues arising in capital punishment cases.

The Eighth Amendment prohibits "cruel and unusual punishment." For a brief period in the 1970s the Supreme Court appeared poised to rule the death penalty unconstitutional. But beginning in 1976, the Court reversed direction, and in a long series of cases since then it has repeatedly rejected efforts to have the death penalty eliminated in America on constitutional grounds.

Running parallel to the death penalty saga is the story of the rise and fall of the federal writ of habeas corpus. Known as the "Great Writ of Liberty," federal habeas corpus is a procedure that permits a federal court to examine the conviction of a prisoner to determine if the prisoner's confinement or terms of punishment comports with the requirements of the Constitution. In its heyday federal habeas corpus was an actively used form of "collateral review" of state court convictions. State prisoners who believed their rights had been ignored in their state trials could petition a federal court to review the state proceedings to determine if any constitutional rights of the defendant had been violated.

There has always been a tension in the application of the habeas corpus. On the one hand, the Supreme Court has recognized the importance of the Great Writ as a safety valve against miscarriages of justice. On the other hand, the Court has been concerned with interference with the state criminal justice system by federal courts, and the danger that desperate prisoners abuse the writ by flooding federal courts with frivolous petitions. A string of Rehnquist Court cases in the 1990s dramatically restricted the use of federal habeas corpus to review state prisoner convictions.

Unhappy with giving prisoners a "second bite at the apple" through federal habeas corpus review, conservatives on the Court have argued that a prisoner's constitutional rights are adequately protected by the opportunity of the prisoner to appeal his or her conviction through the normal avenues of review available in the state court system, which is perfectly competent to hear claims of constitutional violations.

In the *Herrera* case, these two strains of criminal law jurisprudence came together in an extraordinarily dramatic setting: a state prisoner alleged that new evidence established his innocence. The state of Texas was unconvinced and was determined to execute him. The question before the Court, as explained in Marcia Coyle's compelling account, was whether a "mere" claim of innocence was the type of claim that federal courts could hear in habeas corpus petition.

—Editor

A Question of Innocence

MARCIA COYLE

No matter how careful courts are, the possibility of perjured testimony, mistaken honest testimony, and human error remain all too real. We have no way of judging how many innocent persons have been executed, but we can be certain that there were some.—Justice Thurgood Marshall in *Furman v. Georgia,* which found the death penalty unconstitutional in 1972

There is no basis in text, tradition, or even in contemporary practice (if that were enough), for finding in the Constitution a right to demand judicial consideration of newly discovered evidence of innocence brought forward after conviction.—Justice Antonin Scalia in *Herrera v. Collins* in 1993

At 4:39 A.M., on May 12, 1993, before dawn in eastern Texas, state prison officials injected a lethal combination of pancuronium bromide, potassium chloride, and sodium thiopental into both arms of Leonel Herrera Jr., a convicted cop killer.

Only minutes earlier, Herrera, forty-five, secured to a prison gurney in the Huntsville execution chamber, told those waiting to watch him die: "I am innocent, innocent, innocent. Make no mistake about this. I owe society nothing. I am an innocent man and something very wrong is taking place tonight."

About ten minutes after the lethal injection, Herrera was pronounced dead. In the eyes of Texas law, he was a Johnny-come-too-lately with his claim of innocence—first raised in court papers eight years after his conviction for the shooting death of a rookie Los Fresnos police officer. A convicted criminal in Texas can use newly discovered evidence to attack his or her conviction or sentence only if the evidence is produced within thirty days of trial.

And when Herrera, barred by law from presenting his evidence in Texas courts, turned to the federal courts—the ultimate guarantors of federal constitutional rights—he was shut out again. His case went onto a legal track more than one hundred years old, but redirected and greased by the Rehnquist Court to hasten the pace of executions in America by bringing finality to seemingly interminable death row appeals.

In a question that struck the weak spot in the nation's strong support of capital punishment, Herrera then asked the United States Supreme Court: Does it violate the Constitution to execute a person, convicted of murder, who is innocent?

How was it possible that after nearly two decades of rulings designed to ensure fairness in the imposition of the death penalty, the Supreme Court could face such a question? It happened because an increasingly intricate legal web had been woven by the high court in the previous five years, and Herrera found himself caught in it.

Led by Chief Justice William H. Rehnquist, lobbyist on and off the bench for strict limits on death row appeals, the Court's conservative majority has actively retooled the legal doctrine of habeas corpus. Prisoners now face a difficult array of procedural hurdles before federal courts can look at alleged constitutional errors in their convictions and sentences. Herrera was a man without a court in which he could raise belated evidence of his innocence.

For a majority of the Justices, Herrera's question would not find a simple or unambiguous answer. At one end of the spectrum, Justice Antonin Scalia would describe the question as "embarrassing," because the Constitution obviously did not offer anything to someone in Herrera's position. But in the eyes of Justice Harry A. Blackmun, a "no" reply by the high court to Herrera's question would come "perilously close to simple murder."

Herrera was not exactly the poster boy candidate to raise in the United States Supreme Court a question that could, some death penalty abolitionists believed, jolt the complacency of Americans supporting capital punishment.

Leonel Torres Herrera was born September 17, 1947, the second of five children, at the home of his paternal grandparents in Edinburg, the county seat of Hidalgo County, Texas, about ten miles from the United States–Mexico border. Hidalgo County is in the Rio Grande Valley, which produces much of Texas's citrus fruits and vegetables. It is one of the poorest regions in the nation, with a population over 80 percent Hispanic and unemployment locked in high double digits.

Both of Herrera's parents were Mexicans who had immigrated to the United States in search of work, primarily as migrant farm laborers.

Herrera's youth was played out against a background familiar to many death row inmates: extreme poverty and repeated physical abuse by an alcoholic parent. His father, José, was known as a street fighter and a womanizer who carved a path of violence for the next two generations of Herrera men.

Despite his bleak home life, Leonel Herrera did reasonably well in school and excelled in football. But he dropped out of high school in eleventh grade, and shortly afterward, in 1967, joined the Navy. He was stationed in Vietnam on board a nuclear-powered ship, the USS *Long Beach*. He served for two years, receiving combat medals and a general discharge in 1969.

After his release from the navy, Herrera returned to Edinburg a different man, both physically and emotionally, according to family members. He frequently appeared to be sick and suffered from insomnia and nightmares. He and his brother opened a convenience store, which later, along with medical bills resulting from the premature birth of his daughter, placed the family in heavy financial debt.

Around 1972, his father became involved in illegal drug trafficking in Hidalgo County.

Law enforcement officials say the terrain around Hidalgo County is highly conducive to drug smuggling. The Rio Grande River is shallow enough to wade across at points and the land on both sides of the border is flat for quick and easy landings by small planes. A third of the marijuana and cocaine entering the United States from Mexico moves across the river and through the valley.

Violence and public corruption have followed in the wake of the drug dealing. As law enforcement efforts intensified in the mid- to late 1980s, police officers, state troopers, custom agents, and other public officials were among those charged or convicted of drug-related crimes.

José Herrera recruited his two oldest sons, Raúl Sr. and Leonel, for his drug business and provided them with large quantities of cocaine for personal use. Leonel quickly became addicted.

Raúl was responsible for arranging the deals in which drugs were sold; Leonel's job was to "cut" or reduce the purity of cocaine sold on the streets. By the time of his arrest in 1981 for the murder of Officer Enrique Carrisález, Leonel's cocaine addiction was severe. In a request for a thirty-day reprieve from his 1992 execution date, Leonel's

146   Marcia Coyle

family described him in 1981 as suffering from constant bloody and runny noses, respiratory problems, significant weight loss, and visual and auditory hallucinations. But the worst of his problems were yet to come.

On September 29, 1981, Trooper David Rucker of the Texas Department of Public Safety was killed by a gunshot wound to the head near a rest area near Port Isabel, Texas. There were no witnesses, but Leonel Herrera's Social Security card was found near Rucker's body.

About ten minutes after Rucker was killed, Officer Enrique "Rick" Carrisález stopped a speeding car traveling from the direction of the earlier shooting. After calling in the license plate number, he approached the stopped car; the driver stepped out and shot Carrisález in the chest. The officer died nine days later.

Enrique Hernández, a boyhood friend of Carrisález, was riding with the officer that night. After the shooting, he called in a general description of the car. The next morning, after taking Hernández's statement, the police proceeded to get an arrest warrant for Leonel Herrera. Later that day, they showed Hernández a display of photographs. Hernández chose three, one of which was Herrera. On October 1, the police took only Herrera's photo to the hospital and asked Carrisález if he could identify the man in the photo as the shooter. Carrisález, who could not speak, nodded his head, identifying Herrera as the gunman. The same photo, a mug shot carrying the notation "Edinburg Police Department," was shown by itself to Hernández that day and he also positively identified Herrera as the gunman.

About twenty-five police officers captured Herrera at a friend's home five days after the killings. Local news accounts said the arrest ended "the largest manhunt in the Valley in modern times." On searching Herrera, police found a disjointed letter, handwritten on the backs of several envelopes, in which he discussed the death of both officers. The note read:

> To whom it may concern: I am terribly sorry for those I have brought grief to their lives. Who knows why? We cannot change the future's problems with problems from the past. What I did was for a cause and purpose. One law runs others, and in the world we live in, that's the way it is.
>
> I'm not a tormented person. . . . I believe in the law. What would it be without this men that risk their lives for others, and that's

what they should be doing—protecting life, property, and the pursuit of happiness. Sometimes the law gets too involved with other things that profit them. The most laws that they make for people to break them, in other words, to encourage crime.

What happened to Rucker was for a certain reason. I knew him as Mike Tatum. He was in my business, and he violated some of its laws and suffered the penalty, like the one you have for me when the time comes.

My personal life, which has been a conspiracy since my high school days, has nothing to do with what has happened. The other officer that became part of our lives, me and Rucker's (Tatum), that night had not to do in this. He was out to do what he had to do, protect, but that's life. There's a lot of us that wear different faces in lives every day, and that is what causes problems for all. [Unintellible word]

You have wrote all you want of my life, but think about yours, also. [Signed, Leonel Herrera]

I have tapes and pictures to prove what I have said. I will prove my side if you accept to listen. You [unintelligible word] freedom of speech, even a criminal has that right. I will present myself if this is read word for word over the media, I will turn myself in; if not, don't have millions of men out there working just on me while others—robbers, rapists, or burglars—are taking advantage of the law's time. Excuse my spelling and writing. It's hard at times like this.

The police also found blood in his wallet, on a pair of blue jeans, and in his car that matched Rucker's type A blood, but not Herrera's type O.

The Rucker and Carrisález murders were widely publicized. Shortly after Herrera's arrest, he was hospitalized for severe head injuries following, his attorneys say, a police beating. He pled not guilty to the Carrisález killing and went to trial in January 1982.

The trial received extensive media coverage. Over the objection of Herrera's lawyer, one of the jurors seated was a detective with the Brownsville Police Department who wore his firearm during jury service. This detective lived in Los Fresnos where Officer Carrisález had served as one of four policemen. Another juror was a cook and had been a close friend of Officer Rucker for several years. Yet another had a cousin who was a police officer with Officer Carrisález, and one juror's son-in-law was a Brownsville police officer. Uniformed police officers ringed the courtroom throughout the trial. Twenty-four police officers testified during the guilt-or-innocence phase of Herrera's trial; six testified during the sentencing phase.

During the trial, Hernández identified Herrera's car as the vehicle stopped by Carrisález and Herrera himself as the person who shot Carrisález. Herrera, however, contended his brother, Raúl Sr., had a set of keys to the car and was using it that night. He also claimed he kept his Social Security card in his glove compartment.

But the Hernández and Carrisález identifications, along with the physical evidence, proved overwhelming. On January 20, 1982, the jury convicted Herrera. The next day, the trial judge imposed the death penalty. No evidence was offered by Herrera's lawyer to mitigate the sentence, such as his military service, employment record, or his mental and physical health.

While he was awaiting trial in the Rucker murder, Herrera, according to his lawyers and hospital records, was again severely beaten by police and hospitalized. Shortly afterward, he entered a guilty plea in the Rucker case and, during that plea, stated he was guilty of the Carrisález murder.

Herrera later appealed his conviction and death sentence in the Carrisález murder, arguing, among other things, that the identifications by Hernández and Carrisález were unreliable and improperly admitted into evidence at his trial. But the Texas Court of Criminal Appeals upheld the conviction in 1984, and six months later, the United States Supreme Court refused to hear his appeal.

The first of what were to be six execution dates was set for August 16, 1985.

In 1982, the year in which Herrera was convicted and sentenced to die, there were only two executions across the country. Ten years earlier, the United States Supreme Court had effectively struck down all existing death penalty laws because they were imposed in a "wanton and freakish" pattern that violated the Eighth Amendment's ban on cruel and unusual punishments. In 1976, the Justices revived the death penalty after a number of states had moved to make their laws less arbitrary and conform more closely with the Constitution.

By 1977, thirty-five states had capital punishment on their books. During the next five years, they had executed a total of six persons.

The execution pace picked up somewhat after 1982, with the yearly toll hovering slightly below or above twenty executions.

During the same period, however, states' death rows were ballooning. At the beginning of 1980, states housed about 600 inmates on death row, but by the end of 1989, the number had increased to more than 2,200.

Noted death penalty scholar Franklin E. Zimring of the University of California at Berkeley has described capital punishment in the 1980s in America as a "stalemate pattern" in which there were high death sentence rates but very few executions performed outside of those states that historically had high execution rates. For example, he notes that from 1977 through 1989 more than 70 percent of all executions took place in just four states: Texas, Florida, Georgia, and Louisiana.

The slow pace of executions in the early 1980s may have offered small comfort to Herrera, then on Texas's death row cell block located about sixteen miles northeast of Huntsville. But it clearly angered and frustrated one member of the United States Supreme Court, then Associate Justice William H. Rehnquist.

In an otherwise unremarkable death penalty case from Georgia in 1981, Rehnquist targeted what he believed was frustrating the ends of justice, as demanded by the majority of Americans, and he presented a remarkable plan for curing the problem.

In *Coleman v. Balkcom,* a man convicted of the brutal killings of six members of a family was asking the high court for the second time to hear his case. He had lost his direct challenge to his conviction in the Georgia courts, and the United States Supreme Court had refused to hear that appeal. Coleman then went back into the state court system, this time arguing he should have been granted a change of venue in his original trial because of prejudicial pretrial publicity. He lost again and was making his second pitch to the nation's highest court.

Rehnquist urged the Court to take Coleman's case, but not because he thought the state courts had erred earlier or the case raised an important legal question. He wanted to take this case and others like it and, without oral arguments, affirm the state court's decision. By acting on the merits at this stage, instead of simply declining to hear the case, the Court would short-circuit Coleman's next step of going into the federal court system with his claim.

Even though the high court had reinstated the death penalty in 1976 with its decision in *Gregg v. Georgia,* he wrote, the penalty had become "virtually an illusion." He accused the majority of the Court of "surrounding capital defendants with numerous procedural protections unheard of for other crimes." Since 1976, he charged, "hundreds of juries have sentenced hundreds of persons to death, presumably in the belief that the death penalty in those circumstances is warranted, yet virtually nothing happens except endlessly drawn out legal proceedings."

The Court declined to follow the course he was charting. A year later, in another death case that the Court refused to hear, Rehnquist reiterated, "A potential murderer will know that even if he is convicted and sentenced to death, he will very likely not be put to death. If he litigates the case long enough, the odds favor his finding some court which will accept a legal theory previously rejected by other courts."

Although he was losing those early, post-*Gregg* battles, Rehnquist was both persistent and patient. The Reagan years had begun. The death penalty, always controversial, was to become a centerpiece of the new administration's anticrime program. The Court's makeup, too, was about to change. Soon Rehnquist would have two forums—Congress and the Supreme Court—in which to press for reform of what he saw as a major flaw in the criminal justice system.

Rehnquist had taken his seat as a Justice in 1972, two weeks before the Court heard arguments in the landmark death penalty challenge, *Furman v. Georgia,* the case that led them to strike down the death penalty. Rehnquist dissented. Today, he and Justice Harry A. Blackmun are the only present members of the high court who have witnessed all the changes in the death penalty, from its being struck down as unconstitutional in 1972, to its reinstatement in 1976, to the Court's ongoing effort to monitor its implementation by the states according to the demands of the Constitution. Blackmun, who also dissented in *Furman,* has changed his view of the death penalty considerably over the years; Rehnquist has not.

Looking back over the last two decades, many Court experts agree that Rehnquist, along with retired Justice William J. Brennan Jr. and the late Justice Thurgood Marshall, have been the most consistent of the Justices in their approaches to capital punishment. The latter two Justices became known for their often solitary, unshakable opposition to the death penalty as cruel and unusual punishment under the Eighth Amendment. And Rehnquist, seeing no bar to the death penalty in the Constitution and no specific restraints on its implementation, has preached almost total deference to states' policies in this area.

This consistency over time is a hallmark of Rehnquist's jurisprudence, not only in the death penalty area but in most other areas of the law. In fact, some who have known him for many years say that his approach to the law is today much as it was when he was a law student at Stanford University more than four decades ago, which prompts some to speculate humorously that he sprang from the womb with a fully developed jurisprudence. Rehnquist has stood firm even as the nation and the Court itself have changed around him.

Rehnquist was born October 1, 1924, in Milwaukee, Wisconsin. His father was a wholesale paper salesman who never went to college, and his mother was a graduate of the University of Wisconsin.

Rehnquist went to Kenyon College on a scholarship but soon dropped out to enlist in the Army Air Corps meteorology program in 1943. He served in North Africa at the end of World War II and was discharged in 1946 with the rank of sergeant.

After his discharge, he went back to school to complete his college degree, enrolling in Stanford University. He majored in political science and graduated in 1948. After earning a master's degree in political science from Harvard in 1950, he returned to Stanford to study law and graduated first in his class in 1952.

Rehnquist headed east in early 1952 to begin a clerkship at the United States Supreme Court with Justice Robert Jackson. When the clerkship ended in June 1953, he set out for the southwest, settled in Phoenix, Arizona, and spent the next sixteen years building a successful general law practice.

During that same period, he also began to build a political persona. He worked for Republican candidates and wrote and made speeches critical of the liberal Warren Court. In 1957, for example, he wrote in a national magazine that the Warren Court decisions were typified by "extreme solicitude for the claims of Communists and other criminal defendants, expansion of Federal power at the expense of state power, great sympathy toward any government regulation of business."

In 1964, he vigorously supported Arizona senator Barry Goldwater's bid for the presidency. Although Goldwater was unsuccessful, Rehnquist had been noticed, and the payoff came when, four years later, Richard Nixon won the White House.

Nixon brought another Phoenix lawyer to Washington, Richard Kleindienst, who was tapped to be the deputy to the new attorney general, John Mitchell. Kleindienst, in turn, brought Rehnquist with him to the Justice Department. He became head of the Office of Legal Counsel, advising the president and other top law enforcement officials on the legality of their actions.

Rehnquist soon became a very visible and effective spokesman for the Nixon administration on many criminal law issues. In regular appearances before congressional committees, he endorsed, among other controversial positions, the elimination of the exclusionary rule, which bars the admission at trial of evidence illegally obtained by the police. He defended warrantless wiretapping of alleged subversives and vigorous government surveillance of Vietnam War protesters.

After nearly three years in the Office of Legal Counsel, Rehnquist, in January 1971, was tapped by Nixon for one of two vacancies on the United States Supreme Court. The other slot went to Lewis F. Powell Jr., a former president of the American Bar Association, from Richmond, Virginia.

In announcing Rehnquist's appointment, Nixon criticized Supreme Court decisions that had weakened "the peace forces as against the criminal forces in our society" and emphasized that law enforcers be given the "legal tools they need to protect the innocent from criminal elements." In Rehnquist, he had found a champion of the first order.

His confirmation did not go as smoothly as Nixon had hoped. Not surprisingly, Rehnquist drew opposition from liberals because his record indicated a strong conservatism on civil rights and civil liberties issues. The Leadership Conference of Civil Rights led the opposition. The American Civil Liberties Union also announced its opposition— the first time it had ever opposed a high court nominee.

Charges surfaced that in 1964, as a Republican poll watcher, he had harrassed black voters. But he denied those charges. He also ran into trouble for a 1952 memo he had written as a clerk to Justice Jackson. In that memo, he argued that "separate but equal" public schools— those segregated by race—were constitutional and should be upheld. He told the Senate committee the memo had been requested by Justice Jackson as a rough draft "of a statement of his view" and did not represent Rehnquist's personal views. He announced his support of the legal reasoning and rightness of the Court's later decision in *Brown v. Board of Education,* dismantling the separate but equal doctrine.

Counterbalancing some of the criticism, however, was Rehnquist's undisputed reputation for legal brilliance. After a week-long floor debate, the Senate confirmed his nomination by a vote of sixty-eight to twenty-six. At age forty-seven, he became one of the youngest Justices to serve on the Court.

In his early years on the Court, Rehnquist alone was the voice of the extreme ideological right. In reviewing his first four terms as Justice, Harvard's David Shapiro concluded that Rehnquist's philosophy had three basic tenets: (1) Conflicts between an individual and the government should, whenever possible, be resolved against the individual; (2) conflicts between state and federal authority, whether on an executive, legislative, or judicial level, should, whenever possible, be resolved in favor of the states; and (3) questions of the exercise of federal jurisdiction, whether on the district court, appellate court, or Supreme Court level, should, whenever possible, be resolved against such exercise.

That pattern continues to this day, but it was not a dominant pattern until Ronald Reagan began to put his imprint on the high court. When he was nominated by Reagan in 1986 to succeed Warren E. Burger as Chief Justice, Rehnquist was known as the "Lone Ranger," a nickname stemming from the fifty-four lone dissents he had written, a Court record. But Rehnquist had persevered in his conservatism and the tide was changing.

The 1988–89 term marked the first term of the fully constituted Rehnquist Court. Three Reagan appointees were on the bench—Sandra Day O'Connor, Antonin Scalia, and Anthony M. Kennedy—giving Rehnquist a working conservative majority. In a series of dramatic rulings on abortion, job discrimination, and separation of church and state, the term marked a fundamental shift in how the Court viewed its role.

The decisions reflected a strong belief that judgments of the political process in general and of legislatures in particular should be presumed correct, and that past Courts had strayed too far from the plain words of those judgments.

"That's a point of view that's been present on the Court for decades, but it has not prevailed since the Vinson Court in the forties and fifties," said Court scholar A. E. Dick Howard of the University of Virginia School of Law.

Rehnquist was an important player in the shift in direction because he "held the fort over the years," said Howard. In his own sometimes isolated conservatism, he added, Rehnquist has served as a bridge between the conservatism of Felix Frankfurter, who served on the Court from 1939 to 1962, and the Court's direction today. His position over the years makes the 1988–89 term "seem like less of a break than it was," said Howard.

In a 1985 interview with the *New York Times,* Rehnquist described himself as an advocate of judicial restraint rather than an activist with conservative goals:

> Every time that we say a law of Congress is unconstitutional, that a state law is unconstitutional, we are overriding a democratically reached decision. Now the Constitution requires us to do that, but it requires us to do it only with great caution and circumspection. . . . I don't know that a court should really have a sense of mission. I think the sense of mission comes best from the President or the House of Representatives or the Senate. They're supposed to be the motive force in our government. . . . The idea that the Court should be way out in front saying, "Look, this is the way the country ought to go," I don't think that was ever the purpose of the Court.

But Rehnquist's words rang hollow for those involved in battling the death penalty before the high court. The note he had sounded in the *Coleman* case in 1981 was, from their perspective, more activist than restrained. And, as time and events would show, he had a very strong sense of mission about the federal courts' role in capital punishment cases.

When the United States Supreme Court refused to hear Herrera's appeal in 1985, his conviction, in the eyes of the law, was final. He now had basically two options. He could await his execution or he could go back into the state courts—and, if unsuccessful there, into the federal courts—and challenge the process by which he was convicted.

If he could convince a judge that an error violating his constitutional rights had been made by the trial judge, his lawyers, or the prosecutor—for example, if the prosecutor withheld evidence that tended to exonerate him—Herrera could win a stay of his execution and ultimately a new trial, a reduced sentence, or even freedom.

Herrera chose the second option, and began an eight-year odyssey through state and federal courts for what is known as a writ of habeas corpus. It was this process, in which death row inmates go back and forth between state and federal courts, seeking relief for alleged constitutional errors in their cases—claims that have nothing to do with their guilt or innocence—that Rehnquist argued against in the *Coleman* case and decided to change.

In a 1990 speech, Rehnquist said:

> The system at present verges on the chaotic. The (average) eight years between conviction in the state court and final decision in the federal courts is consumed not by structured review of the arguments of the parties, but in fits of frantic action followed by periods of inaction. . . . This system cries out for reform. I submit that no one—whether favorable to the prosecution, favorable to the defense, or somewhere in between—would ever have consciously designed it.
>
> The essence of the question is not the pros and cons of capital punishment, but the pros and cons of federalism. . . . What is the proper balance between the lawful authority of the states and the role of the federal courts in protecting constitutional rights?

The writ of habeas corpus, also known as the Great Writ of Liberty, is perhaps the most important, and now most controversial, of writs used by the federal courts. Its roots go back hundreds of years to English common law where it was an order from a court to "have the body" of a prisoner presented so the court could investigate the legality of his physical detention. In time, it became available to anyone in England jailed without due process of law.

For American colonists the privilege of the writ was one of the fundamental rights for which the Revolutionary War was fought. Today, federal and state constitutions protect the writ. The United States Constitution states the privilege of the writ "shall not be suspended, unless when in Cases of Rebellion or Invasion the public safety may require it."

Before retiring from the high court, Justice William J. Brennan Jr., in a 1963 decision, said the writ's history is "inextricably intertwined" with the growth of personal liberty. "Its root principle is that in a civilized society, government must always be accountable to the judiciary for a man's imprisonment; if the imprisonment cannot be shown to conform with the fundamental requirements of law, the individual is entitled to his immediate release."

For much of the nineteenth century, the federal courts made limited use of the writ. The Judiciary Act of 1789 authorized those courts to use the writ only on behalf of federal prisoners. But in 1867, during the Reconstruction era, Congress extended the power of federal courts to issue writs to state prisoners whose detentions violated federal law.

During the next fifty years, habeas was not very controversial for the simple reason that there were not many federal rights that state prisoners could claim. Most of the Bill of Rights had not yet been applied to protect people against actions by the states and the United States Supreme Court took a narrow view of what federal rights did exist.

How narrow a view the high court took was tragically demonstrated in the 1915 case of Leo Frank, convicted of murdering a thirteen-year-old girl in a trial dominated by mob violence and anti-Semitism. The Court in *Frank v. Mangum* refused to examine the merits of Frank's claims that prejudice and violence had poisoned his trial, and looked only at the process by which the state courts had reached their conclusions. Frank was later dragged from his jail cell by a mob and hung. He received a posthumous pardon seventy-one years later, based on the testimony of a man who said as a young boy he saw the janitor in Frank's family-owned mill carry the limp body of the girl to the mill's basement.

Nearly a decade after the *Frank* case, the Court began to shift away from this narrow view of habeas corpus. The playing field soon was to be leveled—some would say it was tilted in the opposite direction—with the arrival of the Warren Court.

In a 1953 North Carolina case, *Brown v. Allen,* in which a convicted rapist claimed racial discrimination in jury selection and challenged the use of a coerced confession at his trial, the high court said that federal courts, in any case raising a constitutional claim, must examine the facts to determine whether a state court reached the correct result. Justice Felix Frankfurter wrote that this view of the scope of federal habeas corpus was compelled by Congress in the 1867 law extending the writ to state prisoners. The only negative voice raised was that of Justice Robert Jackson, for whom the young William Rehnquist was clerking.

Almost on the heels of this expansive view of habeas corpus, the Warren Court in the 1960s began a steady expansion of the rights of criminal suspects and defendants under the Fourth, Fifth, Sixth, Eighth, and Fourteenth Amendments. Federal courts now could provide habeas relief for many more constitutional errors than previously subject to review.

Besides the expansion of rights and habeas review, one other factor would contribute to Rehnquist's very accurate prediction in 1980 that death row inmates would aggressively pursue habeas petitions in the federal court—the Court's own death penalty decisions.

From 1976, when the Court revived the death penalty, to date, the Justices have struggled to ensure it is administered by the states in a constitutional way. They have considered substantive challenges involving what classes of people can be executed—minors, rapists, the mentally retarded, the insane—and structural challenges involving racism and what factors juries can consider as mitigating or aggravating in weighing a penalty of death.

By the 1980s, the nation was witnessing more inmates on death row, more habeas review, more constitutional rights as well as wrongs, and more controversy.

Law enforcement officials became increasingly vocal in their criticism of habeas petitions, arguing they were time-consuming, costly, repetitive, and mostly frivolous. Some federal judges complained about the number of filings to review, even though most can be dismissed without evidentiary hearings. State officials decried the delay in finality of punishment. And, state courts resented having their judgments reexamined by federal courts.

Habeas corpus is the principal impediment to enforcement of the death penalty, insisted Kent S. Scheidegger of the Criminal Justice Legal Foundation in Sacramento, California, which has litigated and lobbied on habeas issues. "From the very beginning until 1953, it was understood habeas corpus was not a substitute for appeal. When you present your claims to state courts, that's the end of it." Independent review of state court judgments by the federal courts, he said, was to be the exception, not the rule.

But for the defenders of habeas corpus as it has existed since 1953, the American Civil Liberties Union, the NAACP Legal Defense and Educational Fund, the American Bar Association and others, the costs associated with it are a price that must be paid, particularly if states continue to use the death penalty. Recent studies have shown federal courts have found a significant percentage of constitutional errors in state court convictions, across the board. In capital murder cases, according to one study, the error rate was as high as 40 percent.

The core problem in habeas, its supporters argued, was not repetitious, frivolous, last-minute petitions by death row inmates, but, as the studies were showing, bad state trials. Capital defendants were frequently represented by appointed lawyers who were ill-trained, un-prepared, and lacked the resources to do proper investigations, they insisted. Federal habeas review by independent, life-tenured federal judges, its supporters argued, is the safety net as long as this system persists.

"If we're going to execute people, we have to live with all the ineffi-ciencies that come with safeguarding that people be legally executed," said Seth P. Waxman, a death row litigator with the Washington firm of Miller, Cassidy & Larroca, in an interview with the *National Law Journal* four years ago. The Supreme Court itself, he noted, has found reasons to give a prisoner habeas relief sometimes on his third or fourth federal petition.

But the political costs in 1993 were very different than in 1953. "When you could only remedy two and a half constitutional defects, who cared?" said habeas scholar Vivian Berger, vice dean of Columbia University Law School. "But when you plugged in the Warren Court revolution, with its steady expansion of the rights of criminal defen-dants under the Bill of Rights and the Fourteenth Amendment, well, then the conservative ox was gored."

With his August 16, 1985, execution date rapidly approaching, He-rrera filed his first state habeas petition, which was denied by the Texas Court of Criminal Appeals on August 2. Five days later, he filed a fed-eral petition in the federal district court in Brownsville, once again challenging the reliability of the identifications used against him at his trial. The federal court on August 12 entered a stay of his execution, but did not rule on his petition, incredibly, for four more years.

Although lawyers for death row inmates have been blamed by Rehn-quist, other federal judges, Republican presidents, lawmakers, and others for prolonging litigation in the courts in order to delay execu-tions, in Herrera's case, the federal court itself was responsible for the longest delay. Texas assistant attorney general Margaret Griffey, who later argued against Herrera before the Supreme Court, said such court delays are not unusual. "Some courts are just slower than others," she said.

In 1989, the federal court denied Herrera's request for relief and dis-solved the stay of execution. He appealed to the United States Circuit Court of Appeals for the Fifth Circuit, which, on June 25, 1990, also rejected his claim. On October 15, the United States Supreme Court refused to hear his appeal of that ruling. A Texas trial court then set a new execution date for Herrera: December 17, 1990.

During those five years in which Herrera was pursuing his first round of state-federal habeas petitions, the legal and political landscapes of federal court review of habeas petitions were changing dramatically for death row inmates.

The Reagan and Bush administrations, backed by state and local prosecutors, aggressively, but unsuccessfully, pushed Congress to enact limits on habeas petitions by death row inmates. They made repeated attempts in anticrime bills to prohibit federal court review when a death row inmate's claim had received "full and fair" review in the state courts. This approach, habeas supporters contended, would have returned the scope of habeas corpus to the days of Leo Frank.

While Congress hemmed and hawed on habeas, Rehnquist upped the political ante. As Chief Justice, Rehnquist is head of the Judicial Conference of the United States, the policy-making arm of the federal judiciary. In 1988, he appointed an ad hoc committee, chaired by retired Justice Lewis F. Powell Jr., to recommend reforms of federal habeas in death penalty cases.

The Powell Committee presented its recommendations in 1990, urging that prisoners be limited, in most instances, to one federal habeas petition and that it be filed within six months of their convictions becoming final on direct appeal. If the states wanted to take advantage of these new limits, the committee recommended a quid pro quo: the states must provide lawyers for prisoners in state habeas proceedings. (The Constitution only guarantees criminal defendants a lawyer at trial and on direct appeal.)

But Congress soon stalemated over these proposals as well. The same Congress that received the Powell report went on to enact a crime bill without habeas corpus provisions. And Rehnquist, who was saying in speeches that the scope of habeas "is a question of policy for Congress to decide," was no longer waiting for Congress.

Rehnquist was not alone in his impatience with the use of habeas corpus petitions by death row and other prisoners. Justice O'Connor, second only to the Chief Justice in her devotion on the Court to federalism, or states' rights, also was critical, saying habeas corpus frustrated "both the States' sovereign power to punish offenders and their good faith attempts to honor constitutional rights." And, Justice Byron White, while not as openly hostile, took a strict view of the writ's scope, saying that federal courts are not "forums in which to relitigate state trials."

In more than a dozen decisions beginning in 1989, the Court's conservative majority, over vigorous dissents by Justices William J. Brennan, Thurgood Marshall, Harry A. Blackmun, and John Paul Stevens, effectively accomplished most of what Rehnquist sought from the Powell Committee and Congress. Those decisions erect a series of complicated and nearly insurmountable hurdles for prisoners seeking federal court review of constitutional errors. Among the most daunting of those obstacles are rulings virtually limiting prisoners to one federal petition and prohibiting them from taking advantage of favorable new constitutional rules announced by the high court if their convictions are final.

But in its march toward finality, the high court held out one strand of hope: All of these obstacles could drop by the wayside and a federal court would examine a constitutional claim if a prisoner could make a credible showing of actual innocence.

Two weeks after the trial court set December 17, 1990, as his second execution date, Herrera was back in state court with another habeas petition, but this time, among other claims, he argued for the first time that he was actually innocent of the Carrisález murder, based on newly discovered evidence.

For his second round of habeas petitions, Herrera had a new lawyer, Mark Olive of Tallahassee, Florida. Olive was a veteran death row litigator. He had been director of the Georgia Death Penalty Resource Center, one of fourteen federally funded centers created by Congress to recruit counsel for indigent death row inmates. In 1975, before any resource centers had been created or much envisioned, he had helped to set up a prototype resource center at Florida State University. Quiet and deliberate-spoken, Olive is described by colleagues as very smart, diligent, and a guerrilla fighter in the trenches.

In the fall of 1990, Olive got a phone call from Robert McGlasson, then head of the Texas Resource Center. McGlasson was looking for lawyers to help with the next group of inmates facing execution dates. Texas, with nearly four hundred inmates on death row and the highest execution rate in the nation, "was and is under water" in its need for postconviction lawyers, said one death row lawyer-volunteer.

McGlasson basically put all the upcoming cases in a hat and drew names. Olive got Herrera. No one knew much about Herrera at that point, except that he was convicted of a cop killing in the Rio Grande Valley, and if any case was a "bad case" politically, this was the case.

After accepting the case, Olive and the resource center began their investigation of Herrera's case. The first few times the lawyers met with Herrera, he steered them away from any inquiries into his innocence. He didn't want them talking to his nephew or other family members, they recalled, because he felt his family was in jeopardy.

Eventually, Herrera's lawyers heard through various sources that Hector J. Villarreal, a former Edinburg state district judge, had information about the murders. Villarreal told the lawyers that in 1984, while representing Leonel's brother, Raúl Sr. on a charge of attempted murder, Raúl had confessed that he, not Leonel, had killed Officers Rucker and Carrisález.

In previous talks with Villarreal, Raúl had told the lawyer that he, Leonel, and their father were involved in drug trafficking with the county sheriff, Brígido Marmolejo. Rucker, the first officer killed in 1981, was also part of the ring, he claimed, and acted as security when Leonel cut the cocaine on South Padre Island.

On September 29, 1981, Raúl told Villarreal, Leonel was supposed to go to the island with a drug dealer from the East, cut the cocaine for the dealer, and leave. But that night Leonel was too "coked up" to drive to the island, so Raúl, who had his own set of keys to Leonel's car, took his place. Rucker wasn't pleased by the switch. He didn't know Raúl and had a bad argument with him. The deal did not go down. As Raúl and the dealer left the island, Rucker pulled them over; another argument ensued, and Raúl shot Rucker. About ten minutes later, Carrisález pulled over the speeding car, and Raúl said he shot Carrisález. Raúl told Villarreal he had expected Leonel to be acquitted, so he kept quiet.

After Leonel's conviction, Raúl told Villarreal, he began blackmailing the sheriff. While in jail on the attempted murder charge, he threatened to "spill the beans" on the sheriff.

Marmolejo reportedly was a target of an FBI investigation in the mid-1980s that identified him as one of several Valley residents suspected of drug trafficking. However, the sheriff was never indicted or charged with any crimes as a result of the investigation.

Shortly before Raúl's trial was to begin, while he was out on bail, Raúl was shot in the back of the neck and killed by José López, a business partner, who later pleaded guilty to attempted manslaughter and received a probated ten-year sentence.

While checking Villarreal's story, the resource center lawyers found a back-up to his account. Juan Franco Palacious, who shared a cell with

Raúl in 1984 in the county jail, said Raúl told him then he had shot Rucker and Carrisález.

Herrera's lawyers used affidavits from Villarreal and Palacious to back Leonel's claim of actual innocence in his second state habeas petition. Before the court ruled, it modified Herrera's execution date to January 23, 1991. The trial court denied relief on January 14, finding that "no evidence at trial remotely suggested" that anyone other than Herrera killed Carrisález. The Texas Court of Criminal Appeals affirmed on May 21, 1991, and denied a rehearing on September 18, 1991. A fourth execution date was set: February 19, 1992.

Villarreal later said he had told Raúl's story to Leonel's trial lawyer after Raúl was killed and did not know why that lawyer did nothing with the information. The lawyer could not be questioned because he was dead, shot by the jealous husband of one of his divorce clients.

But if the Herrera family was running drugs with law enforcement officials in the county and a lawyer tried to expose it, suggested some close to the case, he probably would have gotten the same treatment as Leonel. "This is a rough community," said one lawyer. The second attorney in Herrera's murder trial would not meet with resource center lawyers in the area; he insisted on coming to Austin.

For Herrera's family and friends, the fear then and to this day, said those close to him, was that by saving Leonel, others might be killed. For his part, Leonel was prepared to go to his death to protect those people, they added.

But gradually others did come forward. Raúl Herrera Jr., nine years old at the time of the killings, told the lawyers he was in the car that night with his father, as was López, and had witnessed the killings. He said, in an affidavit, that no attorney for Leonel had ever asked him anything about the murders. He also claimed he had told his story to a local police office and was told in return never to say anything about it. And José Ybarra Jr., a schoolmate of the Herrera brothers, said that Raúl Sr. had told him one summer night in 1983 that he had shot the two police officers.

Herrera's lawyers first attempted to get his conviction reviewed again in state court, but to no avail. A state court denied Herrera's state habeas corpus application, finding that there was no evidence at trial that remotely suggested that anyone other than Herrera had committed the crime. Herrera's lawyers took their affidavits into federal court on February 16, less than three days before his scheduled execution. The petition went to Judge Ricardo Hinojosa, a Reagan appointee who had been mentioned as a possible Supreme Court nominee. Hinojosa was a conservative jurist who had presided for almost ten years in the border area of south Texas where the crime occurred.

The next day, Hinojosa granted a stay of execution so that Herrera could present his claim of innocence and affidavits in state court and explained he did so "in order to ensure that Petitioner can assert his constitutional claims and out of a sense of fairness and due process." The judge also scheduled an evidentiary hearing on a related claim made by Herrera.

The stage was now set for exactly the kind of last-minute, chaotic maneuvering that Rehnquist and other judges had been complaining about for years. Herrera was scheduled to die before dawn on February 19.

The state attorney general's office immediately appealed Hinojosa's stay to the Fifth Circuit. At 8:30 P.M., February 18, a three-judge panel overruled Hinojosa. The panel rejected all of Herrera's constitutional claims. As for his claim of innocence, the panel said, "The rule is well established that claims of newly discovered evidence, casting doubt on the petitioner's guilt, are not cognizable in federal habeas corpus." Even assuming Herrera was innocent, the court thus ruled a claim of innocence alone was not enough to justify a writ of habeas corpus.

At 11 P.M., Herrera's lawyers filed a request for a stay of execution in the United States Supreme Court. While waiting for the high court to act, recalled McGlasson, he was in Austin on the phone trying to find a state judge who would issue a stay. Olive was in Houston contacting federal judges. At about 1:30 A.M., the Supreme Court denied a stay of action. The lawyers needed five votes, but only got four—Justices Blackmun, Stevens, O'Connor, and Souter.

The lawyers then informed the state that they would ask the high court to convert their stay application into a petition for certiorari, a request that the Supreme Court take the case. At 4:15 A.M., the Court denied that request, with the same four Justices stating they would grant the motion and grant certiorari.

While five votes are needed to stay an execution, only four votes are needed to grant a petition of certiorari. At this point, Herrera's lawyers knew they had four votes for certiorari. The question they would ask the high court to review seemed to leap off the pages of the Fifth Circuit's opinion. The appellate court had said innocence didn't matter, period. No other court had gone so far.

While the resource center staff kept Herrera on the phone outside the execution chamber, Olive worked on drafting the petition. At 4:30 A.M., McGlasson notified the state attorney general's office that he was going to file a certiorari petition and it was likely to succeed; he was told, in turn, that the state would proceed with the execution at 5 A.M. because no stay was in effect.

On the basis of the likelihood the Supreme Court would take Herrera's case, a federal judge then issued a stay of execution. But the state immediately went to the Fifth Circuit, which at 5:45 A.M. vacated that stay.

Herrera's claim of innocence was "just newly discovered evidence, without a constitutional claim, as the Fifth Circuit said," insisted Texas assistant attorney general, Robert Walt, head of the state's death unit. And, under Texas law, state courts are barred from reviewing newly discovered evidence if produced thirty days after trial. "You can't just walk in at the last minute with an affidavit and say, 'I'm innocent.'"

At 6:15 A.M., the United States Supreme Court agreed to take Herrera's case and decide his question: Does the Constitution prohibit the execution of a convicted person who is innocent? But the Court again refused to stay the execution. At 6:20 A.M., the Texas Court of Criminal Appeals stepped forward and issued an order vacating the execution date.

Herrera's case was slated for argument in October 1992. But he was not safe yet.

Shortly after the high court granted review, Walt insisted that the execution stay was not really a stay. The state appellate court simply vacated the execution date, he explained, leaving the trial court free to set a new date. "It wouldn't surprise me at all if the trial court set a new execution date, about thirty-one days out," he predicted at the time.

Two weeks later, the trial court did exactly that; it set April 15, 1992 as the new execution date for Herrera.

Herrera's evidence of his innocence, said Walt, was "contrived and not credible in any fashion. The affidavits don't jive with the physical evidence in the case."

Lawyers on both sides then went back to the Texas Court of Criminal Appeals. The court issued a formal stay prohibiting Herrera's execution until his Supreme Court case was decided. In an obviously pained decision, Judge Morris Overstreet wrote:

"This Court finds itself in the unenviable position of having a Texas death row inmate scheduled to be put to death while his case is pending review by the highest court in the land. . . . Because of the 'rule of five,' that Court, which agreed to hear this case on the vote of four justices, but refused to stay the execution, once again creates the ultimate dilemma regarding a Texas death row inmate. Once again a death row inmate needlessly has a carrot dangled before him."

Judge Overstreet noted that in 1990 another Texas death row inmate was executed while his case was pending before the Supreme Court. Ironically, the Justices later dismissed his case as moot because of his death. Quoting the late Justice Thurgood Marshall in that case, Judge Overstreet said that according to established practice at the high court, a vote to grant review "should have triggered a fifth vote to grant petitioner's application for a stay of execution." Such was the practice until the retirement in 1987 of Justice Lewis F. Powell Jr., who often provided that fifth vote.

The *Herrera* case was an inevitable headline grabber. Although in the public's mind Herrera was asking the high court a question shocking in its simplicity—does it violate the Constitution to execute an innocent person—the Justices in reality faced a more complex and technical issue.

At its legal core, *Herrera v. Collins* was about forum and procedures. Where and how could Herrera assert his claim of innocence based on newly discovered evidence when state courthouse doors were locked because of Texas's thirty-day rule, and federal courts, at this stage, could not redetermine a jury's verdict of guilt?

The Court was caught between the public's perception of the case and the legal reality. And, as oral arguments and the ultimate ruling would show, some Justices were not happy at all to be stuck in a web that they themselves essentially had woven.

In 1992, the possibility that innocent persons could be executed seemed more likely than ever as recent news accounts reported a growing number of death row inmates being released or having sentences commuted because of new evidence or questions of innocence. Randall Dale Adams and Clarence Brandley of Texas; Gary Nelson of Georgia, and James Richardson and Joseph Brown in Florida had all been freed when evidence of their innocence came to light.

While the case's outcome was obviously crucial to Leonel Herrera himself, it also was very important to those involved in the death penalty debate.

"We all thought this was the next wave in the anti-death penalty battle," recalled North Carolina assistant attorney general Joan Byers. "The whole name of their game is delay."

But the *Herrera* case, insisted John Blume of the South Carolina Death Penalty Resource Center, presented in "its starkest form" the ramifications of the high court's habeas revisions.

"The whole thrust of the habeas decisions has been to say habeas should remain only as a safety valve for those actually innocent," he explained. "I thought Mr. Herrera was going to the Supreme Court to say, 'If you're really serious, well, here I am.'"

Both sides had less than eight months to write briefs and prepare for the October 7 oral arguments. Olive and Blume took on the brief-writing chores, but they and other lawyers involved in the case wanted someone with national stature in the Court's eyes to argue on behalf of Herrera.

Talbot "Sandy" D'Alemberte, in mid-term as president of the American Bar Association, was a civil trial lawyer in the Tallahassee office of Steele, Hector & Davis, about two blocks away from Olive's office. He had known Olive since the mid-1970s when, as dean of Florida State University's law school, he had recruited Olive to help start the death penalty resource center at the school. He also had worked with Olive later on a couple of death penalty postconviction cases.

D'Alemberte got a phone call from Olive asking him to join the Herrera legal team and argue the case. "I don't consider myself an expert in these cases," he later said. "I'm basically a civil litigator, a libel and press access lawyer. I also don't have the tolerance for these cases that others do. It just burns me out emotionally. Leonel's case was probably the worst I've ever had in that sense."

Before agreeing to argue the case, D'Alemberte wanted to do his own investigation. He went to south Texas and talked with Valley lawyers about the case, the possibility of police involvement in the murders and drug trafficking. He also met with Herrera and his nephew, Raúl Jr.

"I don't know of any place quite like south Texas," he recalled. "But I actually came away thinking Leonel was innocent and I ought to take the case."

In the Texas attorney general's office, Assistant Attorney General Margaret Portman Griffey was tapped to write the state's brief and make her first Supreme Court argument. She had been handling death cases for five years. Law was her second career; earlier in her life, she had been an artist, an expert weaver.

Griffey was immediately aware of the legal and political significance of the *Herrera* case. If the Justices directed federal habeas courts back into the fact-finding process in these cases, she thought, it would be the largest expansion of the Great Writ yet, with important ramifications for the interaction of federal and state courts. And, the way in which her opponents had downplayed the physical evidence in the case and distorted the legal question for the public, she said, made clear the political agenda behind the case.

But she too felt compelled to do her own investigation. Griffey went to south Texas; traveled, along with police and the prosecutor, over the murder route; combed through police and prosecutorial files, and questioned local drug enforcement authorities. While it was clear from the trial record that Herrera was guilty, she said, it was clear now in her mind too.

A third player also was at work on the case. The solicitor general of the United States had decided to support Texas before the Supreme Court. *Herrera*'s issue directly affected the constitutionality of a federal rule that bars federal courts from considering claims of newly discovered evidence two years after a conviction.

The government's brief was assigned to a veteran assistant to the solicitor general, Paul Larkin Jr., who, interestingly, had gone to Stanford University School of Law in order to study with Anthony G. Amsterdam, the noted anti-death-penalty advocate. Amsterdam unsuccessfully argued against the constitutionality of Georgia's death penalty in the 1976 case, *Gregg v. Georgia*. As with D'Alemberte and Griffey, the possibility of Herrera's innocence touched a raw nerve with Larkin, who ultimately would devote more time to preparing this case than any other in his seven years as an assistant. He would share ten minutes of Griffey's argument time before the Court.

In their brief to the high court, Herrera's lawyers made basically four arguments:

The Eighth Amendment's bar against cruel and unusual punishment prohibits the execution of an innocent person. Citing key Supreme Court rulings, they argued, the death penalty can be imposed only on those who "killed, attempted to kill, or intended that a killing take place or that lethal force be used" or whose actions constituted "major participation in a felony, combined with reckless indifference to life." Actual innocence triggers the Eighth Amendment's protection.

The Fourteenth Amendment's Due Process Clause, they argued, demands that a claim of innocence be heard somewhere. If, as the high court has said, the Due Process Clause prohibits government actions that "shock the conscience," then convicting and executing an innocent person is such an action.

Federal habeas review must be available if state law closes all avenues, as it had in Texas, for presenting an innocence claim based on newly discovered evidence. And relief should be granted if a defendant can show a fair probability that under all of the evidence, there was reasonable doubt as to guilt.

The state countered, in its brief, that there was no Eighth Amendment issue. That amendment, it argued, applies only to issues of punishment, and Herrera's newly discovered evidence relates to his guilt or innocence. His due process rights also were not violated, the state contended. The United States and thirty-four states strictly limit the time for bringing forward claims based on newly discovered evidence, and those time limits have withstood challenge.

Federal habeas review, it argued, is not available here because habeas exists only to remedy constitutional errors, not to correct errors of fact. Herrera had only a freestanding claim of innocence.

In preparation for oral arguments, D'Alemberte went through two mock arguments and was critiqued by a network of experienced death row litigators and habeas corpus scholars. Griffey too went before skilled state prosecutors as well as Paul Larkin Jr., assistant to the solicitor general.

On Wednesday, October 7, 1992, the third day of the new term, the Court took up the *Herrera* case as the second case of the morning session. D'Alemberte was first at the podium.

Regardless of what followed, he knew he had one point to get across: a federal judge should be allowed to make the threshold decision as to whether a claim like Herrera's should get a hearing. "Here we had Judge Hinojosa, appointed by Ronald Reagan, a mature judge, no wild-eyed liberal, looking at this and saying, 'I'm disturbed enough I want to hear it.' For the appellate court to say he can't is really arrogant," D'Alemberte recalled.

D'Alemberte also knew that if Herrera was to have any hope of winning, he would have to convince Justices O'Connor and Kennedy who, as they had in the past, could moderate the extreme views on the right and left wings of the Court.

D'Alemberte barely made his opening statement that Herrera's case turned on the question of whether a hearing must be held before some-one "with a colorable claim of innocence" can be executed when the Justices' questions began to flow fast, and in some cases, furiously.

Justice White and the Chief Justice asked a series of questions forcing D'Alemberte to clarify terms he was using and the phrasing of the questions in Herrera's certiorari petition. Justice O'Connor soon interjected, briskly insisting that Herrera, while alleging innocence, was before the Court as a guilty defendant. Most states, she pointedly added, had time limits for considering newly discovered evidence, and Herrera was making his claim many years after his conviction.

She also noted that Texas has a clemency process for people in Herrera's position. D'Alemberte conceded Herrera was legally guilty. As for a clemency request, he said, "It has been done, although there is not any great history of clemency or pardon in Texas."

Justice White asked D'Alemberte if he would be arguing his case if Texas had a five-year instead of a thirty-day limit on newly discovered evidence. Repeating a theme of his argument, D'Alemberte replied, "Innocence ought to be of paramount value," overcoming any time limit.

He told Justice White that over the years, evidence of innocence had been discovered many times, many years after a conviction. The Great Writ, he said, is the "safety valve" to prevent fundamental miscarriages of justice.

But, interjected Chief Justice Rehnquist, the safety valve has been in the context of "claims of innocence traceable to a constitutional violation," not in the context of free-standing claims of innocence.

Justice O'Connor abruptly demanded, "Exactly what is the constitutional rule you would have this Court adopt?" D'Alemberte first replied the rule against cruel and unusual punishment prohibits "barbaric" punishment, including the execution "of someone who is innocent."

But Herrera is a "guilty person here," again insisted Justice O'Connor. "What rule do you propose?" D'Alemberte quickly answered, "We would suggest the rule that says an inmate with a colorable claim of innocence may not be executed without provision for a hearing on that claim."

At that point, it was clear D'Alemberte wanted a rule only for prisoners facing death. But Justice Scalia then insisted if his argument was valid, his rule "should apply to everyone in prison." He warned D'Alemberte that this rule would put an "enormous" burden on the criminal justice system. But D'Alemberte argued he was not seeking a broad rule and the Court could limit it to death cases because, as the Court itself has often said, "Death is different," and different rules sometimes are demanded.

The Justices then began probing the scope of the hearing a federal judge would have to hold to make the threshold decision that a claim of innocence on habeas warranted a full hearing. From D'Alemberte's replies, Justice Souter suggested D'Alemberte's rule was not tied to newly discovered evidence and would allow an inmate to attack his conviction for any reason as long as he raises a probability of his actual innocence. "Innocence is of such paramount value that an inmate should have a hearing on a colorable claim, with or without newly discovered evidence," D'Alemberte argued.

Listening to the Court's exchange with D'Alemberte, Griffey later recalled, "I was glad I wasn't getting some of their questions." It became quickly evident the Justices weren't interested in the facts of the *Herrera* case, only the legal issues. As she stepped up to the podium, she mentally discarded a section of her argument dealing with the trial evidence.

Almost immediately Griffey had much better luck than D'Alemberte. She was able to deliver her full opening statement. The trial is the constitutionally designated mechanism for determining guilt, she told the Justices, and a state's clemency procedure is the proper method for resolving late claims of innocence.

The rule sought by Herrera, she argued, would turn trials into preliminary determinations of guilt. In capital crimes, it would require repeated stays of executions and would force courts to review a cold record and weigh unreliable evidence years after the trial. Late-hour alibis, she reminded the Justices, are inherently unreliable.

Justice Scalia then jumped in, "Isn't innocence paramount?" Griffey later recalled the impact of his question. "I thought, 'Oh, God, it's such a global question. I wasn't prepared for anything so global. Those are the tough questions, the broad ones.' I thought, 'Well, of course the answer is yes.' "

Griffey told Scalia, "Certainly innocence is paramount," but the trial is the properly designated mechanism for determining innocence. And, Griffey stuck to that theme like a bulldog throughout her twenty minutes.

Justice Kennedy then asked Griffey, "Suppose you have a videotape which conclusively shows the person is innocent" and state law or policy does not allow new evidence claims in the clemency process. Is there a federal constitutional violation? "No, there is not," Griffey replied. Would it be unconstitutional then to execute that person? Not under those circumstances, Griffey replied, adding that such a situation was not likely to happen because of the myriad of constitutional protections provided at trial as well as the clemency powers of the governor.

"Clemency and commutation operate to the advantage of the defendant," Griffey argued, explaining the executive branch is not bound by technical court rules and the reasonable doubt standard in those procedures. The Justices then began to explore the frequency of clemency in Texas capital cases, with Justice Stevens remarking, sarcastically, that setting aside death sentences was not one of the Texas Board of Pardons' "favorite things."

Justice O'Connor asked if any clemency requests had been granted in the last fifteen to eighteen years. "No," answered Griffey.

Justice Stevens soon began an exchange leading him to summarize, "The very issue here is if there is sufficiently persuasive evidence of innocence, is there a right under the Eighth Amendment not to be executed?" Griffey replied, "It would not violate the Eighth Amendment as long as the defendant was found guilty in a trial process that did not give rise to a constitutional error."

The assistant to the solicitor general, Paul J. Larkin Jr., had ten minutes of smooth sailing presenting the Bush administration's position. The debate before the high court, he said, was conducted and resolved fifty years earlier with the adoption of the federal rules of criminal procedure. A two-year time limit was put on motions for new trials based on newly discovered evidence, he said, and a special exception for capital cases was abolished. The primary interest served by the rule, he said, was finality of justice.

But, Justice Stevens interjected, "The rule didn't apply to many capital cases. When was the last federal death sentence carried out?" In 1960, replied Larkin, but, he added, "it would be a mistake to say today the balance of interests differs from those 50 years ago. Most states have fixed time periods and there is widespread recognition there must be time limits. It is not fundamentally unfair to set a fixed time limit and thereafter channel innocence claims through the clemency process."

Leaving the courtroom that day, D'Alemberte and his colleagues found it difficult to see five votes for Herrera's argument. Months later, lawyers on both sides recalled the unusually hostile tone of the arguments.

For D'Alemberte, the reason for the hostility was simple. "They didn't want anything to do with the case. This was a subject that scared the hell out of them. They were caught between their fear of opening the floodgates to these claims and their fear of executing an innocent person, and they didn't like it."

But, countered state prosecutor Joan Byers of North Carolina, "The Court was hostile because Herrera was not the case it was billed to be. Every time the Court ratchets down rights it's because there's been some abuse of the process."

On January 25, 1993, the high court affirmed the Fifth Circuit's ruling that Herrera's claim of actual innocence does not entitle him to federal habeas relief.

Writing for a six-member majority, the Chief Justice said, "Claims of actual innocence have never been held to state a ground for federal habeas relief absent an independent constitutional violation occurring in the underlying state proceeding." Federal courts, he explained, are not forums in which to relitigate state trials. Society's resources, he added, are concentrated at trial to determine a person's guilt or innocence.

Few rulings would be more disruptive of the federal system than to require federal habeas review of freestanding claims of innocence, he insisted. Federal courts would have to hear testimony from witnesses who testified at trials taking place years ago and who made affidavits, and would then have to determine guilt or innocence once again.

Traditional habeas relief for such a prisoner would require the state to retry him, added Rehnquist. "Yet there is no guarantee that the guilt or innocence determination would be any more exact. To the contrary, the passage of time only diminishes the reliability of criminal adjudication."

Herrera's claim, according to the majority, did not fit into a recent series of high court decisions allowing a showing of innocence to be used as a gateway to federal review of alleged constitutional errors that would otherwise have been barred from review. And, the majority added, it did not fit into the doctrine of cases in which the Eighth Amendment requires increased reliability of the process by which the death penalty is imposed.

However, Herrera's claim did belong in the clemency process, the majority said. "Clemency is deeply rooted in our Anglo-American tradition of law, and is the historic remedy for preventing miscarriages of justice where judicial process has been exhausted."

In perhaps the strangest part of the majority opinion, Rehnquist then assumed "for the sake of argument in deciding this case," that in a capital case "a truly persuasive demonstration" of actual innocence made after trial would render the execution of a defendant unconstitutional and warrant federal habeas relief "if there were no state avenue open to process such a claim."

The threshold showing for a death row prisoner would have to be "extraordinarily high," the majority said, and Herrera's evidence "falls far short of any such threshold."

Justice O'Connor, joined by Justice Kennedy, wrote separately, agreeing with the majority opinion's reasoning and result, but emphasizing, "the execution of a legally and factually innocent person would be a constitutionally intolerable event. Dispositive to this case, however, is an equally fundamental fact: Petitioner is not innocent, in any sense of the word." She then proceeded to dissect the credibility of Herrera's evidence, emphasizing the weight of the evidence pointing instead toward Herrera's guilt. O'Connor emphasized the letter Herrera had written in which he acknowledged responsibility for the murders, the blood sample evidence, and the suspicious nature of the affidavits upon which Herrara attempted to rely at the eleventh hour, noting that they "conveniently blame a dead man." Justice O'Connor even criticized the federal judge who initially granted an execution stay.

Justice White too wrote separately. He concurred in the majority's result, but not its reasoning. He assumed it would be unconstitutional to execute someone who has made a persuasive showing of innocence, but to be entitled to relief, a prisoner would have to show that "no rational trier of fact could find proof of guilt beyond a reasonable doubt."

Only Justices Scalia and Thomas were willing to say that the Constitution permits executions in cases in which postconviction assertions of innocence are based upon newly discovered evidence. "There is no basis in text, tradition, or even in contemporary practice (if that were enough), for finding in the Constitution a right to demand judicial consideration of newly discovered evidence brought forward after conviction," wrote Justice Scalia.

Nonetheless, the two Justices said, they were joining the majority opinion because there was no legal error in assuming for the sake of argument, as the majority did, that a right to review exists. And, they added, they understood "the reluctance of the present Court to admit publicly that Our Perfect Constitution" lets stand any injustice.

"With any luck," added Justice Scalia, "we shall avoid ever having to face this embarrassing question again, since it is improbable that evidence of innocence as convincing as today's opinion requires would fail to produce an executive pardon."

Justice Blackmun led the dissent, joined by Justices Stevens and Souter. The protection of the Eighth Amendment, he insisted, does not end after someone has been validly convicted and sentenced. And, he added, the execution of an innocent person is the ultimate "arbitrary imposition" forbidden by the Fourteenth Amendment's Due Process Clause.

"Whatever procedures a State might adopt to hear actual innocence claims, one thing is certain: The possibility of executive clemency is not sufficient to satisfy the requirements of the Eighth and Fourteenth Amendments," he wrote. "The vindication of rights guaranteed by the Constitution has never been made to turn on the unreviewable discretion of an executive official or administrative tribunal."

Justice Blackmun also called the majority's view "perverse" in light of what the Court has done with federal habeas rulings. Even as it has increasingly erected barriers to federal review of prisoners' claims in order to bring finality to their cases, he said, the Court, beginning with a trio of cases in 1986, had adopted the view that there should be an exception to this concept of finality. And that exception, he said, is when a prisoner can make a colorable showing of innocence.

After adopting an actual innocence requirement for review of otherwise barred claims, explained Justice Blackmun, the majority was now taking the position that the claim of actual innocence itself was not a constitutional claim but simply a gateway through which a prisoner must pass to get review of his claims on the merits.

"In other words, having held that a prisoner who is incarcerated in violation of the Constitution must show he is actually innocent to obtain relief, the majority would now hold that a prisoner who is actually innocent must show a constitutional violation to obtain relief. The only principle that would appear to reconcile these two positions is the principle that habeas relief should be denied whenever possible."

Justice Blackmun ended the dissent on a very personal note. He reiterated his past "disappointment" with the Court's "obvious eagerness" to eliminate restrictions placed on the states' power to execute as well as his recent doubts about the continuing constitutionality of the death penalty in the absence of those restrictions.

"Of one thing, however, I am certain," he concluded. "The execution of a person who can show that he is innocent comes perilously close to simple murder."

After the decision was announced, D'Alemberte recalled, he felt "shattered." The majority did appear to leave the door open to federal courts for truly persuasive claims of innocence, he said, but no one was really certain of the legal impact of the majority assuming "for the sake of argument" in an opinion.

"I think they have left the door open because they had to," said D'Alemberte. "My hope always was the Court would be too embarrassed to go down the track Scalia would have them go." He felt shattered by the decision, he explained, because even though he and Herrera's other lawyers may have preserved a constitutional principle, they had in all likelihood lost Herrera's life.

Griffey, too had problems with Rehnquist's assuming "for the sake of argument" that a constitutional right to review would exist with an extraordinary showing of innocence. "There really is no support in the Constitution for that," she said. "On the other hand, as a citizen, I'm quite comfortable with that. I know that within the system as it operates now, there is always that consideration [for the possibility of innocence] in the mind of anyone who does this kind of litigation."

But some court experts doubt the Justices have left the door open to federal review of a truly compelling claim of innocence. "The decision, like a coin, has two sides," explained one expert. "The last two pages say 'yes,' but everything leading up to it is a refutation of every argument someone could make."

Although the Supreme Court had concluded Herrera's case, his lawyers were not done. The majority's trashing of Herrera's new affidavits, they worried, would lead to them being told to "get lost" wherever they went next for relief, including the Texas Board of Pardons and the Texas governor.

That trashing, done by Justice O'Connor and Chief Justice Rehnquist, was particularly unfair, they felt. As Justice Blackmun noted in his dissent, federal courts routinely rely on affidavits at the preliminary stage of habeas proceedings. Cross-examination and credibility determinations are made at the hearing, assuming the court grants one. Herrera never got that far because of the Fifth Circuit ruling.

In focusing on the trial record evidence, as the majority also did, the defendant always looks guilty, said John Blume, just as Randall Dale Evans and James Richardson did.

Herrera's lawyer gave polygraph tests to their witnesses in an effort to bolster his case and presented the results to state and federal courts as well as to the governor and Board of Pardons, but to no avail. On Wednesday, May 12, 1993, Herrera was executed. In late August, federal agents of the Drug Enforcement Administration raided the office and luxury home of Sheriff Brigído Marmolejo, who Herrera's brother had claimed was part of their drug business, in a prelude to a rumored drug-related indictment.

In the federal courts, the *Herrera* case really hasn't changed anything, said lawyers on both sides of the issue. Because actual innocence is virtually the only gateway to federal review of otherwise barred constitutional errors, more habeas claims raising actual innocence are likely, but that trend was expected before the Herrera decision.

In general, the Supreme Court is viewed by death row litigators as a hostile place in which to bring a claim of any kind. That is not likely to change until the high court's composition changes. The Court's newest justice, Ruth Bader Ginsburg, had no experience with death claims while sitting on the appellate court in the District of Columbia, so her views are untested.

As for freestanding claims of innocence by death row inmates, no one is sure what will follow *Herrera* in terms of numbers. The public is hearing more recently about innocent men released from death row because, said John Blume, "In the last few years, for the first time in the history of the death penalty, there have been adequate resources to investigate capital cases. Resource centers can put the state's case to the test. It was a system run on the cheap for a long time."

Clemency is still a rare grant to death row inmates in this country. In 1992, there were two grants of clemency.

And no one is certain how the courts will respond to cases like Herrera's. What is a "truly persuasive" demonstration of actual innocence?

Referring back to Justice Kennedy's hypothetical question in the *Herrera* argument on whether it would be unconstitutional to execute someone who has a videotape conclusively proving his innocence, one lawyer said, "I think you're going to need the videotape."

CHAPTER SEVEN

The philosophical conflicts between "libertarian" and "communitarian" views of law are visible in raised relief in the debates over controls on racist speech. For communitarian thinkers, racial equality and tolerance are not just good ideas, they are the law of the land, the declared public policies of the United States. Communitarians, convinced that people's actions proceed from their opinions, are likely to believe that racist opinions lead to an atmosphere of race hate and insensitivity, fostering acts of palpable violence and discrimination.

Libertarians, by contrast, emphasize the primacy and independence of the individual. The libertarian is generally loath to permit government to engage in lawmaking designed to build community by making persons more tolerant or more sensitive, instead emphasizing the liberty of individuals to do whatever they please as long as their actions do not cause harm to others.

In free speech cases, one of the most difficult problems is what American society should treat as a "harm" justifying regulation or abridgment of speech. Is it enough that speech harms the community by insulting some symbol or belief that the community holds sacred—such as the American flag? Is it enough that the speech harms individuals, or members of certain groups, by insulting them on the basis of their race or religion?

Communitarians are likely to see such harms as justifying penalties on speech, because such speech causes severe injury both to the values that glue society together and to the individuals who must endure these insults to their dignity and peace of mind. Libertarians, on the other hand, are likely to treat such harms as insufficient to justify laws abridging speech. For the libertarian, insults to community values or individual sensibilities are part of the price of social life. The only way to preserve the libertarian freedom to speak one's mind just because it is one's mind, or to allow breathing space for dissent and iconoclasts, is to tolerate speech that most in the community loathe.

The Supreme Court's First Amendment decisions have, in recent times, tended to side more with the libertarian than communitarian vision of freedom of speech. Freedom of speech has been, indeed, an area in which "conservative" Justices have often seemed more zealous libertarians than their liberal counterparts.

In its 1989 flag-burning decision, *Texas v. Johnson,* a majority of the Supreme Court claimed as a "bedrock principle" of modern American free speech jurisprudence the proposition that controls on speech may not be justified solely on the grounds that the content of the speech will shock or offend some who are exposed to it. The lineup of Justices in *Texas v. Johnson* did not follow any predictable ideological pattern. The decision was written by the Court's most indefatigable liberal, Justice William J. Brennan, who was joined by Justices Thurgood Marshall and Harry Blackmun, two other routinely liberal votes. Justice Antonin Scalia (a strong conservative) and Anthony Kennedy (a moderate conservative), however, also joined the Brennan opinion. Among the dissenters in *Johnson* were the normally liberal Justice John Paul Stevens and the normally conservative Chief Justice Rehnquist.

The flag-burning decision demonstrated the resolve of a majority of the Court to adhere to the "bedrock principle" even when most people in the community would feel the shock and offense—indeed, when the speech foments virtually universal disgust and revulsion. *Texas v. Johnson* also illustrates a second principle of current First Amendment orthodoxy: no cleavage may be drawn between the emotional and intellectual components of speech. Speech does not forfeit its protection under the First Amendment merely because it is graphic, shocking, or laced with hate or vulgarity.

These free speech principles have been forced in the last several years to contend with an increase in racist incidents, particularly at colleges and universities, incidents that have led to calls for clamping down with legal penalties on racist speech. These calls have generated a crisis in conscience and Constitution, for they place the constitutional and moral imperatives of racial tolerance and equality squarely in conflict with freedom of speech.

The spate of racial attacks on campuses—where freedom of speech is by tradition particularly treasured—sorely tests the principle that our free speech rules should be neutral, that it should not "pick and choose" between "good speech" and "bad speech" based on society's collective judgment concerning the propriety of the message. The almost irresistible temptation to penalize racist speech is nourished by our most progressive and generous instincts—our hopes for tolerance and harmony among all racial, ethnic, and religious groups in our pluralistic culture. If the temptation to penalize racist speech begins in our hopes for tolerance, it becomes twice as strong when, out of compassion, we attempt to view the attacks from a victim's eyes.

The city of St. Paul, Minnesota, passed an ordinance against hate speech that grew out of the growing national disquiet over racist speech. David Savage's essay tells the story of the legal challenge to that ordinance.

The Supreme Court held that hate speech laws such as the St. Paul ordinance were unconstitutional because they were a form of "viewpoint discrimination." Hateful speech denigrating others on the basis of certain viewpoints about race or sex or religion was made illegal, while hateful speech denigrating others on the basis of other viewpoints was not. Looking at the matter from the perspective of First Amendment doctrines, the St. Paul case was particularly intriguing because it involved a category of speech, so-called fighting words, that many had previously thought not to be protected at all. The Court appeared to hold that while it is permissible to have a "fighting words" law, it is not permissible to have a "fighting words" law in which certain classes of fighting words (those falling within the particular types of hate speech the law proscribes) are penalized while others are not.

Prior to the St. Paul case, in addition, the Court was divided on whether it even made sense to think of free speech cases in terms of some "categories" of speech that were protected forms of expression and others that were not. Several prior opinions had begun to undermine the assumption that "fighting words" referred to a neat and easily definable category of words that were unprotected by the First Amendment. Rather, it had begun to appear that the term "fighting words" was simply a shorthand for situations in which speech was uttered in contexts intended to precipitate imminent lawless action.

As David Savage's account explains, however, one of the difficulties in the St. Paul case was that the speech at issue did indeed take place in a context in which lawless action might imminently ensue. The speech, in fact, was part of an act of lawbreaking: hoodlums entering the yard of an African American family at night to burn a cross. The Supreme Court resolved the conundrums of the St. Paul case with the announcement of rules that appeared to tolerate no viewpoint-based discrimination, even when the speech was uttered in a context in which the speech would normally not be protected. While the hoodlums could be prosecuted for criminal trespass, and could have been further prosecuted under a viewpoint-neutral fighting words law, they could not be prosecuted under the hate-speech fighting words law that had been enacted by St. Paul.

The decision in *R.A.V. v. City of St. Paul* was followed in the next term by a decision in a case arising from Wisconsin that raised the question of whether it was constitutional to enact laws aimed not directly at *hate speech* but at *hate crimes*. May a state, for example, make a battery based upon racial animus a crime subject to a higher penalty than a common battery not motivated by racial hatred? The defendants argued that this was yet another form of viewpoint-based discrimination, because the thoughts in the perpetrator's head at the time of the battery determined the severity of the crime. Characterizing hate crimes laws as efforts at thought control, the defendants sought to invoke the St. Paul decision to persuade the Court that such hate crimes laws are unconstitutional.

The Supreme Court, however, refused that invitation, distinguishing hate crimes laws from hate speech laws. Hate crimes laws, the Court held, are not grounded in the content of speech. Rather, like most criminal laws, they gauge the severity of the criminal act by the intent of the criminal at the time the act is committed. Words may be used as evidence of the perpetrator's intent, but the words themselves are not the subject of the law's penalty.

Some were persuaded by the distinctions drawn by the Court in these two cases, believing that the Court had drawn intelligible distinctions among the concepts of "actions," "thoughts," and "speech." Others thought these distinctions were metaphysical at best. Critiques of the Court's distinctions came from both the Right and the Left. From the Right, a number of critics argued that "a thought crime is a thought crime," in the guise of legislation against either hate speech or hate crime, and that all such laws should be deemed unconstitutional under the First Amendment. From the Left, a number of critics argued that discriminatory action is discriminatory action and the government should be permitted to penalize it, whether the discrimination is accomplished entirely through disparaging words, or through more palpable forms of discrimination or violence.

David Savage's account traces these decisions, setting them against the broader "culture wars" of which they were part.

—Editor

Hate Speech, Hate Crimes, and the First Amendment

DAVID SAVAGE

If there is a bedrock principle underlying the First Amendment, it is that the Government may not prohibit the expression of an idea simply because society finds the idea itself offensive or disagreeable.—Justice William J. Brennan, for the Court in *Texas v. Johnson*

Let there be no mistake about our belief that burning a cross in someone's front yard is reprehensible. But St. Paul has sufficient means at its disposal to prevent such behavior without adding the First Amendment to the fire.— Justice Antonin Scalia, for the Court in *R.A.V. v. City of St. Paul*

Consider this rogue's gallery. Start with Larry Flynt, the porno publisher. Each month, his *Hustler* magazine features a nauseating concoction of bestiality, mutilation, and raunchy humor, as well as the obligatory photos of nude women. Then take Gregory "Joey" Johnson, who, two decades after it had gone out of fashion, took to the streets in the 1980s to condemn "Amerika" as a fascist, militaristic regime. A self-proclaimed Maoist, Johnson said he wanted to spit in the face of Republican warmongers like Ronald Reagan and George Bush. And finally, there's Henry Hill, an old-fashioned career criminal. Over twenty-five years Hill committed an astonishing array of crimes, from setting up a point-shaving scandal at Boston College to stealing $6 million in cash from Lufthansa Airlines.

What these three rogues have in common was that they had court judgments against them overturned on First Amendment grounds by the Rehnquist Court. In the 1988 case of *Hustler v. Falwell,* the Justices unanimously threw out a $200,000 judgment won by the Baptist minister Jerry Falwell in a suit arising from a mock interview published by *Hustler,* in which Falwell supposedly described the "first time" he had sex—in an outhouse with his mother. In the 1989 case of *Texas v. Johnson,* the Court in a five-to-four vote overturned the protester Joey

Johnson's conviction for burning an American flag outside the Republican Party convention in Dallas. And a unanimous Court in the 1991 case of *Simon & Schuster v. New York Crime Victims Board* overturned the so-called Son-of-Sam law and ruled that the state may not confiscate the book and movie profits from Harry Hill's life story simply because he was a convicted criminal.

To do so, wrote Justice Sandra Day O'Connor in the "Son-of-Sam" case, would permit the government to "single out" one type of speech for punishment, in this instance, speech about crime. "The government's ability to impose content-based burdens on speech raises the specter that the government may effectively drive certain ideas or viewpoints from the marketplace," wrote O'Connor, and "the First Amendment presumptively places this sort of discrimination beyond the power of the government."

These were remarkable decisions from a conservative Court. They laid down a simple, but sweeping rule: No matter how offensive the expression—whether it is spitting on the flag or glorifying a life of crime—the government may not punish the speaker just because it disagrees with his or her message. Even Earl Warren and his legendary liberal court had refused to go so far as to strike down the laws against flag burning. These days, with William H. Rehnquist as Chief Justice, the high court often takes a more authoritarian line, siding with prosecutors and upholding state or federal laws against many constitutional challenges. While the Court certainly does at times sustain constitutional claims in the civil rights and civil liberties area—there have been notable victories upholding the right to obtain an abortion, finding violations of the First Amendment's requirement of separation of church and state, and vigorously enforcing constitutional and statutory prohibitions on gender-based discrimination—on the whole the Court under Chief Justice Rehnquist has moved toward the right.

The First Amendment's ban on laws "abridging the freedom of speech" was an exception to this general move to the right. Even in a conservative era, the principle of free speech in America stands as solidly as one of the marble pillars that prop up the Supreme Court building.

Why is this so? Literalists such as Justice Antonin Scalia can point to the words of the First Amendment. It does not say the government should put no "unreasonable" restrictions on speech, or should not go "too far" in limiting speech. It commands that Congress "shall make no laws . . . abridging the freedom of speech." This principle of free expression has become embedded in Court precedents developed over many years; it was not a notion coined by the Rehnquist Court. Rather, the majority stuck by this principle in cases that were bound to provoke controversy.

Still, the recent First Amendment rulings from the Rehnquist Court challenge the assumption that political conservatives grudgingly accept the free speech principle while political liberals enthusiastically champion it. That may have been so in the 1960s, when protesters demonstrated for civil rights and against the Vietnam War and conservatives could be counted upon to stand up for law and order and, if need be, restrictions on speech and protest. But in the 1980s and today, protesters in many areas are most likely to be opponents of abortion. And on college campuses, faculty members on the political left are more inclined to favor restricting racist utterances on campus.

Just a few years ago, the Justices of the Supreme Court split along familiar lines in most free speech cases. Liberals such as William J. Brennan and Thurgood Marshall could be counted upon as staunch defenders of free speech and individual rights, while William Rehnquist would just as predictably take the government's side. But the lines are not so predictable today. The Court's newer generation of conservatives, including Justices Scalia, Anthony Kennedy, and David Souter, seem to reflect the heightened appreciation for free expression. In most constitutional cases, these appointees of Ronald Reagan and George Bush will defer to government decision makers and reject claims of individual rights, but not where the First Amendment is concerned. Even for the staunchest of conservatives, a free speech claim can be a winner.

In 1992, the newest member of the rogue's gallery came to the Court to test the outer limits of free expression. He was a seventeen-year old skinhead named Robert A. Viktora. His case began on the night of June 20, 1990, when Viktora met up with several friends at a home on Earl Street in a white working-class neighborhood of St. Paul, Minnesota. The friends got together to do some drinking and smoke marijuana. According to one participant, Viktora suggested they cause some "skinhead trouble" in the neighborhood.

Across the street sat a large, brown stucco bungalow, a four-bedroom house with a fenced-in yard. Just three months before, Russ and Laura Jones had moved in with their five children. They were the first African American family in the neighborhood, and already they had had some unpleasant moments. One spring morning, they awoke to find their tires slashed. After that, a window of their station wagon was shattered. One afternoon, Laura Jones heard a local teenager call her nine-year-old son with a racial slur. It was about to get worse.

"Do you want to burn some niggers?" one of Viktora's friends suggested. The Earl Street skinheads decided upon a rather pathetic imitation of a Ku Klux Klan raid. They would spread midnight terror by burning a small, makeshift cross on the neighbor's yard. Viktora and friends took apart an old chair and taped the wooden legs together to form a cross. About 2:30 in the morning, they snuck into the Jones' yard, planted their little cross, poured paint thinner on it and lighted it. When Russ Jones awoke to see the burning cross outside his window, he called the police.

It didn't take long for St. Paul detectives to round up the suspects. Several of the young men had bragged about their crimes, and they implicated the others. They could have been charged under local laws with trespass and assault, or under state law, with making a terroristic threat. But Ramsey County prosecutor Tom Foley decided to put to use an antibias law that had been enacted earlier, but never employed. The actions of Viktora and friends, Foley said, fit the definition of a bias crime if ever there was one.

The St. Paul ordinance said "disorderly conduct" includes "whoever places on public or private property a symbol, object, appellation, characterization or graffiti, including but not limited to a burning cross or Nazi swastika, which one knows or has reasonable grounds to know arouses anger, alarm or resentment in others on the basis of race, color, creed or religion or gender." Violators were charged with a misdemeanor.

The broad wording of this ordinance could obviously raise some constitutional objections. Viktora and his friends could have been charged under the ordinance, for example, had they simply burned the cross in their own yard. A passing pedestrian could have complained that he was angered by it, leading to a criminal prosecution. Or suppose several Arab Americans moved into the neighborhood and complained about the Star of David on display outside a local temple. Could they assert that such a symbol of Judaism arouses in them anger and resentment, and on this basis, press prosecutors to charge the local rabbi with "disorderly conduct" under the St. Paul ordinance?

In the case of the cross burning on Earl Street, however, Foley didn't see a free speech problem. In his view, the law did not stop citizens from expressing an offensive opinion or uttering loathsome words. "Nothing in this St. Paul ordinance will deter anyone from marching in a parade, picketing or demonstrating on behalf of an unpopular cause," Foley claimed. "These youths demonstrated, not for a cause, but for a purpose—to threaten and intimidate a specific African American family." The legal protection for free speech is broad, Foley added, but it doesn't give a license to "engage in terroristic acts in the middle of the night."

But an assistant public defender named Edward J. Cleary saw it differently. He was assigned Viktora's case and immediately decided to challenge the ordinance as violating the First Amendment. On behalf of his client now known as "R.A.V." (in Minnesota, the full names of youths are not used in proceedings against juveniles), Cleary submitted a brief to a juvenile court judge contending that the law was unconstitutionally broad. The St. Paul law set out to punish "unpleasant and unpopular expression," he said, without regard for the values embodied in the First Amendment.

Both attorneys cited an array of the Supreme Court's First Amendment pronouncements, but during a hearing on July 13, 1990, Judge Charles A. Flinn Jr. wasted little time in considering the nuances of the First Amendment or parsing the precedents. It looked like an easy case to him. Just four weeks earlier, the Supreme Court had reaffirmed its flag-burning decision of a year earlier, and in the case of *United States v. Eichman,* had struck down a hurriedly enacted federal law against flag desecration.

Judge Flinn told the lawyers he wasn't much interested in exploring the depths of the "overbreadth" doctrine, or the "fighting words" cases for that matter. He wasn't even certain of the facts in R.A.V.'s case, but it seemed obvious to him that cross burning was a lot like flag burning.

"I have a terrible time in this case sort of laying [the ordinance] alongside the line of cases culminating in *Eichman,* and *Johnson,* the two flag-burning cases and their progeny—I can never remember the names, but the Skokie cases and all of those," Flinn told Assistant County Attorney J. Lindsay Flint from the bench. "Should I read some more of the facts of this case, or shouldn't I? I don't know. All I know about it is it's flag burning."

"Cross burning," Ms. Flint corrected.

"Cross burning," the judge continued, "and I don't know anything

other than that. . . . It seems to me the ordinance has a lot of resem-
blances to the flag-burning lines of cases. I don't know how much all
of our talking and flapping our gums is going to help."

With that, Judge Flinn declared the St. Paul ordinance invalid and
unconstitutional under the First Amendment. A few months later,
prosecutors won a more sympathetic hearing from the Minnesota Supreme Court. Where Judge Flinn seemed to care not a whit about why
the state would want to protect its flag or prohibit cross burning, the
state supreme court justices began by endorsing the state's contention
that racist, hateful expressions must be attacked and suppressed.

"Burning a cross in the yard of an African American family's home
is deplorable conduct that the City of St. Paul may without question
prohibit," wrote Justice Esther M. Tomljanovich for a unanimous court.
"The burning cross is itself an unmistakable symbol of violence and
hatred based on virulent notions of racial supremacy."

The Minnesota cross-burning case did not involve any college campus, nor did it involve directly any of the controversy concerning hate
speech and "political correctness" sweeping the nation's campuses. But
by the time the case reached the Minnesota supreme court, it had
become a symbol for those causes. Indeed, in a footnote, Justice Tomljanovich cited a *Michigan Law Review* article by Mari Matsuda entitled
"Considering the Victim's Story." Matsuda is among a group of American law professors who are avid proponents of new laws and university
policies that punish "hate speech"; their arguments gained wide attention on university campuses during the late 1980s. University officials
deal directly with what Matsuda and others claimed was an outbreak of
campus racism, an outbreak that coincided with increases in the numbers of black, Hispanic, and Asian students. These minority students
deserved a civil atmosphere on campus, Matsuda argued. To them, she
claimed, an official tolerance for racist graffiti or overt slurs based on
their race or ethnic heritage suggested an official acceptance of hate
and hostility. Spurred by these arguments, an estimated two hundred
colleges and universities adopted new policies or amended their student conduct codes so as to punish hateful expressions based on race,
gender, religion, national origin, or sexual orientation.

In the 1989 article cited by the Minnesota court, Matsuda said there
are "certain symbols and regalia that in the context of history carry
a clear message of racial supremacy, hatred, persecution and degra-
dation of certain groups" which should not be tolerated in a civilized

society. As examples, she cited the swastika, Klan robes, and the burning cross. The St. Paul ordinance followed this reasoning, and it won an endorsement from the state's highest court. Not only is it permissible for government officials to outlaw cross burning, "it is the responsibility, even the obligation, of diverse communities to confront such notions [of racial supremacy] in whatever form they appear," wrote Justice Tomljanovich.

But what about the supremacy of the First Amendment and free expression? The Minnesota court had a ready answer, the same answer relied upon by most proponents of "hate speech" laws. It came from the so-called fighting words doctrine set in the 1942 case of *Chaplinsky v. New Hampshire.* A Jehovah's Witness, Chaplinsky was distributing literature on the street in a small New Hampshire town when an angry crowd gathered. Fearing a disturbance, a town marshal took Chaplinsky by the arm and led him away. "You are a God damned racketeer" and a "damned Fascist," the angry man told the marshal. For those comments, Chaplinsky was charged with a breach of the peace. In an opinion that sounds distinctly dated, the Supreme Court did not condemn the marshal for infringing upon Chaplinsky's free speech right to pass out his literature, but instead upheld his conviction for disturbing the peace. In doing so, the Court announced an exception to the First Amendment. "There are certain well-defined and narrowly limited classes of speech, the prevention and punishment of which have never been thought to raise any Constitutional problem," wrote Justice Frank Murphy for the Court. "These include the lewd and obscene, the profane, the libelous and the insulting or 'fighting' words—those words which by their very utterance inflict injury or tend to incite an immediate breach of the peace." Justice Murphy said that a face-to-face insult, such as Chaplinsky calling the marshal a racketeer and a fascist, has so little value as free speech that it can be banned in the interest of social "order and morality."

Justice Murphy viewed the "fighting words" exception as narrow, but his language could be interpreted more broadly. "Words . . . which by their very utterance inflict injury" could also cover graffiti scrawled upon a sidewalk, or for that matter, a burning cross. It had been already accepted that the Free Speech Clause covered more than words. It protected "expression," the Court said, and certain actions ranging from saluting to thumbing your nose, or displaying symbols such as a flag were understood as expressions covered by the First Amendment. The

Minnesota Supreme Court noted that the St. Paul law did not ban all cross burnings, only those that "arouse anger, alarm or resentment in others" based on their race or religion. In this sense, the law banned only symbols "which by their very [display] inflict injury." Thus, as "narrowly construed," the St. Paul law was constitutional, the state court ruled.

But in Ed Cleary's view, the state court had strained to uphold the cross-burning law, and in doing so, had bent the First Amendment out of shape. After all, the notion that the state can proclaim which words or symbols are and are not permissible in public sounds more like the law in North Korea or the People's Republic of China than in the United States. Imagine what fun politicians could have if given the power to define which words "arouse anger and resentment" and which by "their very utterance inflict injury." North Carolina senator Jesse Helms would no doubt be satisfied with being called a "principled conservative" or "defender of traditional values." But the labels "right-winger" and "Neanderthal" tend to arouse anger and inflict injury. Helms might wonder, Why not make them illegal?

On college campuses, the new hate speech codes made it clear that students could be punished for uttering certain derogatory terms which offended others based on their race, religion, or sexual orientation. Publicly, administrators were loath to say which words were off-limits. Privately though, they were willing to concede that using words like "nigger," "bitch," or "fag" would violate the codes. Beyond that, the consensus ended. I have pressed officials at the University of California, Stanford, and other universities to discuss which other words and phrases would trigger a violation of the student codes, and they have steadfastly refused. They appear to have realized that not everyone agrees on what words are offensive.

That became clear in the spring of 1993 when officials at the University of Pennsylvania brought charges against a white freshman who, on a cold night in January, sought to quiet black sorority girls singing outside his dormitory. He leaned out the window and called down, "Shut up, you water buffalo." To the young women who brought the charges, his comment amounted to racial harassment. A Penn official who investigated the case agreed. In her explanations, the Penn official mangled geography, along with the First Amendment. Calling someone a water buffalo is racist, she said, because water buffalo are "large, black animals living in Africa." Actually, water buffalo are found in Asia. The embarrassing controversy illustrated, if nothing else, that there is wide dispute on which words "arouse anger" in a reasonable person based on race.

Campus officials do readily concede, however, that many derogatory terms, indeed most, are not covered by the speech codes. This is so because the policies are based on the peculiar proposition that a slur based on your group identification, such as your race or religion, hurts more than one that focuses on you as individual. The awkward, shy freshman who walks through a dormitory and is called "nerd" or "twerp" has not been harassed under the terms of most speech codes, nor is the student who is called a "blimp," a "redneck," or an "asshole." Unquestionably, campus officials, like the lawmakers in St. Paul, have singled out one type of speech for punishment, and are proud for having done so.

But Ed Cleary thought the entire enterprise was unconstitutional, and in the spring of 1991, he appealed R.A.V.'s case to the Supreme Court. The case raised two distinct issues for the Justices, one a technical issue of law and the second a broad issue of social policy.

First, the Minnesota court's reliance on the out-dated *Chaplinsky* decision revealed a long-standing conflict in First Amendment law. In 1969, the Justices had finally and unequivocally adopted the so-called clear and present danger test for free speech that Oliver Wendell Holmes had set forth in dissent in 1919 in *Abrams v. United States.* During the early decades of this century, the high court had regularly upheld laws that imposed stiff punishments for the advocacy of dangerous and hateful ideas, such as Communism or, in *Debs v. United States,* involving the labor leader Eugene Debs, criticism of the military draft. For a speech in which he said workers were "cannon fodder" for the military, Debs was given ten years in prison, a sentence upheld by a unanimous Supreme Court. Then, prosecutors did not have to prove that a speech or a leaflet caused any harm or was likely to do so, only that it advocated dangerous ideas, and *might tend* to cause real harm.

But Holmes argued instead that speech should be protected from punishment unless it posed a "clear and present danger" of causing violence or disruption. Gradually, during the 1930s, his test won the Court's majority's allegiance, but it did not become the clear position of the court until the 1969 case *Brandenburg v. Ohio* decided in the waning days of the Warren Court. A Ku Klux Klan leader, Clarence Brandenburg, had spoken to a rally held on a farm outside of Cincinnati. His blustery, rambling remarks would have been neither much noted nor long remembered, but for the miracle of television. A local TV crew showed up and recorded Brandenburg saying, "We are not a revengent [sic] organization, but if our President, our Congress, our Supreme Court, continues to suppress the white, Caucasian race, it's possible that there might have to be some revengeance [sic] taken."

Hearing this, Ohio prosecutors took some "revengence" of their own, and charged Brandenburg with violating the state's criminal syndicalism statute. This measure from the World War I era made it unlawful to advocate "crime, sabotage, violence or unlawful methods of terrorism" as a way to change the government. But in a brief opinion, the Court overturned Brandenburg's conviction, struck down the Ohio law, and overruled its previous opinions upholding such statutes. Under the First Amendment, the Court ruled, the government may not punish the advocacy of dangerous ideas, including the use of force, "except where such advocacy is . . . likely to incite or produce . . . imminent lawless action." Had Clarence Brandenburg made his racially incendiary comments in a setting that genuinely posed the threat of imminent violence, the result might have been different. If the speech had been made at a Klan rally in downtown Cincinnati in front of City Hall, in a context in which it appeared that Brandenburg was exhorting his followers to storm the building and begin taking out their "revengence," police could have arrested him on the grounds that his words were "likely to incite" violence. But on a farm miles from town, Brandenburg was entirely free to shout hateful words into the country air.

But what then about Chaplinsky? Among his recorded rantings, Brandenburg had also spoken about "burying the nigger" and "sending the Jews back to Israel." Since these are words which tend to "inflict injury by their very utterance," they arguably could be declared unprotected by the First Amendment if the Court followed the rule set forth in the Chaplinsky case. So, when considering laws against hate speech and cross burnings, which precedent stood as the law: Brandenburg or Chaplinsky?

R.A.V.'s case also clearly raised the broad question of social policy. Should the government, whether a city or a state university, single out one category of speech and make it illegal?

This question split civil liberties groups like the American Civil Liberties Union. Typically, its members were devoted to two principles— equality for all and freedom for individuals—but the "hate speech" issue managed to drive a wedge between those two ideas. On one hand, groups such as African Americans, Jews, and gays could not be accorded civil equality in our society if, on college campuses or city streets, they could be subjected to threatening and hateful slurs. On the other hand, how could the principle of free speech survive if the government is empowered to select and ban certain words and phrases?

While the ACLU and its affiliates struggled over the hate speech question, conservative commentators relished the opportunity to denounce what they saw as liberal hypocrisy. They noted that for years, ACLU activists, liberal judges, and left-leaning academics had voiced the words "free speech" to defend all manner of unsavory characters and offensive expressions: the protester who spits on the flag and insults the president, the painter who mocks Jesus Christ, the smelly patron who enters the public library, the homeless person who wants the right to camp in Lafayette Park, or the panhandler who wants the right to stick his face and his hand in front of subway riders. If a question arose over whether black nationalist Louis Farrakhan should be given a college platform to condemn Jews and the state of Israel, or whether Robert Mapplethorpe's photos of explicitly homosexual activity should be publicly displayed, liberals could be counted upon to say that the right to free expression must prevail. The offense to public sentiments did not figure in the equation.

Suddenly, a different rule seemed to apply—at least among some liberals—when blacks, feminists, or gays were offended by certain phrases or symbols. While it was okay to spit on the American flag, flying the Confederate flag was deemed unacceptable. On many campuses, liberal academics, including members of the law faculty, maintained that university officials should punish students who made racist, sexist, or homophobic comments or otherwise offended minority students by their actions. It was said, for example, that fraternity boys who hold a mock "slave auction" must be officially reprimanded to show that such offensive expressions will not be tolerated.

The *Wall Street Journal*'s editorial writers, who sharpen their teeth on such liberal hypocrisies, proclaimed a new wave of "political correctness" was overtaking the nation, especially its college campuses. That term, quickly accepted, was soon known by the shorthand, "PC." If in the early 1980s, every college student came to know that "PC" stood for a personal computer, students by the end of the decade knew the initials stood for a particular mindset on the political left.

In a strict legal sense PC and campus speech codes had nothing to do with R.A.V.'s case, which merely involved the prosecution of the skinhead Robert A. Viktora under a city's criminal statute. But in the larger sense, the case has everything to do with hate speech. In the 1990s, race had become as supercharged an issue as Communism was in the 1950s. Then, the Court was pressed to decide finally whether the First Amendment permitted the government to punish people just because they once had spoken favorably of Communism. Now, the Court would have to decide finally whether the First Amendment permitted the government to punish someone just for saying something unfavorable about African Americans.

Just to make sure the Court got the point, Cleary noted in his brief the controversy over speech codes on campus and the fact that a federal judge, Lawrence H. Silberman, had recently "compared today's climate to the McCarthy era of the 1950s." (Judge Silberman, of the U.S. Court of Appeals in Washington, is a close friend and ideological ally of Justices Antonin Scalia and Clarence Thomas.) In a letter to the Dartmouth Club, Judge Silberman heaped scorn on the liberal academics who endorse today's speech codes, considering how they had railed against earlier attacks on supposed leftists. "The senator from Wisconsin sought to disarm his opponents by calling them communist or communist sympathizers," the Judge Silberman wrote. These days, he continued, faculty members loosely toss around terms such as "racist" and "sexist" to brand their opponents, he said. "I find both approaches equally offensive."

Just a few weeks after Cleary's petition arrived in the spring of 1991, the Court announced it would review the case of *R.A.V. v. St. Paul.* The oral argument was set for December 4. And the outcome would be driven by Silberman's friend and the Court's conservative theoretician, Antonin Scalia.

In his first five years on the court, "Nino" Scalia had made himself into something of a legend, revered by young conservatives, reviled by many liberals, and admired widely as the current Court's brightest star. Anyone who visited the court to listen to oral arguments soon learned why. From the bench, he could be cutting and caustic in his questions, witty in responses, and penetrating in his observations, all within a brief exchange with a lawyer. He was rarely silent.

In person, Scalia does not look formidable. He is about five foot six, rounding in the middle, with jet-black, receding hair. But his eyes have the supremely confident look of someone who says to himself, "I'm the smartest person in this room." Of that fact, Scalia never appears in doubt.

The only child of two Italian immigrants, Scalia was born March 11, 1936, in Trenton, New Jersey, but grew up in Brooklyn. His father was no fish merchant on Fulton Street, however: S. Eugene Scalia was a professor of Romance languages at Brooklyn College and a translator of Dante. Young Nino was a star student in the Catholic schools, a top graduate of the Harvard Law School, and a law professor at the Universities of Chicago and Virginia before he was discovered by the Reagan administration. In 1982, he was sent to the administration's top farm club, the U.S. Court of Appeals for the District of Columbia, and, in 1986, was elevated to the Supreme Court.

Scalia's deportment on the high court reflects his varied background. At various times, he shows the street smarts of a Brooklyn boyhood, the reverence for authority of a young man brought up in the Catholic Church, the penchant for abstract argumentation you would expect of a law professor, and the obsession with words and their precise meaning that you might expect from someone whose father translated great works into English.

To the *R.A.V.* case, Scalia brought two of his other passions: an insistence on clear rules of law and an abhorrence for affirmative action.

Throughout history, there have been Supreme Court Justices who do not care particularly much for clear and precise legal rules but who rather appear to search for the most "fair result" case by case, applying broad legal "standards" rather than crisp and definitive "rules." In modern times, for example, Justices Lewis Powell and Sandra Day O'Connor have tended to eschew application of "clean rules," instead seeking the fairest result in each case. Scalia is adamantly against this approach and had sought to set and follow clear rules of law, regardless of their impact in a particular case. In his first months on the Court, he surprised nearly everyone by casting the deciding fifth vote with the liberal faction to overturn an Arizona man's conviction for stealing a stereo. The facts were these: The police had a warrant to search the man's apartment for several items, including a gun, but not a stereo. But one officer lifted his stereo, took down the serial number from the underside, and recorded it. It turned out the stereo had been stolen, and the man was charged with the theft.

Writing for the majority, Scalia pointed out that the rule is clear:

Police must have probable cause to undertake a search, and they didn't have such cause to look under the stereo. "A search is a search," he wrote, and this one was illegal. The dissenters lambasted him for what they saw as nit-picking, but Scalia was undeterred. For him, adhering to a clear rule counted more than getting what some might see as the most "fair" result.

In 1989, Scalia surprised conservatives again by supplying a key vote to throw out the laws against flag burning in *Texas v. Johnson*. As he understood it, the First Amendment did not permit the government to pass laws prohibiting one type of message—in this instance, contempt for the flag. Is there a "flag exception" to the First Amendment? he asked of the state's attorney. A year later, however, Scalia cast a fifth vote to permit Indiana prosecutors to forbid nude dancing in bars. They did so by enforcing a state law against "public nudity." This law applied to everyone and was not passed with the intent to limit expression, Scalia said. The nature of the law settled the matter, in his view. If it was a measure designed to limit expression, it was presumptively unconstitutional. If not, it could stand, even if it had the effect in some instances of infringing the right to free speech.

Scalia had nearly as much contempt for affirmative action as for hazy, legal balancing tests. In his view, giving official preferences to blacks because of their race was just as wrong as disfavoring them because of their race. "Isn't this what we're trying to get away from?" he once asked an attorney defending a government affirmative action program.

In 1979, while he was still a law professor, he told a revealing story during a panel discussion on affirmative action. Scalia took exception to a comment by a federal judge who said these preferences were a form of "restorative justice" for African Americans. This reminded him, Scalia said, of the story of the Lone Ranger and his faithful Indian companion, Tonto. One day, they came upon an Indian war party. "Ugh, ride um west," Tonto called out as the pair made their escape. But their path was blocked by even more Indians. "Ride um south," Tonto said. It was still no good; they were surrounded by Indians. Alarmed, the Lone Ranger turned to his companion. "What do we do now?" he says. "What do you mean 'we', white man?" Tonto replied.

"I have somewhat the same feeling," Scalia said, on hearing people "talk of the evils that 'we' whites have done to blacks and that 'we' must now make restoration for. My father came to this country when he was a teenager. Not only had he not profited from the sweat of any black man, I don't think he had ever seen a black man," he said. If support for affirmative action depended on white guilt, Scalia had proclaimed himself not guilty.

The hate speech issue had many parallels to affirmative action. On campus, many liberals had supported giving preferences to blacks in admission and hiring, putting aside their earlier opposition to any form of racial discrimination. In recent years, they had put aside their concerns about restrictions on free speech and supported campus speech codes because of what they saw as an urgent need to protect black students from hurtful slurs. To Scalia, neither idea made any sense.

At the oral argument in the case of *R.A.V.*, Ed Cleary began by conceding that R.A.V.'s actions were "reprehensible" and his message of racial hatred "abhorrent," but the First Amendment ensures there is "freedom for the thought we hate," he said, echoing Holmes.

Predictably, the Justices shunned the rhetoric and honed in on the legal issue at hand. The *Chaplinsky* case had said the government may punish "fighting words," and perhaps burning a cross in someone's front yard is akin to fighting words, Justice O'Connor suggested.

Even if the cross burning was not a face-to-face insult, it was close to it, noted Justice Kennedy. "Can the government proscribe threats that cause violence?" he asked. Cleary argued that St. Paul went much further. Moreover, it was unclear what exactly was prohibited, leaving the discretion almost entirely to prosecutors. Neither Kennedy nor Scalia looked satisfied by the answer. With Cleary treading water, Scalia came to the rescue.

"Mr. Cleary, isn't one of your complaints that the Minnesota statute . . . punishes only some fighting words and not others?" he asked. (Often, if an attorney fails to make the argument Scalia favors, the Justice simply intervenes and takes over the argument.)

"It is, Your Honor," Cleary quickly replied. Even if the subcategory of speech is unprotected, as is the case with obscenity or "fighting words," the government "must not betray neutrality," he said.

When Cleary's thirty minutes were finished, he sat down, and county prosecutor Tom Foley arose to defend the St. Paul law. In his brief, he urged the Justices to look at the facts in R.A.V.'s case. Even if the wording of the statute could be considered overbroad, the seventeen-year-old had been charged, not with a speech crime, but a targeted attack on a black family's home. But Scalia soon returned to his argument. The St. Paul law "doesn't cover fighting words that are not limited to words on the basis of race, color, creed, religion or gender," he said.

"That's correct, Your Honor," the attorney nodded. "Why is that,

Mr. Foley?" the Justice asked. Obscenity, like fighting words, "is not protected by the First Amendment. Now I assume that it would be bad, would it not, to have an ordinance that says you cannot use obscene photographs to advertise . . . I don't know, the Republican Party?" That brought laughter in the courtroom, but Scalia was not finished. "If you want to prohibit obscenity, prohibit obscenity," he said. "It's the same here. If you want to prohibit fighting words, prohibit fighting words. But why pick only these particular purposes—race, color, creed, religion and gender? What about other fighting words?"

Foley countered that city officials believe bias crimes are particularly hurtful to the community. "I think the city has an absolute right and purpose to try to regulate the harm that [affects] its citizens. And certainly this bias-motivated conduct and violence is much more harmful—"

"—That's a political judgment," Scalia interrupted. "I mean, you may feel strongest about race, color, creed, religion or gender. Somebody else may feel strong about philosophy, economic philosophy, about whatever."

By the end of the hour, it was clear Scalia would vote to strike down the St. Paul law, and so it seemed would a majority of the Court. But on what grounds? Because the law was unclear in its reach? Because it went beyond "fighting words?" Or would the Court go further and deal a blow to the hate speech movement as a whole?

The answer came on June 22, 1992, a few days before the end of the term. While all nine Justices voted to strike down the St. Paul law, they divided badly over the reasons why. Five Justices, led by Scalia and including the Justices usually counted as the Court's most conservative members (Scalia's opinion was joined by Rehnquist, Kennedy, Souter, and Thomas), favored a broad attack on the entire concept of hate speech laws. The four remaining Justices (Blackmun, O'Connor, Stevens, and White) complained bitterly that the majority had gone too far. Not surprisingly, Justice Scalia stood at the epicenter of the conflict.

Assigned the task of writing the majority opinion by Chief Justice Rehnquist, Scalia cut a broad swath. The government may not impose "selective limitations" on types of speech—in this instance, "messages of bias-motivated hatred," he wrote. He chose not to challenge the Minnesota Supreme Court's conclusion that St. Paul's law punished only "fighting words," which are not shielded by the First Amendment. To do so would have plunged him into a debate over the minor issue of what is and is not a "fighting word." Instead, Scalia wanted to go further and forbid governments from outlawing some types of expressions simply because they dealt with subjects such as race. Officials may not impose "special prohibitions" on words and symbols that "express views on disfavored subjects," he wrote. The St. Paul law does not simply outlaw fighting words, he said, because it does not, for example, punish those who insult others "on the basis of (their) political affiliation, union membership or homosexuality."

In Scalia's view, the St. Paul law suffered from the same flaw as the Texas law that prohibited flag burning and the New York law that prohibited a criminal from getting paid for his story. All three were "facially unconstitutional," he said, because they discriminated against "speech solely on the basis of the subjects the speech addressed." In practice, the St. Paul ordinance was doubly flawed, he said, in that it employed both "content discrimination" and "viewpoint discrimination" against free speech. It punished a type of speech because of its content—that is, expressions concerning race or religion. Moreover, the speakers were punished for asserting a particular viewpoint on the subject. A person standing alongside a St. Paul street carrying a sign with Rodney King's message—"We've All Got to Get Along"—would not be arrested, but a person carrying a sign that said "Blacks: Get Out of St. Paul!" would violate the law.

Among the group of Justices who joined the Scalia opinion—Rehnquist, Kennedy, Souter, and Thomas, the most interesting vote was cast by the Chief Justice. Over the years, he has taken a stingy view of the free speech law. Consider his recent record. He dissented strongly in the *Texas v. Johnson* flag-burning case in 1989 and wrote the five-to-four opinion rejecting the free speech claim in the nude dancing case of 1991, *Barnes v. Glen Theatre, Inc.* Where Scalia and Kennedy had taken the same view on cross burning as they had on flag burning, Rehnquist's stand was harder to explain. But like Scalia, Rehnquist had regularly opposed affirmative action laws and other special preferences for minorities.

Notably, Scalia's opinion said nothing about the problem of racist slurs and anti-Semitic attacks, except to note in a concluding paragraph that "burning a cross in someone's yard is reprehensible." He quickly added, however, that "St. Paul has sufficient means at its disposal to prevent such behavior without adding the First Amendment to the fire." For R.A.V., it meant prosecutors could try him for an assault or making a terroristic threat, but not simply for burning a cross.

The concurring opinions of the other four Justices read like dissents. They agreed only that the St. Paul law was too broadly worded. But, speaking for Harry Blackmun, John Paul Stevens, and Sandra O'Connor, Justice Byron White slammed Scalia's opinion as a "radical revision of First Amendment law" which "will surely confuse the lower courts." According to those Justices, local governments and state colleges can "restrict the social evil of hate speech." Scalia's opinion, by contrast, "legitimates hate speech as a form of public discussion."

Blackmun angrily accused the majority of reaching out to "decide the issue of politically correct speech." For his part, he added, "I see no First Amendment values that are compromised by a law that prohibits hoodlums from driving minorities out of their homes by burning crosses on their lawns."

In a third long opinion, Stevens attacked Scalia's notion that free speech cases can be settled by neat categories and clear lines. "The categorical approach seems to be something of an adventure in doctrinal wonderland," he commented. In Stevens's view, content and context count. "Special harms may be prohibited by special rules. Lighting a fire near an ammunition dump or a gasoline storage tank is especially dangerous; such behavior may be punished more severely than burning trash in a vacant lot," he said. Like the others, Stevens predicted that the Court majority had headed down a path it would regret having taken.

But the Supreme Court had spoken, and the message from the R.A.V. case seemed clear. The government cannot selectively punish expressions of "bias-motivated hatred." Laws and state university policies that punish someone for displaying a swastika, burning a cross, and scrawling graffiti that demeans blacks, Jews, or gays are unconstitutional and void.

The decision spoke powerfully, but soon its message was heard beyond even what the majority intended.

On the day Scalia's opinion in the R.A.V. case was announced, the Wisconsin Supreme Court had before it a constitutional challenge to a different sort of hate crimes law. Where the St. Paul law made it a crime to burn a cross, the Wisconsin law increased the punishment for a criminal who "intentionally selects" his victims "because of race, religion, color, disability, sexual orientation, national origin or ancestry."

The Anti-Defamation League (ADL) had championed this approach in its attack on hate crimes, and such laws had been adopted in twenty-six states. They worked like this: Suppose a thug attacks a person leaving a bar one night and beats him senseless. If arrested and convicted of such an assault, the perpetrator might get a two-year prison term. But if the victim was picked because he was gay—or black, Jewish, Asian, or whatever—the prosecutor could ask that the thug's sentence be increased to four years in prison. Unlike the St. Paul statute, the ADL model law did not create a new crime but "enhanced the penalty" for an existing crime. However, it was largely based on the same premise—that hateful actions based on bias and bigotry deserve special punishments.

The case before the Wisconsin court was a textbook example, except for one fact. In this instance, the perpetrator was black and the victim white. It happened on October 7, 1989, when a group of young black men and boys had gathered outside an apartment complex in Kenosha, Wisconsin. Several of them had just seen the movie *Mississippi Burning,* in which a white man beats a young black boy who is praying. "Do you feel hyped up to move on some white people?" Todd Mitchell, a nineteen-year-old, asked the others. A short time later, Gregory Reddick, a fourteen-year-old white youth, came walking by on the opposite side of the street. "You all want to fuck somebody up? There goes a white boy; go get him," Mitchell said. The gang attacked Reddick, beat him senseless and stole his tennis shoes. When police found him, he was unconscious. Though the youth survived, he suffered permanent brain damage. A jury convicted Mitchell of aggravated battery, which under Wisconsin law carried a maximum penalty of two years in prison. But prosecutors said, and the jury agreed, that Mitchell had chosen his victim because of his race. Based on that conclusion, the judge sentenced him to four years in prison.

Mitchell's attorney, however, contended the hate crimes law that imposed the added sentence was unconstitutional, and on June 23, 1992, the day after the *R.A.V.* ruling, the Wisconsin Supreme Court agreed, in a five-to-two vote.

"Without a doubt, the hate crimes statute punishes bigoted thought," said the state's chief justice, Nathan Stewart Heffernan. It "violates the First Amendment directly by punishing what the legislature had deemed to be offensive thought and violates the First Amendment indirectly by chilling free speech."

State attorneys had argued that the law punishes "conduct"—the selecting of a victim. It didn't matter whether Mitchell hated white people or liked them. Perhaps, he secretly liked whites, but wanted to demonstrate his macho to the gang. Even so, he could be punished under the law because he had intentionally selected his victim because of his race.

But the state court was entirely unmoved. Repeatedly, Heffernan characterized the law as creating a "thought crime"—invoking George Orwell in adjectival form to condemn the notion. "A statute specifically designed to punish personal prejudice impermissibly infringes upon an individual's First Amendment rights, no matter how carefully or cleverly one words the statute," he wrote. The law also "chills" speech, he added, because citizens will have to think twice about uttering racial slurs. Should they later beat someone of another race senseless, those comments could be used against them, Judge Heffernan reasoned.

Within weeks, the Ohio Supreme Court issued a similar decision striking down its hate crimes law. This seemed to carry to its logical extreme one strand of Scalia's opinion in the *R.A.V.* case—the notion that laws may not "select" certain "disfavored viewpoints" for punishment. Unquestionably, lawmakers had enacted the ADL statutes because they viewed racism, anti-Semitism, and homophobia as reprehensible.

On the other hand, the Wisconsin law did *not* actually punish *speech* or expressions—or for that matter, *thought*. It punished only the *act* of selecting a target for an assault based on biased motivation. If neither speech nor expression was directly punished, was the First Amendment violated?

The Wisconsin Supreme Court's ruling that such bias-based crimes were unconstitutional had profound implications. If sustained, the Wisconsin ruling raised the specter of undercutting the nation's key civil rights laws. The Civil Rights Act of 1964 made it illegal for employers to fire a worker "because of race, color, religion, gender or national origin." By that standard, a supervisor may dismiss a worker because he is fat, balding, or a smoker, but not because he is black, Hispanic, or Asian. In that sense, Congress enacted a "statute specifically designed to punish personal prejudice." If the Wisconsin bias crime law was unconstitutional, did it follow that the nation's civil rights laws would also be toppled?

The possibility certainly existed, for if any law that is geared to the intent of the actor, and phrased in terms of such motivations as racial or gender bias, was a form of "viewpoint discrimination," then it was difficult to see how such laws could survive the strict no-viewpoint-discrimination-allowed doctrines of *R.A.V. v. City of St. Paul.*

Not surprisingly, when Wisconsin's state attorney general, James E. Doyle, appealed the state court ruling, the Justices agreed to review the case of *Wisconsin v. Mitchell.* The fate of hate crimes law, and perhaps the civil rights statutes, hung in the balance. "The Wisconsin penalty enhancement statute quite simply does not punish thought, and it does not punish expression of any idea or belief," said Doyle, launching his argument on the morning of April 21. "It punishes criminal conduct. Mr. Mitchell was and is free to think any thought he wants to think."

The state attorney continued uninterrupted for several minutes, usually a good sign. (If the Justices sit quietly during the latter half of an argument, they may have given up on the attorney, or have nodded off. But usually they will interrupt an attorney who leads off on a false note.)

But Scalia could not resist for long. "Is there any limit on the reasons for selections that the state can specify for higher punishment? Could it say, 'If you select a victim on the basis of whether or not he believes in the holes in the ozone layer . . .' Could you do that? Or whether he believes that the earth revolves around the sun?"

Doyle replied that it would depend on whether lawmakers saw a serious problem with attacks on "flat earth people." A few minutes later, a Justice Department attorney who was there to support Wisconsin's argument noted that the state hate crimes law follows the reasoning of the federal antidiscrimination laws.

"So you have to be an equal opportunity criminal. Is that it?" Scalia cracked.

When the attorney mentioned the categories covered by the law, including race, color, religion, disability, sexual orientation, and ancestry, Scalia interrupted again.

"Disability? Have we had a rash of people going around beating up on the handicapped? I'm not aware of that," he said. Clearly, Justice Scalia was not concerned about being politically correct, nor was he enamored of laws designed to punish crimes of bias.

But significantly, no one else on the bench seemed troubled by their constitutionality.

As soon as Milwaukee attorney Lynn Adelman rose to defend the state supreme court ruling, he ran into trouble. The Justices simply refused to buy the notion that Todd Mitchell was punished for his "thoughts." Rather, he was punished for targeting a particular victim, they said.

By the end of the half hour, even Scalia joined the attack. He cited the example of treason laws. "I'm certainly entitled to wish the enemy well in a war that my country's engaged in. But if I perform an act with the intention of helping the enemy . . ."

"Intention is different from motive," Adelman interjected. "Intention is different from motive?" Scalia replied, nonplussed. "Okay, then strike it. I do it with the motive of helping the enemy." Suppose he disclosed secret information. "The only thing that makes it treason is that I do it with the motive of giving aid and comfort to the enemy," Scalia said.

While Adelman tried to wiggle away from the example, Scalia honed in on the parallel. In both instances, the government punishes an action taken for what it deems to be an intolerable reason.

"I don't see any difference between that and what's going on here," Scalia concluded.

The Court's decision, issued on June 11, only confirmed what had seemed apparent during the argument. By a unanimous vote, the high court reversed the Wisconsin ruling and upheld the hate crimes laws.

In his brief opinion for the Court, Chief Justice Rehnquist disposed of Mitchell's arguments. By tradition, sentencing judges have considered a variety of factors before imposing a punishment, including "the defendant's motive for committing the offense." For example, some state laws recommend a death sentence for the murderer who kills for "pecuniary gain." If a reason such as this can be the basis for increasing the penalty, states can also impose harsher sentences on those who attack their victims because of their race, religion, or ancestry. While the defendant cannot be punished for his "abstract beliefs," he can be punished for acting on them, the Chief Justice said.

The ruling in the St. Paul case does not compel a different result, Rehnquist added. "Whereas the ordinance struck down in *R.A.V.* was explicitly directed at expressions (i.e., 'speech' or 'messages') the statute in this case is aimed at conduct unprotected by the First Amendment," he wrote. Leaders of the Anti-Defamation League and other civil rights groups breathed a sigh of relief. The government at all levels could continue to attack harshly those who commit crimes because of racial or religious animus. But the laws must first punish conduct and crime, not expression. In the end, the Court rested on the rigid distinction

Scalia had suggested earlier in the cases involving flag burning and nude dancing. Laws cannot single out one type of expression for punishment, but a general law banning certain conduct can stand, even if it has the effect of infringing free expression.

The issue of hate speech and hate crimes has posed the most difficult free speech challenges of recent years. A society committed to the belief that all persons are created equal cannot permit some of them to be targeted for violence simply because of their color, ancestry, or religion. But this nation has also been unwilling to sacrifice the notion that each one of us can express opinions and views, no matter how extreme or silly they may be. While those two notions can stand in conflict, the Court has showed that neither need be sacrificed. With remarkable dispatch in 1992 and 1993, the Justices confronted the dilemma of bias crimes and emerged with their principles intact.

CHAPTER EIGHT

The struggle for racial justice is a central theme, perhaps *the* central theme, of the American constitutional experience. Debate over slavery nearly scuttled the Constitutional Convention in Philadelphia. An ignominious but unavoidable compromise made nationhood possible, permitting the South to keep its slaves. But the moral abomination of slavery finally led to the Civil War. After the war, the Constitution was amended to provide for racial equality. The Supreme Court, however, emaciated the post–Civil War amendments, rendering emancipation an empty victory by endorsing the insidious racism of "separate but equal."

The Court finally redeemed itself with *Brown v. Board of Education,* the 1954 school desegregation case that generated the most important social revolution in American history, ending, at least in law, the decades of apartheid that had followed the centuries of slavery.

In the forty years since *Brown* the Supreme Court has labored to define the contours of the equality principle declared in it. During this time two competing notions of "equality" have surfaced in American public discourse. "Process equality," which might also go by the name "individualist equality," is a competitive, individualist, survival-of-the-fittest form of equality, a conception that emphasizes the integrity and fairness of the rules of the game. When a process equality thinker uses a term like "equal opportunity," he or she normally means nothing more than freedom of choice or open competition in a marketplace free of any discrimination.

"Outcome equality," on the other hand, is a conception of equality that focuses on results. This is more a "group rights" conception of equality, a conception that emphasizes representation and participation. This version of equality does not look solely at the formal rules of the game to make sure that they are fair; it goes beyond that and measures the degree of diversity and shared power that results from the game.

Process equality thinking and outcome equality thinking are both well established in American culture, and the two versions of equality constantly vie against each another in the civil rights laws passed by legislatures, in the affirmative action programs created by public and private institutions, and in the decrees rendered by courts. Many Americans are not either "pure process" or "pure outcome" equality thinkers but, rather, have impulses and intuitions that include strains of both approaches. And most of the civil rights laws passed by Congress, the states, and local governments, most of the hiring and admissions policies adopted by private corporations, government agencies, or universities, seem to partake of both process and outcome equality elements.

The Supreme Court's decisions interpreting the Fourteenth Amendment's Equal Protection Clause have also contained a blend of process and outcome approaches to equality. In the area of school desegregation, for example, many school boards responded to the *Brown v. Board of Education* ruling first by dragging their feet or resisting and then finally, often more than a decade after *Brown,* by adopting "freedom-of-choice" plans that let school children enroll in any school in the school district. A freedom-of-choice plan is ostensibly a perfect form of equality and to a pure process thinker may seem like all any school board could ever be asked to do. The problem, however, is that in most of those freedom-of-choice school districts black children continued to attend the exclusively black schools and white children the exclusively white schools, and so it appeared in reality as if nothing had changed.

In *Green v. New Kent County School Board,* the Court in 1968 announced that simply moving to a freedom-of-choice regime was not good enough. If a school district had been guilty of intentional segregation of its students, and thus guilty of a constitutional violation under *Brown,* the remedy must be more aggressive; the school district was under an "affirmative duty" to dismantle the vestiges of the discriminatory system "root and branch." The Court wanted results; it wanted them now.

But what should this mandate mean when translated to the context of higher education? In the old segregationist days before *Brown,* many Southern states had created an entirely separate system of state colleges and universities for black students. What should happen to those historically black institutions after *Brown?* Kay Kindred's narrative explores this question in the context of *United States v. Fordice,* a case that put the Mississippi higher education system, and the future of historically black state institutions, on trial.

—Editor

Civil Rights
and Higher Education

KAY KINDRED

In light of the sorry history of discrimination and its devastating impact on the lives of Negroes, bringing the Negro into the mainstream of American life should be a state interest of the highest order. To fail to do so is to ensure that America will forever remain a divided society.—Justice Thurgood Marshall, concurring in part and dissenting in part in *Regents of the University of California v. Bakke*

We do not foreclose the possibility that there exists "sound educational justification" for maintaining historically black colleges as such. Despite the shameful history of state-enforced segregation, these institutions have survived and flourished. Indeed, they have expanded as opportunities for blacks to enter historically white institutions have expanded. . . . I think it indisputable that these institutions have succeeded in part because of their distinctive histories and traditions; for many, historically black colleges have become a "symbol of the highest attainments of black culture." Obviously, a State cannot maintain such traditions by closing particular institutions, historically white or historically black, to particular racial groups. Nonetheless, it hardly follows that a State cannot operate a diverse assortment of institutions—including historically black institutions—open to all on a race-neutral basis, but with established traditions that might disproportionately appeal to one race or another.—Justice Clarence Thomas, concurring in *United States v. Fordice*

What becomes of a dream deferred? Langston Hughes, "Harlem", 1951

It is December of 1992. Sixty-four-year-old Lillie Ayers sits in the warm kitchen of her home in Glen Allan, Mississippi, and wonders if she'll ever see an end to the fight for educational equality. "To me, it seems plain as day. . . . They don't treat the black schools the way they treat the white schools. They never have. Anybody can see that."

Her husband Jake did. On January 28, 1975, Jake Ayers, a former sharecropper, and several other black residents, filed suit against the state of Mississippi claiming that Mississippi systematically under-funded historically black public colleges and universities and maintained a segregated system of higher education.

On June 26, 1992, seventeen years after the suit began, nearly forty years after the Supreme Court issued its landmark ruling in *Brown v. Board of Education* that the doctrine of "separate but equal" in public education is unconstitutional, and thirty years after the University of Mississippi opened its doors under court order to admit its first black student, the United States Supreme Court declared in its decision in the case of *United States v. Fordice* that the state of Mississippi had not met its affirmative constitutional obligation to eradicate the remnants of racial segregation in its eight public colleges and universities. (The name of the case when it reached the Supreme Court was *United States v. Fordice* because the United States Justice Department had intervened on the side of Ayers, and Fordice had become the governor of Mississippi.)

But had the plaintiffs really won? The Court's decision in *United States v. Fordice* had seemed cause for celebration when it was issued in June, but it soon became a source of great concern for the plaintiffs and their supporters. For while the Court agreed that Mississippi continued to operate a segregated and unequal university system, it rejected the plaintiffs' proposed remedy—that the historically black institutions be brought up to parity with the historically white institutions in the state. What, everyone wondered, would be the effect of the decision?

The immediate impact of Mississippi's continuation of a de facto separate but equal policy is obvious at the historically black institutions in the state. Classrooms go unpainted, roofs leak, steps crumble, the sewage system stops up, buildings are mostly stark cinderblock with none of the manicured lawns that sprawl across the predominantly white university campuses. Since the Court declared that parity was not the answer, how could the state fulfill its obligation to dismantle its dual system?

In October 1992 the Mississippi Board of Trustees of State Institutions of Higher Learning, which governs the public four-year universities in the state, approved an alternative plan to resolve this long-standing dispute. Under its proposal, only one of the three historically black institutions would be left intact. The others would be closed or merged into one or another of the white institutions. (As this book was being prepared, the contending plans for the future of higher education in Mississippi were still in litigation in the lower courts, where the case was remanded [sent back] by the Supreme Court.)

"It was never our intention for there to be talking about closing black schools", says Mrs. Ayers, mother of nine and a civil rights activist in her own right. "All we wanted was for them to be given the same things the white institutions were given. That's what Jake wanted. That was his dream."

It is a dream Jake Ayers will never see, because he died in 1986, at the age of sixty-six. "A few days before he died, I remember he told me he thought . . . that the Supreme Court would rule in favor of our case." But Lillie Ayers fears that after her husband's lifelong commitment to civil rights, which ran the gamut from marching with Dr. Martin Luther King Jr. to organizing picket lines against job discrimination, what stands as his greatest victory may also prove a bitter defeat.

Byron R. White

The majority decision in *Fordice* was written by Justice Byron R. White. Interestingly, Justice White also wrote, six years earlier, the majority view for the Court in *Bazemore v. Friday,* which held that a state agricultural service did not violate the Fourteenth Amendment by sponsoring single-race clubs if the racial imbalance of the clubs was the result of private voluntary decisions—an opinion that the *Fordice* Court relied on heavily. The two cases take apparently dissimilar positions on a state's equal protection obligation, but it is neither surprising nor inconsistent that White agreed with both, since he is noted for his independent, case-by-case approach to constitutional adjudication.

Byron "Whizzer" White, appointed to the United States Supreme Court by President John F. Kennedy in 1962, ended his thirty-one years on the Court at the end of the 1992–93 term. He served the ninth longest tenure of the 107 Justices to serve on the Court. Summarizing that tenure is not an easy task. He has been referred to at times as a "conservative" and at times as a "moderate," yet, for many of the lawyers and legal scholars who follow the Court, Justice White cannot be described as an "ideological" Justice—one who thought in terms of an overarching judicial philosophy. During his thirty-one years on the Court, he was never certain to be a member of any alliance but decided cases on their own merits, guided by pragmatism rather than dogma.

It is unclear what expectations President Kennedy had of White when he appointed him in March 1962 as a replacement for retiring Justice Charles Evans Whittaker. Byron White was known for his keen intellect, rigid integrity, and steadfast independence in his work as a private lawyer, as head of a Citizens for Kennedy organization in 1960, and later as deputy attorney general under Robert Kennedy, where his most publicized moment occurred in May 1961, when he confronted Alabama governor John Patterson over the presence of armed federal officers sent to the state to protect freedom riders from racial violence. Those characteristics were reflected throughout his years on the high court. While his 1962 appointment made him a member of the Warren Court, he remained judicially and intellectually independent from it, choosing to join certain of its landmark decisions, dissenting from others.

When White assumed office, the Court was in the midst of a criminal procedure reformation. It had just decided its first reapportionment case (in *Baker v. Carr*), ennunciating the "one man one vote" principle, and had declared school segregation unconstitutional. White's position on these issues initially reflected his roots as a Kennedy-appointed moderate. He voted with the liberals on the Court on most civil rights and reapportionment issues and in 1972 voted to strike down the death penalty though he voted to reinstate it in 1976. His support for law enforcement led him to dissent from many decisions strengthening the rights of criminal defendants, such as *Miranda v. Arizona,* where he wrote that the ruling would prevent interrogations, reduce the number of confessions and guilty pleas, and slow down investigations and apprehensions in those cases where time is of the essence. His position on rights of criminal defendants remained consistent through the years, as he participated in the rollback of many of those rights in the early and mid-1980s, as reflected in his opinion for the majority in *United States v. Leon,* in 1984, which allowed the use of evidence obtained under a defective search warrant as long as the police had acted in good faith.

White's position on civil rights did shift with respect to affirmative action, "minority set-asides" (in *City of Richmond v. J. A. Croson Co.*), and "quotas," although he supported affirmative action in college admission in the *Bakke* case in 1978 and joined a five-to-four majority in *Metro Broadcasting v. FCC* in 1990, upholding minority preference policies published by the Federal Communications Commission. He consistently dissented from abortion rights rulings, beginning with his pointed dissent in *Roe v. Wade.* In perhaps his most controversial opinion, Justice White wrote for a five-to-four majority upholding a state antisodomy statute in *Bowers v. Hardwick.* He called the claims of homosexual rights in the case "at best, facetious."

Despite his shifting perspectives on certain civil rights issues, he never wavered in support of strong remedies to dismantle school desegregation. During his second term on the Court, he cast a vote in favor of James Meredith's petition for admission to the University of Mississippi. Ironically, thirty years later, in the *Fordice* decision, he told the state of Mississippi it still had not done enough to end segregation and, writing for the majority of the Court, required stronger measures to dismantle segregation in public higher education. In the intervening years he voted to uphold interdistrict busing in Detroit in *Milliken v. Bradley* in 1974 and to uphold a Court-ordered tax increase to finance desegregated schools in Kansas City, Missouri, in *Missouri v. Jenkins* in 1990.

Critics of White say that he limited his long-term influence by taking a narrow approach to opinion writing. His opinions are said to resolve the particular case, but not to suggest abstract principles capable of generalization to a number of cases. For that reason he is not identified with any famous line of cases or any particular doctrine. Admirers point to that approach as a strength—describing White as a legal realist who built his jurisprudence from one concrete case to another, with respect for the judicial process and a deference to precedent.

United States v. Fordice: *The Decision in Brief*

The Supreme Court's eight to one decision in *Fordice* represents a critical development in desegregation law as it applies to higher education. Although the Court had revisited the question of desegregation in the context of public elementary and secondary schools many times since its decision in *Brown,* it had never before addressed the question in the context of higher education.

Fordice is significant for what it says . . . and for what it does not say. It reaffirmed the desegregation principles of *Brown v. Board of Edu-*

cation and established that the duty imposed on states under *Brown* applies to higher education. The Court made it clear that a state cannot meet its constitutionally mandated obligation to dismantle what was once a legally sanctioned, segregated university system just by implementing race-neutral admissions policies. Perhaps most significantly, the Court established a new standard for determining when a public university has met its duty to desegregate. In so doing, it rejected the lower courts' assessment that a "freedom-of-choice" approach to college admission was sufficient in a system that was once segregated by law. The new standard requires an assessment of the causes of a college's racial makeup: if that makeup is the result of the state's earlier segregation laws, then the new *Fordice* standard applies.

As articulated by Justice Byron White, who wrote the decision, the standard says that policies holding over from the days of segregation that continue to have discriminatory effects must be reformed "to the extent practicable and consistent with sound educational practices." But the Court left to the lower courts the burden of examining Mississippi's system in light of the standard and offered no specific guidance in its application.

The Court also left unanswered questions about the future of the historically black colleges in Mississippi and elsewhere in the South. It said that the historically black institutions were not constitutionally entitled to increased financial support if the purpose was "solely so that they may be publicly financed, exclusively black enclaves of private choice." But it left open the possibility that the lower courts could order increased funding to the institutions as part of an overall effort to make the historically black institutions stronger component parts of a state system open to all students.

The Dual System in Historical Context

In 1862, through the Morrill Land Grant Act, the United States government provided the states with land to establish public institutions for teaching liberal arts and practical skills. Slavery, which kept blacks illiterate, and the segregation that followed the Civil War effectively excluded blacks from access to those institutions.

The changes began in 1865, when the federal government created the Freedmen's Bureau. While the 1862 Morrill Act did not specifically authorize use of funds for the education of freed slaves, the first commissioner of the new bureau appointed a general superintendent of schools to work with the black churches, Northern missionaries, and private philanthropic organizations who, with limited resources, had undertaken to provide education through private black institutions.

In 1866 Congress provided the bureau with funds to be used for education. With the help of the new funds, these private institutions worked to provide basic education to freed blacks, and, as the education level of black students increased, the institutions extended the level of education provided to include college work. But, unlike white students in former slave states, until 1890 and the enactment of the second Morrill Act, blacks in Southern and border states had no publicly supported colleges available to them. The limited resources of the private black institutions were inadequate to meet the heightened demand. With the enactment of the second Morrill Act, Congress required states with dual higher education systems to provide land grant (or public) colleges for blacks as well as whites. As a result, sixteen black institutions were designated land grant colleges. Nonetheless, the endowment for these black institutions was substantially less than that of the institutions set up under the earlier Morrill Act, and public black colleges have been systematically underfunded ever since.

Mississippi began its state-supported university system in 1848 with the establishment of the University of Mississippi (commonly referred to as "Ole Miss"), an institution dedicated exclusively to the education of white students. Under its original charter, Ole Miss was designated a comprehensive institution with professional and specialized degrees.

Thereafter, the state established additional postsecondary, single-race higher education institutions, beginning with Alcorn State University. Alcorn University received its original charter in 1871. Renamed Alcorn Agricultural and Mechanical College after passage of the second Morrill Act in 1890, it was designated an agricultural college for black youth and first began to admit blacks. In 1878, the state legislature chartered Mississippi State University as an agricultural and mechanical school for white males only (it became coeducational in 1930). Mississippi University for Women was founded in 1884, exclusively for "the education of white women in the arts and sciences." In 1910, the legislature created the University of Southern Mississippi to train white students as teachers for white public elementary and secondary schools. Delta State University opened its doors in 1924 to provide a liberal arts program for white students. In 1940, the state established Jackson State University "to train black teachers for black public schools." Shortly thereafter, in 1946, Mississippi Valley State University was created to educate black teachers primarily for rural and elementary schools and to provide vocational instruction to black students.

At the time of the Supreme Court's ruling in *Brown v. Board of Education,* Mississippi had operated a dual system of higher education for eighty-three years. The first black student to attend the University of Mississippi, James Meredith, was not admitted until 1962, and only then by court order. For the next twelve years, the segregated dual system remained largely unchanged. Mississippi State, Mississippi University for Women, the University of Southern Mississippi, and Delta State each admitted at least one black student during that period, but the student bodies of each university remained overwhelmingly white. During the same period, Jackson State and Mississippi Valley State University were exclusively black. By 1968, Alcorn State had admitted five white students.

In 1969, the United States Department of Health, Education, and Welfare (HEW) requested, pursuant to Title VI of the Civil Rights Act of 1964, that Mississippi devise a plan to desegregate in fact a university system that was once segregated by law. In June 1973, the Board of Trustees of State Institutions of Higher Learning, the governing body for the Mississippi public university system, submitted a plan to improve educational opportunities for all Mississippi citizens by setting numerical goals for the enrollment of students of other races at state universities, hiring multiracial faculty, and instituting remedial programs and special recruitment measures.

The department rejected the plan for failure to comply with Title VI because it was inadequate in the areas of student recruitment and enrollment, faculty hiring, elimination of unnecessary duplication, and did not go far enough in its institutional funding practices to ensure that a student's choice of one institution or another would be based on criteria other than race. Despite protestations by the board that the Mississippi system was in compliance with Title VI, the racial composition of the state's universities had changed only marginally from the nearly exclusively single-race levels of 1968. In fact, HEW noted that for the 1974–75 school year, black students comprised 4.1 percent of the full-time undergraduate enrollments at the University of Mississippi, 7.5 percent at Mississippi State, 8.0 percent at the University of Southern Mississippi, 12.6 percent at Delta State University, and 13.0 percent at the Mississippi University for Women. In contrast, the percentage of black students at Jackson State was 96.6 percent, at Alcorn State 99.9 percent, and at Mississippi Valley State, 100 percent.

Although HEW refused to accept the plan, the board adopted it nonetheless. Any potential effectiveness of the plan in eliminating the inequities was further compromised when the state legislature refused to fund it until fiscal year 1978, and even then at well under half the amount requested by the board. Jake Ayers and his fellow plaintiffs filed suit in 1975 in federal district court in Mississippi, shortly after HEW rejected the board's plan.

The Lower Court Decisions

Jake Ayers and other black citizens of Mississippi alleged that the State of Mississippi had maintained the "racially segregative effects" of its "prior legally mandated dual system of higher education," in violation of the Fifth, Ninth, Thirteenth, and Fourteenth Amendments of the United States Constitution, of 42 U.S. Code, sections 1981 and 1983, and of Title VI of the Civil Rights Act of 1964. Soon after the case began, the United States intervened on the side of the plaintiffs.

For twelve years after the initiation of the litigation, the parties attempted to resolve the suit through "voluntary dismantlement" of the segregated system. In 1981, the Board of Trustees issued revised "mission statements" identifying the purpose of each public university. The missions were reclassified and clustered into three categories: comprehensive, urban, and regional. "Comprehensive" universities were those with the greatest existing resources and program offerings. The three institutions classified as comprehensive were the University of Mississippi, Mississippi State, and Southern Mississippi, all of which were exclusively white institutions under the prior de jure system. The board authorized each comprehensive institution to continue offering doctoral degrees and to assume leadership in certain disciplines. Jackson State University, a historically black institution, was given the only "urban" university designation. As such, it was assigned a more limited research and degree mission, geared toward an urban setting. The "regional" classification was for institutions that the board envisioned as primarily undergraduate in role. Thus, the term "regional" was somewhat of a misnomer: these universities were defined more by their academic mission than by the geographical locality in which they were based. Institutions designated as regional included both those that had been either exclusively white—Delta State and Mississippi University for Women—or exclusively black—Alcorn State and Mississippi Valley.

As of 1987, the parties in the law suit had not reached agreement on whether the state had taken affirmative steps to dismantle its prior dual system, so they proceeded to trial. Both sides presented evidence on admissions standards, faculty and administrative staff recruitment, program duplication, on-campus discrimination, institutional funding disparities, and satellite campuses. The plaintiffs argued that the state continued to sustain historic, race-based distinctions among its institutions of higher learning. The state alleged that it had fulfilled its duty to dismantle its state-imposed segregative system by developing and maintaining good-faith, race-neutral policies in student admissions, faculty and staff hiring, and operations, and that the continued existence of racially imbalanced institutions alone was not unlawful in light of the varying objectives of the state's eight institutions and the student's freedom of choice with respect to which institution to attend.

The Mississippi district court concluded that where a state has previously maintained a racially dual system of public education as a matter of law (de jure), it assumes an "affirmative duty to reform those policies and practices which required or contributed to the separation of the races." The court held that although the affirmative duty to dismantle a racially dual structure applies to the higher education context no less than to elementary and secondary schools, in the higher education context "the affirmative duty to desegregate does not contemplate either restricting choice or the achievement of any degree of racial balance." The district court concluded that student enrollment and faculty hiring patterns should be reviewed but that "greater emphasis should be placed on current state higher education policies and practices in order to ensure that such policies and practices are racially neutral, developed and implemented in good faith, and do not substantially contribute to the continued racial identifiability of individual institutions." Applying that standard to the Mississippi university system, the court found no violation of federal law and held that the state of Mississippi had fulfilled its affirmative duty to disestablish its former de jure segregated system.

The United States Court of Appeals for the Fifth Circuit reheard the case and affirmed the decision of the lower court on August 18, 1992. It agreed that Mississippi was constitutionally required to eliminate invidious racial distinctions and to dismantle its dual university system. It concluded that duty had been met since Mississippi had "adopted and implemented race neutral policies for operating its colleges and universities and that all students have real freedom of choice to attend the college or university they wish." The Supreme Court had ruled in *Green* that merely adopting such "neutral" policies as free choice would not meet a school district's constitutional obligation to dismantle a dual system of primary or secondary schools. Nonetheless, the court of appeals refused to follow that same standard in the context of universities. The court determined that because universities were fundamentally different from lower schools, the State of Mississippi had discharged its affirmative obligation to dismantle its segregated higher education system by simply moving to such neutral policies.

United States—*The Supreme Court's Decision*

On appeal, the Supreme Court confirmed, without equivocation, that a state's constitutionally mandated obligation to dismantle former de jure dual systems of education, established in *Brown* and its progeny, applies to its system of higher education. With this ruling, the Supreme Court said, for the first time, that the mandate of *Brown* is applicable at the university level no less than at the elementary and secondary level. Unless a state can meet its burden of proof on this issue, it continues in violation of the Fourteenth Amendment. Since the State of Mississippi had conceded that it was subject to the obligation, the primary issue before the Supreme Court was whether or not it had met that duty.

Under the *Fordice* standard, a state must do more than merely implement race-neutral admission policies in order to discharge its constitutional obligations. Where college attendance is by choice rather than assignment, the college a student eventually attends is determined by a number of factors in addition to admissions policies. Other policies, held over from the era of segregation, may still be in force, substantially restricting a person's choice. If they are, they must be reformed "to the extent practicable and consistent with sound educational practices."

Under this standard, if present-day discrimination can be traced to a system that once legally mandated segregation, plaintiffs need not prove intentional discrimination on the part of state officials to establish that the Equal Protection Clause of the Fourteenth Amendment has been violated: discriminatory intent is presumed. However, if current policies are not derived from the past system, the plaintiffs must present evidence that the discriminatory impact of the new policies is the result of intentional state action.

Applying its newly articulated standard to the findings of the district court, the Supreme Court concluded that several features of Mississippi's old segregation policies were still in place, contributing to the current racial identity of its institutions. So, although they seemed neutral, those policies were constitutionally suspect. The State of Mississippi, it decided, is obliged to justify those policies as educationally sound or to eliminate them. The Court did not attempt to render an exhaustive list but focused on aspects of Mississippi's system that it deemed clearly remnants of the prior system: its admission standards, program duplication, institutional mission assignments, and the continued operation of all eight public universities.

The Admissions Policies. The district court had conceded that the 1963 admissions policies of the three flagship, historically white universities—the University of Mississippi, Mississippi State University, and University of Southern Mississippi—which required all entrants to achieve a minimum composite score of fifteen on the American College Testing Program (ACT) test, had a "discriminatory taint" by virtue of the fact that, at that time, the average ACT score for white students was eighteen and the average score for black students was seven. It concluded, however, that present admissions policies emanated from policies enacted in the 1970s to redress student unpreparedness, rather than from the 1963 policies. The court of appeals affirmed this conclusion. But the Supreme Court dismissed the "student unpreparedness" rationale as a "mid-passage justification" for the perpetuation of a policy originally enacted to discriminate against black students and, as such, insufficient to lessen the constitutionally suspect nature of current admissions standards. The Court found that not only are current policies traceable to the prior segregated system and to policies originally adopted for discriminatory purposes, but they also continue to have present-day discriminatory effects.

Under current admissions policies, every Mississippi resident under twenty-one years of age seeking admission to the state university system must take the ACT exams. Any applicant who scores at least fifteen qualifies for automatic admission to any of the five historically white institutions, with the exception of Mississippi University for Women, which requires a score of eighteen for automatic admission. Those scoring less than fifteen, but at least thirteen, qualify for automatic admission to the historically black Jackson State, Alcorn State, and Mississippi Valley State universities. The Supreme Court found that these requirements restrict the choices of entering students in such a way as to perpetuate segregation. Since those scoring thirteen or fourteen are, as a general matter, precluded from attending any of the five historically white institutions, they must choose one of the historically black institutions (or attend a junior college with hope of transferring to a historically white institution) if they wish to obtain a college education.

While the district court may have been correct in its finding that few black students are actually denied admission to a Mississippi university for failure to achieve the minimal ACT score, the Supreme Court determined that this finding failed to take into consideration the inherent self-selection precipitated by the automatic admission standard. "It is logical," the Court observed, "to think that some percentage of black students who fail to score fifteen *do not* seek admission to one of the historically white universities because of the automatic admission policy." Since proportionately more blacks than whites face this choice, the current admissions policies contribute to the continuing racial imbalance of Mississippi's universities.

The Court also found segregative effects in other present policies. Historically white and historically black institutions with the same institutional mission—the "regional" universities—have different minimum automatic entrance scores, they noted. So do institutions with different programmatic emphases that perpetuate historical mission assignments—the so-called comprehensive and regional universities.

The Court found similarly suspect the state's use of the ACT test score as the sole determinant of automatic admission, without consideration of the applicant's high-school grades. The disparity between black and white students' high-school grade averages was shown to be much narrower than the gap between average ACT scores. That fact, considered in light of reports by the American College Testing Program, the administering organization of the ACT, that ACT scores used as the sole admissions criterion presented an incomplete picture of an applicant's ability to perform adequately in college and that the ACT requirement was originally adopted by the universities for discriminatory purposes, led the Supreme Court to conclude that the current requirement is traceable to that decision and continues to have segregative effects.

Program Duplication. The second aspect of the Mississippi university system warranting review was the widespread program duplication found between the historically black and historically white institutions. The district court defined "unnecessary program duplication" as "those instances where two or more institutions offer the same non-essential or noncore program." Under this definition, all duplication at the bachelor's degree level of nonbasic liberal arts and science courses and all duplication at the master's level and above were deemed unnecessary. The district court found that 34.6 percent of the twenty-nine undergraduate programs at the historically black institutions are unnecessarily duplicated at the historically white institutions, and that 90 percent of the graduate programs at the historically black institutions are unnecessarily duplicated at the historically white institutions. Despite these findings, however, the district court concluded that there was no proof that the duplication is directly associated with the racial makeup of these institutions and no proof that eliminating the duplication "would be justifiable from an educational standpoint or that its elimination would have a substantial effect on student choice."

The Supreme Court took issue with the district court's conclusions on a number of grounds. First, the district court held that the petitioners had not established that unnecessary duplication was unconstitutional. But, since program duplication was a necessary element of the "separate but equal" notion of the prior de jure dual system, the Supreme Court argued, the present unnecessary duplication is a continuation of that system. By requiring the plaintiffs to prove that it violated the Constitution, the district court had improperly shifted the burden of proof from the state, which, under *Brown,* bears the burden of showing that it has dismantled its prior segregated system. Second, the Supreme Court objected to the district court's holding that, because it lacked direct proof, it could not conclude that eliminating the unnecessary duplication would be educationally justifiable. The Court said that when the lower court found there was *unnecessary* duplication, that fact in itself implied the absence of educational justification. Based upon the district court's own findings that the duplication "cannot be justified economically or in terms of providing quality education," the Court concluded that some if not all duplication could be eliminated. Finally, when the district court considered the issue of program duplication separately from other policies of the higher education system (such as differential admissions), it failed to consider the combined effects of the policies in judging whether Mississippi had met its duty to dismantle the prior dual system.

Institutional Missions. During the de jure segregated period, the University of Mississippi, Mississippi State University, and University of Southern Mississippi were the flagship institutions of the state system. As such, they received the most funds, had the most advanced and specialized programs, and maintained the broadest curricula. Each institution was restricted to providing education for white students only. Mississippi University for Women and Delta State University were also restricted solely to whites, but were more limited in scope of function. Both Mississippi University for Women and Delta State University provided undergraduate education in liberal arts and fields such as home economics, education, music, art, and education. By contrast, when they were founded, the three exclusively black institutions were more limited in academic mission than the five all-white institutions, since they served simply as agricultural or teachers' colleges. Funding and curricular decisions during the de jure segregated period were based on the purposes for which the institutions were established.

The Court found fault with the 1981 mission designations of the flagship universities as "comprehensive"; of Delta State, the Mississippi University for Women, Alcorn State, and Mississippi Valley State as "regional" universities; and of Jackson State as an "urban" university.

The Court determined that the 1981 institutional mission designations derived from the historical racial assignments and that the different missions assigned to the universities necessarily limited to some degree a student's choice of which institution to attend. The effect of the mission classifications, it decided, was to maintain the more limited program scope of the historically black institutions. The assignment of differential missions to a state's public universities would not, absent a discriminatory purpose, violate the Equal Protection clause merely because one or more of the institutions remained or became predominately one race. But when the mission designations are combined with the differential admission standards and the unnecessary program duplication, the likely effect would be interference with student choice.

Operation of Eight Public Universities. In evaluating the operation and maintenance of all eight universities, the Court stated at the outset that the existence of as many as eight institutions was undoubtedly the result of state laws mandating separation of the races. Given the close proximity of institutions with essentially the same mission and the limited financial resources available to the state for higher education, the Court concurred with the district court's assessment that maintaining all eight institutions was wasteful and irrational.

The Court surmised that closing one or more institutions would, in light of the system's program duplication and the institutional mission and admissions policies, lessen the discriminatory effects of the system. But it declined to say whether such action was constitutionally required. It found the record too incomplete to determine whether one or more institutions should be closed, or whether the constitutional violation could be remedied simply by eliminating program duplication or altering mission assignments. The case was "remanded" (or sent back) to the federal district court in Mississippi to determine whether maintaining all eight universities itself affects student choice and perpetuates a segregated system, whether maintaining each institution is educationally justifiable, and whether one or more of the institutions could be closed or merged with existing institutions.

The Equal Protection Precedents Distinguished. Both the district court and the court of appeals conceded that Mississippi was constitutionally obliged under the Fourteenth Amendment to eliminate the dual school system it had once mandated by law and that the obligation extends to its system of higher education. Where the lower courts and the Supreme Court differed was on whether Mississippi had met that duty simply by implementing race-neutral admissions policies.

The court of appeals found the holding of *Green v. New Kent County School Board* inapposite in the context of higher education. In *Green,* the Supreme Court had ruled that the adoption of a freedom-of-choice plan does not discharge the constitutional duty of a formerly de jure segregated grade-school system if the plan fails to eliminate, or at least significantly decrease, the racial imbalance within the system. Under

Green and its progeny, a racial imbalance, although insufficient in itself to establish a constitutional violation, gives rise to a presumption that a presently identifiable imbalance is the result of intentional state action during the de jure period. As an appropriate remedy, a court may order student reassignments (busing) despite the operation of policies that are ostensibly neutral.

The court of appeals took the position that remedies like student reassignment, upheld in *Green,* are inapplicable in the higher education context, because universities were fundamentally different from lower schools. Relying primarily on the Supreme Court's finding in *Bazemore v. Friday* that state sponsorship of single-race clubs did not violate the Fourteenth Amendment if the racial makeup of the club was the result of voluntary choice, the appeals court held that since college attendance is a matter of choice rather than assignment (unlike school attendance), the adoption and implementation of race-neutral policies sufficed to demonstrate that the state had taken all affirmative steps necessary to fulfill its constitutional obligation.

The Supreme Court found the lower courts' reliance on *Bazemore* misplaced. At issue in *Bazemore* was whether the funding and operational assistance provided by a state university's extension service to voluntary 4-H and Homemaker Clubs was a violation of equal protection when the majority of clubs had single-race membership. The Court also held the *Green* ruling inapplicable, but only in a voluntary choice program when the state has completely abandoned its policy of segregation and there is no evidence of lingering discriminatory effects of that policy, and when the state can demonstrate that any racial imbalance is the result of purely private decision making in which the state plays no role.

So, Mississippi could not take refuge in *Bazemore;* the state would have to face judicial inquiry into whether it had left in place facets of the earlier segregated system that perpetuated racial segregation, whether by influencing student choice or by promoting segregation in other aspects of the university system, without sound educational justification. If it had left such policies and practices in place, the Court decided, they would be in direct conflict with the equal protection mandate of the Fourteenth Amendment.

Implementation of the Standard. The Supreme Court offered little guidance to the lower courts as to how the newly articulated standard

should be implemented. All that was ascertained was that Mississippi's former system of higher education had constrained students' free
choice and that in order to meet its constitutional duty to dismantle
that system Mississippi had to take whatever steps were necessary to
ensure that student choice with respect to higher education would be
truly free.

The continued existence of predominantly one-race institutions was
not in and of itself evidence of the state's failure to fulfill that obligation; the "full range of policies and practices must be examined" and,
if found to contravene the *Fordice* standard, eliminated *where practicable and in keeping with sound educational policies.* Other than to
suggest that implementation of the standard does *not* mean upgrad-
ing the historically black institutions solely to create "more equal" but
nonetheless separate, "publicly financed, exclusively black enclaves by
private choice," the Court offers no direction.

The Separate Opinions. The decision in *Fordice,* written by Justice Byron
White, represented the opinion of an eight-member majority of the
Court. Justices O'Connor and Thomas also wrote separate concur-
rences, elaborating on the standard carved out by the majority, which
offer the lower courts slightly more insight into implementation.

Justice O'Connor sought to clarify how the current policies of a state
might be measured against the Court's standard of educational sound-
ness and practicability of elimination. The circumstances in which a
state with a long history of discrimination may maintain a policy, the
effects of which are the legacy of prior segregation, are narrow. Where
present policies are traceable to the prior de jure system and the state
could accomplish legitimate educational goals through less segregative
means, the courts may infer lack of good faith. If a state shows that
maintenance of certain remnants of its prior system are essential to
meet its legitimate objectives, it still must prove that it has counter-
acted and minimized the segregative impact of those policies to the
extent possible. Only by eliminating any remainder of the prior segregation or by negating (insofar as possible) the segregative impact can
the state satisfy its obligation to prove that it has "taken all steps" to
dismantle the discriminatory system.

Similarly, while agreeing with the Court that a state does not satisfy
its constitutional obligation by implementing race-neutral admission
policies, Justice Thomas emphasized that the standard adopted in *For-

dice is, nonetheless, different in the context of a university system than in the grade-school context, which is governed by the standard adopted in *Green v. New Kent County School Board.*

Justice Thomas wrote that the *Fordice* standard requires a focus on the specific policies said to produce the racial imbalance rather than on the imbalance itself. At the university level, courts cannot order the reassignment of students to eliminate an existing imbalance; they must instead examine whether policies traceable to the de jure era that continue to promote segregation are educationally justified. In Justice Thomas's view, the *Fordice* standard is a narrower and more manageable one than the one imposed by *Green* and its progeny.

The distinction drawn between *Fordice* and *Green* underpins Justice Thomas's main point, that historically black colleges and universities should be preserved. In particular, Justice Thomas wrote that because imposing the *Fordice* standard does not compel the elimination of all observed racial imbalance, "it portends neither the destruction of historically black colleges nor the severing of those institutions from their distinctive histories and traditions."

The *Fordice* standard does not require a challenged policy to be eliminated if it has a sound educational justification. It is on this criterion that Justice Thomas based his argument for historically black institutions. According to Thomas, desegregation remedies must be practical and flexible, reconciling public and private needs. Remedies crafted for the Mississippi system must consider the educational need of the present and future students in Mississippi. When this compelling need is taken into account, Justice Thomas opined that there is sound educational justification for maintaining historically black colleges and universities.

Relying on a 1971 report of the Carnegie Commission on Higher Education, which focused on the state of historically black colleges, Justice Thomas concluded that, despite the history of state-enforced segregation, the historically black institutions have flourished and exercised leadership in developing educational opportunities for black youth at all levels of instruction, especially in the South. They are both a source of pride for blacks who have attended them and a source of hope to black families who aspire to provide their children with higher education. These institutions continue to play a key role in enhancing the general quality of the lives of black Americans.

That these institutions have remained viable is, in large measure, because of their distinctive histories and traditions. The state cannot maintain those traditions by restricting particular institutions, whether historically white or historically black, to one race. However, a state can operate a diverse assortment of institutions—open to all on a race-neutral basis—but with traditions and programs that might appeal disproportionately to one race or another. According to Justice Thomas, institutional diversity is the "sound educational justification" for continuation of historically black universities. Although a state is not constitutionally required to maintain its historically black institutions as such, neither is it forbidden from doing so. For Justice Thomas, institutional diversity is a value worth preserving, for "it would be ironic, to say the least, if the institutions that sustained blacks during segregation were themselves destroyed in an effort to combat its vestiges."

Justice Scalia concurred in the judgment in part and dissented in part. He agreed that Mississippi is constitutionally compelled to remove all discriminatory barriers to access to its public universities and that the state's ACT requirements for admission require further judicial review. He also agreed that the state was under no constitutional obligation to equalize the funding of the historically black and historically white institutions. Beyond that, Justice Scalia and the majority found no common ground. Scalia rejected the imposition of an obligation on Mississippi and other states to demonstrate compliance with the *Brown* mandate in the context of higher education. He also assailed the *Fordice* standard as incomprehensible and contradictory.

First, Scalia took issue with the majority for setting out what he deemed not *one* workable standard but *two*. According to Justice Scalia, the Court initially articulated the standard for higher education to require elimination of all old policies that continue to have segregative effects. The "influencing of student enrollment decisions" was presented, according to Scalia, as only an example of a "segregative effect." But, he argued, as the Court later applied the standard to the facts before it, the test changed. "Influencing student enrollment decisions" became less an example of a segregative effect than a defining feature of segregation. The "second test" articulated by the Court, then, in Justice Scalia's view, was that the policies that must be eliminated are those that are legacies of the dual system, that contribute to the racial imbalance of the state's universities, *and* that do so in a way that "substantially restricts a person's choice of which institution to enter."

For Scalia, the "restricting choice" requirement is, at best, unclear. In his view, it is not apparent from the Court's usage whether the requirement is meant to address strong coercion of student choice by the state, to slight inducement, or to something in between. He suggested that the test is presumably aimed at state action that "affects" choice, since the Mississippi policies called into question included mission designations, program duplication, and operation of eight public universities, all of which, Justice Scalia argued, in no way *restrict* the decision of where to attend college.

Scalia's difficulties with the Court's standard went beyond the "restricting choice" requirement. Assessing when a challenged state practice perpetuates segregation under the standard was equally troubling. Specifically, in evaluating Mississippi's case, he concluded that designating three historically white institutions as the only comprehensive institutions in the state actually encouraged integration. Citing statistics that showed that approximately 30 percent of all black college students attending four-year colleges in the state attend one of the comprehensive universities, Justice Scalia implied that the lack of an alternative meant that any student, black or white, who desired to pursue a "comprehensive" course of study would, by necessity, do so at one of the historically white institutions with comprehensive status. Thus, in his view, Mississippi's mission designations furthered integration. As a general matter, Scalia objected to the "aggregation" of particular practices for a "composite" condemnation, which the majority's standard permitted: the majority's standard, he argued, allowed a particular practice that did not by itself foster segregation to be aggregated with other practices and the composite effect to be condemned. But when a district court should aggregate and when it may consider each practice in isolation was, he contested, left unclear. Finally, Justice Scalia found the concepts of "sound educational justification" and "impractical elimination" too ambiguous to be workable. Such ill-defined terms, he argued, would frustrate and confuse lower courts in their struggles to apply the *Fordice* analysis.

Interestingly, Justice Scalia does not believe that historically black institutions will be more viable after *Fordice*. Scalia, like Thomas, took the position that although the Constitution does not require equal funding for historically black and historically white institutions, it does not prohibit it. But, unlike Thomas, Scalia believed that the majority's decision in *Fordice* would prevent a state from funding more or less equally single-race public educational institutions, even though they

are open to all on a race-neutral basis and only appeal disproportionately to one race or the other by virtue of established traditions and
programs. For, as Scalia saw it, an equal funding policy would continue
segregation by enabling students to attend predominately single-race
schools without fear of sacrificed quality, and the educational diversity
that comes from preserving historically single-race institutions would
not meet the "sound educational justification" exemption of *Fordice*.
Far from encouraging the historically black colleges, Scalia concluded,
in what might be described as an ominous prophecy, "what the Court's
test is designed to achieve is the elimination of predominately black
institutions."

United States v. Fordice—*The Aftermath*

The Supreme Court remanded the case to the federal district court in
June 1992. Judge Neal B. Biggers Jr. instructed the parties to seek an
out-of-court settlement to end the segregation of Mississippi's higher
education system. As this book was going to press, the opposing parties
had made no progress toward settlement, and the case was likely to go
to trial.

In October 1992, the governing board of Mississippi's higher education system proposed a plan that called for closing two of the historically black universities—Alcorn State, the nation's oldest black land
grant college, and Mississippi Valley State—and merging them into
two of the historically white institutions, Mississippi State University
and Delta State, respectively. The third predominately black university, Jackson State, would remain open and add academic programs to
attract more white students.

The merger plan was received by a storm of protest throughout
the African American community of Mississippi and by the country's
forty-two public historically black universities. The plan has generated
a debate over how financially strapped states should restore university systems that have been separate but rarely equal. Educators fear
that states will use court desegregation orders as a rationale to eliminate black institutions rather than spend to improve them. They argue that the loss of historically black institutions offers, as a cure to
segregation, a plan that further damages the victims of the original
segregation by eliminating a part of their cultural and educational heritage. William Sutton, president of Mississippi Valley State University,

and other black leaders have called the plan unfair to black campuses. "Why does desegregation only have to work one way—sending blacks to white schools?"

Educators argue that the success of black colleges cannot be dismissed and the need for maintenance of black colleges as sanctuaries and nurturers continues as a large number of the students who matriculate at those institutions come from inner-city environments, where education is marginal. They believe that more whites would attend these institutions if they had more high-profile academic programs, especially professional schools.

The United States Department of Justice has proposed a plan for Mississippi that appears to mirror that philosophy. It would keep all eight public universities open and give historically black Jackson State University control of the state medical school, currently a part of the University of Mississippi. The plan also recommends (1) giving Jackson State control of Hinds Community College, a two-year institution with seven campuses, one of which is in Jackson and competes for students with Jackson State; (2) renaming Alcorn State University the Alcorn Institute for Applied Science and Technology, with the mission of offering undergraduate and master's degree programs in the sciences; (3) transferring the engineering programs at the University of Mississippi to one of the historically black institutions; and (4) forcing the universities to withdraw from all-black or all-white athletic conferences. The district court can consider the Justice Department proposal in designing a remedy, but it is not required to do so.

In apparent fulfillment of the prophesy of educators and supporters of historically black institutions, the Supreme Court's ruling in *Fordice* has sparked a chain reaction of sorts. The Louisiana District Court has ordered the dismantling of that state's segregated university system by consolidating seventeen public colleges and universities. The order has drawn harsh criticism from two predominately black Louisiana institutions, Southern University and Grambling State University. Said Southern University president Robert Gex: "Suddenly . . . desegregation is a laudable goal, but it is totally unfair to balance the books on the backs of the historical victims."

The seventeen Southern and border states that operated state-sanctioned segregated higher education systems watch closely and await final resolution of the Mississippi case, as do the one hundred five historically black colleges throughout the nation.

CHAPTER NINE

Congress in recent decades has on a number of occasions enacted federal laws providing federal financial assistance for various social and economic programs that require, as a condition of receipt of federal funds, adherence to certain nondiscrimination principles. The principle is quite simple. State and local agencies, or private contractors who deal with the federal government, are told in effect, "We will give you federal money for your program, but in turn you must agree to abide by certain rules." Those rules often involve the protection of civil rights.

One of the most famous examples of such a program is Title IX of the Education Amendments Act of 1972, usually referred to simply as Title IX, a law that prohibits sex discrimination by educational institutions receiving federal financial assistance. The law defines "educational institution" broadly, as "any public or private preschool, elementary, or secondary school, or any institution of vocational, professional, or higher education."

It is one thing to declare such a sweeping policy, and another to enforce it. When an educational institution is guilty of violating Title IX, what happens? Are its funds cut off? Who is responsible for catching violators? The federal government? Individual victims of discrimination? May victims file suit in court to enforce the law? Are victims entitled to receive any compensation? Unfortunately, Congress did not make it very clear in the law what the remedies were to be, and the resolution of that problem has devolved to the Supreme Court, which must attempt to discern the intent of Congress.

In *Cannon v. University of Chicago,* decided in 1979, the Supreme Court held that Title IX is enforceable through what lawyers call "an implied right of action." This means that a private person discriminated against by an educational institution may initiate a lawsuit based on the violation of Title IX. This "cause of action" is deemed "implied" because it is a remedy created by the courts to enforce the congressional statute—Title IX itself does not say anything explicitly one way or the other as to whether such a suit should be permitted.

Although the *Cannon* case held that a private cause of action is permitted to enforce Title IX, it did not explain what remedies were available to the victims of discrimination in such a case. Specifically, *Cannon* did not decide whether victims could seek monetary damages against the school that was responsible for the discrimination.

In *Franklin v. Gwinnett County Public Schools,* the Supreme Court was asked to decide this issue. The case was brought by Christine Franklin, a student in a high school operated by the Gwinnett County school district, claiming that she had been subjected to continual sexual harassment and abuse by a teacher, Andrew Hill. After Christine Franklin's complaint was filed, Hill resigned on the condition that all matters pending against him be dropped, and the school thereupon closed its investigation. Franklin sued for money damages under Title IX, but lost when the lower courts held that Title IX does not authorize damages awards.

In his account of this case, Steve Wermiel describes the extraordinary stress and trauma that such a sexual harassment allegation brings to the persons involved, and to the community in which it occurs. His account provides a striking example of the dramatic interplay between the human side of such a dispute, and the resolution of legal issues that have enormous practical importance in the fields of education and civil rights.

—Editor

A Claim of Sexual Harassment

STEPHEN WERMIEL

No person in the United States shall, on the basis of sex, be excluded from participation in, be denied the benefits of, or be subjected to discrimination under any program or activity receiving Federal financial assistance.—Title IX of the Education Amendments Act of 1972

Sexual harassment which creates a hostile or offensive environment for members of one sex is every bit the arbitrary barrier to sexual equality . . . that racial harassment is to racial equality.—Justice William Rehnquist, for the Court in *Meritor Savings Bank v. Vinson*

As a student at North Gwinnett High School, Christine Franklin ordinarily would not have attracted much attention outside her own circle of friends. Academically, she ranked about in the middle of her class of some 235 students, excelling as a member of the school's band.

But she became the center of attention in the spring of 1988, when the popular and respected head football coach at North Gwinnett High, Andrew Hill, resigned his position amidst allegations that he had sexually harassed Christine Franklin while she was a student and that he had had sexual intercourse with her on several occasions. The resignation and the events that followed shattered the calm of this suburb of Atlanta, some twenty-five miles northeast of the Georgia capital.

Even then, no one thought Franklin's complaint of sexual harassment against the Gwinnett County school district would lead all the way to the U.S. Supreme Court. Before the controversy would drop from the local headlines, however, it produced a federal investigation, a major Supreme Court civil rights ruling, a secret out-of-court settlement, two other lawsuits for damages including one under an archaic Georgia law, and a public rally of parents and former students in support of Hill.

Ironically, although the Supreme Court decision forced hundreds of school districts throughout the nation to adopt procedures and guidelines for handling sexual harassment problems, the high court ruling resolved little in the dispute between Franklin, Hill, and Gwinnett County.

As the school year began in the fall of 1986, these events were unimaginable. The school year was off to a typical start. Franklin was fifteen years old and in tenth grade, living in the community of Buford, not too far from the high school, which was located on the edge of the nearby city of Suwanee. Besides playing the flute in the school band, Franklin was enrolled in standard courses—algebra, English, and biology—and in economics, taught by a teacher who had just arrived at the high school, Andrew Hill. Franklin also had a new boyfriend, Doug Kreeft, a student whom she had known for a while but had just started to date (in 1992, they were married).

What happened next remains in dispute. Eight years after Franklin met Hill and six years after she made public her sexual harassment claim, no court—state or federal—had made a determination of the facts of the case. The out-of-court settlement in 1993 meant that there was never a trial in the federal court case or in one of two state court cases. The other state court lawsuit also faced legal and procedural hurdles that delayed or thwarted any court ruling on the truth or falsity of Franklin's allegations, or on liability for the alleged misconduct.

Nevertheless, it is possible to piece together the conflicting versions of what happened from depositions and other court records and documents.

When Hill began teaching at North Gwinnett High, he was thirty-six years old, an experienced high-school teacher and football coach in a state that cares more about high school football records than about average SAT scores. A 1972 graduate of the University of Georgia, he had taught a variety of high-school subjects and served as an assistant coach in south Georgia. After a few years, he had moved to Gwinnett County, teaching at two other high schools and moving up the coaching ladder to become defensive coordinator. He took the job at North Gwinnett High in 1986 because it gave him his first chance to become head football coach. Married in 1973, he was the father of three children.

Franklin's statements of what happened describe a classic abusive situation in which a teacher, in a position of power, trust, and influ-

ence, took advantage of the emotional vulnerability of an impressionable student. Hill's statements admit none of that and insist that there
was never any sexual or even conversational impropriety on his part.

Franklin told investigators that she and Hill became friends soon
after the school year began in the fall of 1986. She said Hill allowed
her to grade daily quizzes in his economics class and to record the
grades. Hill's office was located in the athletic field house in the rear of
a classroom. Franklin said that he would sometimes give an economics
assignment to work on in class and then take her into the office to talk.

Initially, they talked about her grades, about her flute playing, and
about her boyfriend. Later, she said, he began to ask her sexually explicit questions about her boyfriend and engaged in other suggestive
conversation. She said he asked whether she and her boyfriend had
sex, and asked whether she would consider having sex with an older,
more experienced man. With the door to his office closed, he told her
that his wife would not engage in sex with him after their last child was
born and that two girls at another high school where he had worked
helped out by having sex with him.

These conversations made Franklin feel uncomfortable, and she mentioned them to another teacher. The other teacher assured her that he
and Hill went to the same church every Sunday and that Hill just was
not that kind of man. (In a later statement to school officials, Franklin
said she concluded at the time, "I'm mistaken, he's a good man. He
wants to talk with someone. I should not be offended.")

Rumors began to circulate in the school about her and the coach.
Franklin said she arrived in her tenth grade English class one day and
found an anonymous note on her desk that said, "I heard Coach Hill
is good. Is he better than Doug?" Infuriated, she confronted Hill, who
told her to calm down and then forcibly kissed her on the lips. She
said she then found her boyfriend and told him about the incident.
The boyfriend confronted Hill, who denied that anything improper had
occurred. Franklin and her boyfriend were supposed to be in band
practice at the time, and when they returned, Dr. William Prescott, the
band teacher, insisted on knowing what had detained them. When they
told him, he wrote an anonymous note to Hill. Franklin said the note
told Hill that his conduct was inappropriate, but Hill later maintained
that the note simply said, "Beware of Christine Franklin."

According to Franklin, for the remaining days of the fall semester,
Hill stayed away from her. But the psychological toll was already appar-

ent; she failed algebra and biology. Throughout spring semester 1987, though the sexual tone of the conversations stopped, she continued to meet Hill. "I trusted him again. I thought he really cared about me," she later told investigators.

Hill's version of events up to this point differs sharply from Franklin's. In a deposition in February 1989, Hill said Franklin was one of four or five students in the economics class with whom he used to talk occasionally and who helped him once or twice to grade quizzes. He acknowledged one occasion on which he was about to start class but found Franklin crying outside the classroom. He said she told him she was afraid that she was pregnant. A few days later, they talked again, and he said it was the only occasion he could recall on which he talked to Franklin in his office with the door closed.

In all respects, however, Hill denied Franklin's account. He said he never asked her sexually explicit questions or discussed his own marriage with her. He said he never kissed her and never had a conversation with her boyfriend about any such incident. He said he had little contact with her in the spring, except for one conversation in which Franklin told him she had broken up with her boyfriend and then, moments later, the boyfriend had showed up, looking for Franklin.

After the school year ended, Franklin had little contact with Hill, she said, until late in the summer when the coach called her home and suggested that his wife and family might be going away for a weekend and that he and Franklin might get together. Franklin said that when her mother asked why Hill was calling her, she took Hill's advice and told her mother that he wanted to know the schedule for band practice.

When school started, Franklin, who was now sixteen and in eleventh grade, said that Hill found her course schedule and occasionally waited for her outside her classes to talk. Her boyfriend had left for navy training, and she said Hill would ask her questions about what she was doing to "satisfy" herself. When she protested at such questions, he reassured her that they were friends and that he would never hurt her. Periodically, she said, he wrote notes asking that she be excused from one class or another or asking teachers to excuse her lateness to their classes.

One day in October 1987, Franklin said, Hill asked her English teacher to excuse her from class and walked her to the field house. Once inside, she said, he began to remove her clothes, then his own, climbed on top of her on a couch in his office and had sexual intercourse with her. "I was scared. I could not say anything. I could not move," she said in a statement to investigators.

He continued to wait for her outside her classes, she said, and acted as if nothing had happened. Some days later, she said, he once again asked to have her excused, this time from her American history class. He took her to a room in the field house where the gym mats are stored. "I felt that I would be in a lot of trouble if I didn't do what he wanted and he would somehow tell somebody what was going on," Franklin told investigators. She said that Hill asked her if she wanted her boyfriend or her mother to find out. On this occasion, she said, she removed her pants herself, and he had sexual intercourse with her, lying on a gym mat. After that incident, she asked her English teacher, Lori McDonough, and her history teacher, Edward Winn, to refuse to let Hill take her out of their classes, she said. McDonough would later recall the request by Franklin, although Winn did not.

In early December, there was a third such incident, she said. In her account, Hill once again asked to have her excused from her history class and took her to the press box of the football field, where he started telling her that she could give him an erection just sitting in front of him. She told him that he was scaring her and said that while she was lying on her back, she could see the stairwell they had climbed to get to the press box. Hill then said to her, "Yeah, those stairs do look mighty steep, don't they?" After that, she said Hill had sexual intercourse with her. By the time she was able to leave, history class was over and Hill gave her a note to take to geometry. "A few days later, I told him he was scaring me," Franklin wrote in her March 1988 statement to investigators. "I didn't want someone to find us, I didn't want any more of this."

Later she would describe the effect on her in more profound and emotional terms. "It was a nightmare. It took every ounce of courage just to get up and go to school in the morning," she said on ABC's *Good Morning America* after the U.S. Supreme Court ruled in her case in February 1992.

In his deposition, Hill denied every detail of this story. He insisted that he never called Franklin at her home during the summer, although a school investigator later concluded that he had, and that there were no weekends when his wife and family were away without him. He said Franklin initiated conversations with him in the fall semester, 1987, primarily to talk about her parents' marital problems.

He denied any sexual involvement with Franklin. Indeed, throughout the years of legal maneuvering, Hill has never wavered in maintaining his innocence.

How did this dispute shift from a searing emotional experience for
Christine Franklin to a U.S. Supreme Court case of major national significance? Much happened in the spring semester, 1988. Although it
was not publicly known at the time, Hill said he had informed the
high school principal in January 1988 that he would resign as head
football coach after two losing consecutive seasons for the North Gwinnett football team. (The team record was four to six in fall 1986, Hill's
first season as head coach, and a dismal one to nine in fall 1987.) The
first public word of his resignation came some months later when he
wrote a resignation letter dated April 14, 1988, after Franklin had made
accusations against him and as he faced the prospect of a lengthy investigation. He noted in his letter of resignation that he was stepping
down "pending dropping of all matters against me."

Franklin, who had turned seventeen by then, learned that at least
one other student at North Gwinnett High had complained of virtually
identical sexually explicit conversations with Hill. "I didn't want to see
someone else go through the pain I did," Franklin said in her eight-page
typed statement to school officials on March 28, 1988. Franklin said
she came forward "because I couldn't deal with the pain, the rumors,
by myself anymore. . . . This became too much and too big for me to
handle."

On February 22, 1988, Franklin went to her old English teacher, Lori
McDonough, to tell her of Hill's alleged treatment of her. This touched
off a series of meetings, spanning more than a week, and much hand
wringing by school officials to try to decide what to do about the allegations. McDonough reported her conversation with Franklin to the
guidance counselor, Virginia Lacy. On February 25, 1988, Franklin met
with Lacy, who later reported that Franklin initially told her that "she
willingly had sexual intercourse" with Hill. Franklin's federal court
complaint alleges, however, that Hill "forced himself" upon her in at
least one of the three instances of sexual intercourse and refers to his
sexual "demands" in all three episodes.

Lacy reported the allegations to Dr. Franklin Lewis, the school principal. On March 1, 1988, Lewis and Lacy informed Hill of the allegations, and then on March 2, Lewis met with Franklin to hear her side

of the story. After that, the school initiated a formal investigation of the allegations.

A simple chronology does not really tell the whole story, however. There were other things taking place, subtle pressures and actions that contributed to the climate that led to the lawsuit. For example, the school investigator, Dennis Foster, who was director of safety and security for the Gwinnett County public schools, reported in an April 1, 1988, memo, "Coach Andy Hill was told by Dr. Lewis, the first time we talked to him, to stay away from her. That same day Coach Andy Hill approached Christine and told her to drop the case."

Franklin also told investigators that soon after she made her allegations to school officials, she was approached by Dr. Prescott, the music teacher and band leader, who urged her to drop the matter because she was in a "no-win" situation. Franklin said that he was concerned about the allegations becoming public and warned that her reputation would be sullied if there were coverage in the news media and on television. The music teacher also approached Doug Kreeft, Franklin's boyfriend, according to Franklin, and asked him to help dissuade her.

According to the federal court complaint filed by Franklin's lawyers, there had been earlier examples of the school district allegedly being unresponsive. The court papers alleged that in October 1987, another student complained to an assistant principal at the high school that Hill had made sexually oriented comments to her and that Hill had harassed Franklin, too. The assistant principal chastised the student for her allegations but took no further action, according to Franklin's lawsuit.

Hill continued to deny all allegations. However, the inquiry by the school district's investigator, Foster, seemed to find some plausibility in Franklin's story. In his April 1 memo to Gwinnett school superintendent Dr. Alton Crews, Foster said he had found "some elements of facts where comments made by Coach Andy Hill can be proven as untrue." None of these proved the ultimate question of whether Hill harassed Franklin or forced her to have sexual intercourse with him. But, as Foster observed, "After reading the statements it is obvious that students, teachers and administrators gave Coach Andy Hill ample warning that he was making a mistake and to be wary of any involvement."

One fact that made an impression on Foster and later on a federal investigator was that Franklin knew that Hill had a surgical scar on the left side of his abdomen. Foster said Hill told him that if Franklin's allegations were true, she would know about the scar because she would have seen it during their alleged sexual encounters—and Franklin, in her statement, did mention that she had seen the scar. But in his deposition, Hill said the scar was from gallbladder surgery and that he frequently mentioned it in his classes. The importance of the scar, he said, was twisted by Foster's investigation: many students knew about the scar because he talked about it; if Franklin did not know about it, that would prove her allegations false.

With Foster's investigation complete, school officials considered their options. They later told a federal investigator their choices were to do nothing, refuse to renew Hill's contract, suspend him, or fire him. When Hill submitted his resignation letter on April 14, school officials felt that the matter was concluded.

Far from being concluded, this drama was simply moving from the high-school stage to a new theater, populated by lawyers and judges, one in which the scripts of human emotion are replaced by complaints and briefs.

Not satisfied to let school officials drop the matter, Franklin, with the support of her mother, Nancy, and her boyfriend, Doug Kreeft, hired an Atlanta lawyer, Stephen Katz, who worked at a small Atlanta firm, Weinstock & Scavo, located on the edge of the city's fashionable Buckhead district. In an interview Katz later recalled that "early on, an apology probably would have been enough to end the matter" for Franklin and her family. No apology was forthcoming from school authorities. In August 1988, Katz filed a complaint in Franklin's behalf with the U.S. Department of Education Office for Civil Rights, charging sexual harassment, intimidation after the allegations of harassment, and inadequate grievance procedures for handling sexual harassment complaints.

Why make a federal case out of it? During the fiscal year in which the complaint was filed, the Gwinnett County public schools received $1.8 million in federal aid to education, giving the U.S. Department of Education jurisdiction over the district. The focal point of the complaint—and of the lawsuit that went to the U.S. Supreme Court—was a provision of federal law known as Title IX.

Title IX, or more formally Title IX of the Education Amendments of 1972, is a federal civil rights statute that prohibits sex discrimination in federally funded education programs. The text of the law says, "No person in the United States shall, on the basis of sex, be excluded from participation in, be denied the benefits of, or be subjected to discrimination under any education program or activity receiving federal financial assistance." It is popularly known as the federal law that is forcing colleges to offer equal opportunities to women students in athletic programs, changing the past practice of having fewer women's teams when there were women interested in competing or of scrapping women's teams, but not men's, during budget cutting.

The federal Education Department is the initial line of enforcement of Title IX and issues regulations for enforcement of Title IX that cover sexual harassment under the heading of prohibited gender discrimination. These regulations define sexual harassment as "verbal or physical conduct of a sexual nature, imposed on the basis of sex, by an employee or agent of a recipient (of federal funds) that denies, limits, provides different, or conditions the provision of aid, benefits, services, or treatment protected under Title IX."

Franklin's complaint was handled by an investigator from the Atlanta regional office of the Education Department, Doris Shields. Shields spent a week in the school district in October 1988, interviewing students, teachers and administrators and compiling copies of records and written statements. In a November 1988 report, Shields concluded, "Based on the evidence obtained, we have determined that the District is in violation of the regulation implementing Title IX . . . because the student was subjected, on the basis of sex, to verbal and physical conduct of a sexual nature by a District employee which subjected her to different treatment and limited her enjoyment of an aid, benefit, or service, i.e., an education in a nondiscriminatory environment." The investigation also found that the actions of Hill and Prescott, the music teacher, after Franklin made her allegations amounted to intimidation that interfered with her right to complain about sexual harassment.

However, this significant step for Franklin was short-lived. A letter to Franklin's lawyer on December 14, 1988, from the regional civil rights director for the Education Department, Jesse High, said federal officials had a series of conversations with Gwinnett school administrators during the preceding weeks. In those conversations, Gwinnett school officials pledged to take steps to adopt Title IX sexual harassment grievance procedures and to appoint a Title IX coordinator. Based on those assurances, the Education Department reported, "We, therefore, consider the District to be presently fulfilling its obligations with respect to Title IX and are closing our investigation of this complaint."

That result was totally unacceptable to Franklin and her family. On December 29, 1988, her lawyer, Stephen Katz, filed suit in U.S. District Court in Atlanta. They named as defendants the school district and Dr. Prescott, the music teacher. The lawsuit charged that the school district failed in its responsibility to protect Franklin from the alleged sexual harassment by Hill, and that Franklin was the victim of sex discrimination because of Hill's conduct. The lawsuit also charged that the alleged intimidation of Franklin was a violation of Title IX, as well.

The federal court lawsuit, based on Title IX, was actually the second lawsuit filed. On August 2, 1988, about the time Franklin's lawyer contacted the Education Department, Franklin's mother, Nancy, filed a separate lawsuit in state court against Hill. The lawsuit alleged that Hill violated an archaic state law, the Georgia Seduction of a Daughter Statute. Passed in 1863, the seduction law gives a father, or a mother if the father is no longer available, the right to sue for damages for the seduction of an unmarried daughter living at home. The action is one under the state law of torts or civil wrongs.

Georgia also has a criminal seduction statute. The Gwinnett County district attorney's office looked into the possibility of filing criminal charges against Hill for seduction. In June, 1989, however, the district attorney's office reported to Mrs. Franklin that they would not file criminal charges. Assistant District Attorney Donald Johstono wrote, "It is my personal opinion, after a thorough review of the case, that Christine was the victim of a seduction. . . . However, in order for us to proceed with a criminal charge, we would have to prove beyond a reasonable doubt that force was used by Mr. Hill to make Christine have sex with him. It is my opinion that there is insufficient evidence to establish the element of force as required."

With the tort action pending in state court and the Title IX action in federal court, lawyers had taken over the leading roles in the drama. Occasionally, the action moved back to the school officials, as it did in January 1989, when they began to fight back, perhaps to combat negative publicity, perhaps to strengthen their posture in Franklin's Title IX lawsuit. The Education Department's letter finding a violation of Title IX but subsequent compliance was released to the news media, prompting a story in the January 4, 1989, *Atlanta Constitution,* headlined, "Gwinnett Schools' Lack of Grievance Plan Called Illegal." But the next day, the *Atlanta Constitution* ran a follow-up, entitled, "Schools to Clarify Sexual Harassment Grievance Plan." In the follow-up story, Gwinnett school superintendent Crews explained, "Title IX is one of many federal regulations we must comply with. We had a procedure in place. It just didn't spell out that it applied to that statute. It's really a technicality." And as to Franklin's case, the administrative assistant to Crews, George Thompson, was quoted, saying, "We feel that situation was handled appropriately. Each time something was reported it was referred to the next level. I don't want to leave the impression that we feel we did anything wrong." Thompson was designated to be the Title IX coordinator for the school district.

If there had been any doubt about Franklin's resolve to go ahead with legal action, these developments prompted her to push ahead. But progress on the legal front required the patience of a saint to tolerate the slow pace and the wisdom of a prophet to follow the intricate tangle of legal rules and procedures.

On May 1, 1989, as Franklin was nearing completion of her high-school career, U.S. District Court Judge Orinda Evans dismissed the Title IX lawsuit. Judge Evans found that the claim that the school district had no grievance procedures in place for Title IX was moot because school officials had clarified their policy on sexual harassment and on Title IX generally. "It appears that the relief to which the plaintiff is entitled under Title IX has been obtained and her claim against the school is moot," said Judge Evans.

In a crucial portion of her decision, Judge Evans concluded that implementation of grievance procedures was the only relief to which Franklin was entitled because Title IX did not permit lawsuits by individuals for damages. Relief under Title IX was limited to court orders halting misconduct or ordering school officials to take corrective steps in the future. If school officials refuse to comply, the ultimate sanction is for the Education Department to suspend federal aid. "No authority binding on this court," Judge Evans wrote, "endorses compensatory damages to individuals suing under Title IX. This court declines to enlarge on the existing remedies available under Title IX."

The decision by Judge Evans put the spotlight on a significant legal problem, one particularly acute in sexual harassment cases. Often, by the time a student, teacher, or staff member files a lawsuit under Title IX for sexual harassment, the misconduct has stopped or the student has graduated or the employee has moved to another job. The result is that a student who complains by filing a lawsuit bears the expense and emotional burden of the legal proceeding, only to achieve a result that will be of little or no direct benefit to that individual. For example, had Judge Evans ruled that Gwinnett County had to implement a more detailed or more effective grievance plan and had to stop all sexual harassment in its schools, the ruling would have had virtually no effect on Franklin, who was preparing to graduate. It is often the case that only a lawsuit that allows the student to recover damages for past harm will really provide any relief or personal benefit to that student.

Still, Judge Evans was merely following what she understood to be the law at the time. The language of Title IX says nothing about lawsuits for damages. The U.S. Court of Appeals for the Eleventh Circuit had ruled years earlier that lawsuits for damages were not allowed under Title IX, and Judge Evans was bound by the decision of the appeals court, which sits in Atlanta and covers Georgia, Florida, and Alabama. Franklin's lawyer, Stephen Katz, conceded this point, although he also predicted that the law might change in the appeals court or the Supreme Court. He told the *Atlanta Constitution,* "It is the law today, but it may not be in the future."

In August 1989, a year after initiating legal action with the Education Department and in state court against Hill, the newly graduated Franklin appealed the federal case to the Eleventh Circuit. It would be more than a full year before the Eleventh Circuit rejected her plea and sent the case of Christine Franklin on its way to the Supreme Court. The case was argued in the Eleventh Circuit in February 1990. Franklin's side was argued by Katz and the senior partner of the firm, Michael Weinstock. The school district was represented by Frank Bedinger III of the Atlanta firm of Freeman & Hawkins, which represents the school district's insurance company. Bedinger argued alone, although his brief was written with the school district's lawyer, Victoria Sweeny of the firm of Thompson & Sweeny, located in Lawrenceville, not far from North Gwinnett High School.

By the time of the argument, it was apparent that the legal stakes had grown. There were friend-of-the-court briefs filed by the Georgia and Alabama School Boards Associations, warning of the dangers of allowing school boards to be sued for damages for Title IX violations. There was also a brief filed by the National Women's Law Center, supporting Franklin's position.

On September 10, 1990, the Eleventh Circuit upheld Judge Evans's dismissal of the lawsuit. The decision was written by Judge J. Smith Henley, a federal appeals court judge from Harrison, Arkansas, who was visiting as a senior judge, one who still hears cases but is in semiretired status and has a reduced workload. Joining him in the three-to-zero ruling were two members of the Eleventh Circuit, Judge Frank Johnson of Montgomery, Alabama, who had ruled on numerous important civil rights cases in a distinguished judicial career, and Senior Judge James Hill of Jacksonville, Florida.

One important aspect of the legal issue had already been decided by the Supreme Court and did not need to be resolved by the Eleventh Circuit. The language of Title IX does not say expressly that individuals may sue, leaving open the possible interpretation that only the U.S. Department of Education could go to court to enforce the antidiscrimination law. In 1979, the Supreme Court resolved that ambiguity, ruling six to three that Congress had intended to allow individuals to sue for sex discrimination in education programs. That decision, *Cannon v. University of Chicago,* did not address the question in Franklin's case of what remedies are available when an individual sues under Title IX.

The decision of the Eleventh Circuit was devoted almost entirely to a single question—whether the Supreme Court, in a 1983 decision involving a different but similarly worded civil rights law, had ruled that lawsuits for damages could be implied as a remedy for intentional discrimination when the language of the law did not spell out any such relief. The difficulty in resolving this question was that the 1983 decision, *Guardians Association v. Civil Service Commission,* included five different opinions by the nine-member Supreme Court, making it almost impossible to discern a new legal rule to apply to other cases. The *Guardians* case involved Title VI of the 1964 Civil Rights Act, which prohibits racial discrimination in any program receiving federal funds. The Eleventh Circuit conceded, as Franklin's lawyers argued, that if the Supreme Court had allowed an implied remedy for damages in Title VI cases, there might be enough similarity in the statutes to treat Title IX the same way. In the end, the Eleventh Circuit said that it could not clearly conclude that the Supreme Court had allowed an implied remedy for damages. Judge Henley wrote, "We proceed with extreme care when we are asked to find a right to compensatory relief, where Congress has not expressly provided such a remedy as a part of the statutory scheme, where the Supreme Court has not spoken clearly, and where binding precedent in this circuit is contrary." To Franklin and her lawyers, the Eleventh Circuit decision meant only one thing—next stop, the highest court in the land.

The appeal to the Supreme Court, a petition for a writ of certiorari, was filed on December 10, 1990, using the full ninety days allowed by federal law to appeal to the high court after a lower court ruling. The petition was filed by Weinstock, who had taken over the case when Katz left the law firm, and an associate in the firm, Hillard Quint. When the three-hundred-dollar filing fee required by Supreme Court rules was paid, *Franklin v. Gwinnett County Public Schools* became an official case in Supreme Court records. The case was assigned the docket number 90–918.

Although more than two and a half years had passed since Franklin first complained to school officials, the focus of the Supreme Court appeal was not whether Franklin had been sexually harassed, or whether she or Hill was telling the truth. Rather, the sole question presented by the petition was the legal issue of whether, under Title IX, an individual who files a lawsuit may seek damages. It was a question of enormous practical legal significance, but one that was fairly far removed from the experiences of Franklin. In that respect, however, it was somewhat typical of cases decided by the high court, which often reviews appeals that have more national legal significance than they have impact on the parties to the specific lawsuit. Although Justices, from time to time, assert in speeches that the Court decides specific cases, not issues, the practical result of the Court's actions is often precisely the opposite.

The petition had a potent new weapon working in its favor, which arrived just a few weeks before the petition was due. Weinstock and Quint called attention to it in the very beginning of the petition. They asserted that the Eleventh Circuit's decision finding that no lawsuit for damages could be filed under Title IX directly conflicted with the decision of another federal appeals court, requiring a Supreme Court resolution of the problem. Indeed, the U.S. Court of Appeals for the Third Circuit, which sits in Philadelphia, ruled on November 13, 1990, that Title IX does authorize lawsuits for compensatory damages. The Third Circuit, in *Pfeiffer v. Marion Center Area School District,* acknowledged that its decision "puts us in conflict" with the Eleventh Circuit.

This was a major development. Since the Supreme Court only decides about 110 of the nearly 5,000 appeals that are filed each year, the Justices require some way of sorting out the appeals that are really worthy of their attention. One traditional barometer used by the court is to determine whether there is a "circuit conflict" that needs to be resolved, so that a particular federal law will have a uniform meaning throughout the country. The existence of a genuine and significant circuit conflict substantially increases the chances of having one's appeal heard.

The Gwinnett County public schools were represented by their local counsel, Victoria Sweeny, and by the insurance lawyer, Frank Bedinger. According to federal law and Supreme Court rules, the school system had thirty days to respond to Franklin's petition, and so in January 1991, Sweeny filed a brief in opposition urging the high court to deny review and to leave intact the Eleventh Circuit's ruling. They argued that there was no real circuit conflict and that the Eleventh and Third Circuit decisions differed materially from each other.

Although the Justices of the U.S. Supreme Court hold their conferences to discuss cases in closed-door, secret sessions, with no one else present and no formal record of their conversations, it is likely that Franklin's appeal was discussed very briefly at such a conference on Friday, February 15, 1991. Not infrequently, the Justices find that they are unable to fully assess the existence of a circuit conflict or the importance of resolving it. When this situation arises with a question of federal law enforced by a federal government agency, it is common for the Justices to ask for the views of the executive branch of the federal government. That is what the Court announced in a terse order on February 19, 1991. The Justices asked for a brief on whether they should hear the appeal to be filed by the solicitor general of the United States, a top-ranking official of the Justice Department, who traditionally represents the federal government in the Supreme Court.

In May, Solicitor General Kenneth Starr, a former federal appeals court judge and contender for a Supreme Court vacancy in the administration of President George Bush, advised the Court that there was a circuit conflict that was in need of resolution. That made the next step almost a foregone conclusion. The Justices rarely ask for and then ignore the solicitor general's recommendation on whether to review a question of federal law. On June 10, 1991, the Justices issued a brief order granting the petition and scheduling oral argument for the case in the fall.

The Supreme Court's decision to hear the appeal moved the case on to a whole new plane. *Franklin* perfectly illustrates a major trend in Supreme Court litigation in the past decade—the rise of professional Supreme Court advocates. Once the appeal was granted, Quint and Weinstock decided that they needed the expertise of a lawyer who had experience preparing briefs and arguing in the Supreme Court, one who could tailor the appeal to the Justices. According to Weinstock, the firm received a number of letters from "Supreme Court specialists" who wanted to handle the case. They settled on a very small but prestigious Washington firm, Klein, Farr, Smith & Taranto, and in particular on Joel Klein, a widely respected lawyer who had argued dozens of Supreme Court cases. Klein, who was a law clerk to Justice Lewis Powell in 1974, later became deputy White House counsel to President Clinton in late 1993. Weinstock explained his choice later: "I would have addressed the court as a choir, but Klein was able to address them on an individualized basis."

Gwinnett County's lawyers had a similar idea, although a somewhat different approach. They hired Albert Pearson III, a longtime University of Georgia Law School professor, well known throughout the state. Pearson, who had spent a year as a judicial fellow at the Supreme Court in 1987–88, later left teaching to join a respected Georgia litigation law firm, Butler, Wooten, Overby & Cheeley. For Pearson, it was his first Supreme Court oral argument.

First, there was the matter of the briefs. Klein said in an interview that he faced a strategic decision. "We had to make a very clear judgment about how much her story was featured versus emphasizing the legal conception," he said. "The danger was that if we simply argued that here's a clear wrong that cries out for a remedy, it would be too easy for the court to say, 'Fine, address that in Congress.'" The strategy adopted was to focus on the significance of legal remedies, rather than simply playing for a sympathetic ear. "Clearly, our conclusion was to help the court weave its way through its reluctance to imply rights," Klein said. The brief emphasized the view that once a right of individuals to sue is established, as it was under Title IX in the 1979 *Cannon* decision, then all traditional forms of relief, including damages, should be available. Appealing to an increasingly conservative court, Klein's brief argued that this helps courts avoid usurping the role of the legislature. Allowing all traditional remedies, he wrote, "avoids the need for courts either to nullify legislation because no particular remedy is specified or to decide on an ad hoc basis which remedies would best further Congress's purposes."

Pearson said he got involved after Bedinger and Sweeny were already working on their brief. Their brief took the approach that damages were unnecessary and were inconsistent with the purpose of Title IX. Relief through injunctions and court orders "seeks to promote compliance and to maintain institutional relationships; damages function primarily to punish and tend to stimulate institutional resistance," the brief said.

Other briefs arrived from friends of the court, although the only one on Gwinnett County's side was from Solicitor General Starr and one of his legal staff who also took part in the oral argument, Stephen Nightingale. As Klein had anticipated, they sought to turn the issue into one of judicial activism—unelected judges playing the role of elected legislators. The Justice Department brief argued that the Supreme Court and lower federal courts lacked the power to find implied remedies for implied rights to sue. "In view of the care with which Congress has fashioned statutory remedies in recent decades, there is no empirical basis for a free-floating presumption that the enactment of a statutory prohibition embodies a broad delegation to the courts to fashion whatever remedies they—as opposed to Congress—may consider appropriate," the solicitor general's brief said.

The other briefs filed, somewhat surprisingly, did not include any support for Gwinnett from organizations of school boards or school officials. "It was surprising to me that educational institutions didn't take a position in this case," Pearson said in an interview. Rather, three briefs were filed in support of allowing lawsuits for damages. One was by the Lawyers' Committee for Civil Rights Under Law, which handles many cases under the similar, earlier law, Title VI of the 1964 Civil Rights Act. Another was by a coalition of groups representing disabled Americans, who were concerned with the effect of the case on another, similar federal statute, section 504 of the Rehabilitation Act of 1973, that prohibits discrimination on the basis of handicap in federally funded programs. A third was filed by the National Women's Law Center for a large number of organizations interested in Title IX, including the National Organization of Women, the National Education Association, and the American Association of University Professors.

The oral argument took place at 10 A.M., the first case of the day, on

Wednesday, December 11, 1991. Klein argued first in the sixty-minute session. He sought to bolster his view that damages should be allowed by showing that employees had been permitted by the court to sue for back pay under other, similarly worded federal laws. Chief Justice William Rehnquist failed to see the comparison, calling it "a rather distant implication." Justice Sandra Day O'Connor wondered whether it made any difference that Title IX was based on Congress's power under the Constitution to appropriate funds, "the Spending Clause," rather than on other legislative powers that were involved in some other cases involving implied rights to sue. Klein replied that it would be "strange" to assume "that when Congress provides federal funds to a program it would want a less vigorous or less comprehensive scheme of enforcement with respect to civil rights." Klein also argued that subsequent acts of Congress, since 1972, demonstrated a clear understanding by Congress that damages were an available remedy under Title IX. Overall, the Justices asked comparatively few questions of Klein, who concluded, "It seems to me that we now have a twenty-year relationship, basically from '72 to the present, where the Court and Congress have interacted in a way that indicates at least now that damages are . . . available under Title IX, and I don't think there is any good reason to undo that understanding."

Klein later said the argument "was interesting in that unlike many arguments, I didn't have a good feel for where the Court was going."

Pearson, in contrast, ran into a buzz saw right away in the person of Justice John Paul Stevens. Justice Stevens wondered what kind of court order (called "equitable relief") would provide any benefit to a student like Franklin if damages were unavailable. "What is the possible, even theoretical possible remedy that the individual plaintiff in this case could have available that would motivate even bringing the case?" Justice Stevens asked, pressing the point repeatedly. Pearson explained that the possibility of the Education Department requiring corrective action would provide the motivation. "But that's not responsive to my question," Justice Stevens replied. After Pearson tried again, and Justice Stevens yet again, Justice David Souter interjected, "Isn't your answer to Justice Stevens' question, No, there is no equitable relief which she will seek?" Pearson later recalled, "Justice Stevens really jumped on me at oral argument."

Nightingale also received comparatively few questions, although some gave him a chance to try to refute Klein's arguments. Klein relied on a Supreme Court decision from 1946, *Bell v. Hood,* to show that for more than forty years, the Justices had recognized that federal courts had discretion to adjust the available legal remedies to correct the violation of federally protected rights. One justice asked Nightingale whether "our decision in Bell against Hood is limited to constitutional violations?" He replied, "It is, your honor. That is our position." He also disputed Klein's view of the meaning of subsequent acts of Congress.

Apart from the significance of the case, the oral argument attracted inordinate interest because it was the first involving alleged sexual harassment for the newly appointed Justice Clarence Thomas. Justice Thomas had joined the Court that fall after a bitter confirmation fight in which Anita Hill, a law professor, accused him of sexually harassing her when she worked for him a few years earlier. Justice Thomas disappointed the spectators who packed the court chambers: he did not say a word.

It did not take the Justices very long to reach a decision. On February 26, 1992, almost exactly four years after Christine Franklin first complained about sexual harassment to an English teacher, she won the right to sue the Gwinnett County public schools for damages. The outcome was unanimous, although the Justices divided six to three over their reasons for recognizing the right to sue for damages.

The legal analysis was straightforward. The majority opinion, written by Justice Byron White, concluded that there was a long history— nearly two hundred years—of allowing federal courts to use any available remedy for a legal wrong. He referred to "the long line of cases in which the court has held that if a right of action exists to enforce a federal right and Congress is silent on the question of remedies, a federal court may order any appropriate relief." Justice White also found that Congress took a number of steps in the 1980s to amend Title IX or related laws, including amendments designed to overturn the effects of Supreme Court decisions restricting these statutes. During these legislative corrections, Congress expressed no concern with the existence or scope of the right of private individuals to sue under Title IX or other civil rights statutes, Justice White said.

Justice White also rejected the Justice Department's argument that allowing lawsuits for damages when Congress did not authorize them is usurpation of legislative power. Recognizing new rights to sue may raise that problem, but "the discretion to award appropriate relief involves no such increase in judicial power," Justice White said.

Justice Antonin Scalia, in a separate concurring opinion that was joined by Chief Justice Rehnquist and Justice Thomas, agreed with Justice White that Franklin's lawsuit for damages should be reinstated. Justice Scalia reached his conclusion because of the subsequent legislation. He rejected the Court's argument that courts may invoke all available remedies unless Congress limits those that may be used. He said the Court was wrong to find the right of individuals to sue implicit in the law in the *Cannon* decision, although he conceded that it was too late to overturn that ruling. However, he reasoned that since Congress did not create the cause of action in the first place, it is illogical to say all remedies may be used unless Congress expressly limits them.

Since Franklin's lawsuit alleged that the harassment and intimidation were deliberate, the Court's decision applies primarily to instances of intentional misconduct. The Justices had no reason to decide for sure whether damages may similarly be available if the sexual harassment is unintentional. Also left undecided is the question of whether sexual harassment by one student against another student may lead to the awarding of damages against a school district.

Reaction to the decision was loud, clear, and divided. Women's rights groups lavished praise on the decision. "This is a major win that opens up Title IX dramatically," Marcia Greenberger, director of the National Women's Law Center, told the *New York Times*. "Having a real remedy will give an enormous push for equity" in education, she said.

But in Atlanta, Gwinnett County public schools lawyer Victoria Sweeny sounded a note of caution in the *Atlanta Constitution*, "The people who are going to be paying for these claims—meritorious or not—are going to be the taxpayers of America."

For Christine Franklin, the decision was about the best wedding present she could have been given. Just twelve days earlier, on February 14, 1992, Franklin and Doug Kreeft were married and were living with Kreeft's parents in Suwanee, where North Gwinnett High School is located. Franklin, who had turned twenty-one, had a one-year-old son and said she was still feeling the effects of the sexual harassment. She attended Georgia Southern University for one year on a scholarship to major in music, but dropped out. She told the *Atlanta Constitution* that she had developed sleeping and eating disorders since the alleged harassment. But when she learned of the Supreme Court's decision, she said, "I'm really excited. Actually, I'm walking on air."

Within days, Weinstock, Franklin's lawyer, said he would press for a trial and seek at least $1 million in damages from the school system. "The school had the business, under the law, to protect this particular student. They failed to do it," said Weinstock, who appeared with Franklin on ABC's *Good Morning America*.

Andrew Hill, the coach who resigned, continued to maintain his innocence. By the time the Supreme Court ruled, he had left the teaching and coaching professions and was working as an electrical supplies salesman in the Gwinnett County region. Hill remained silent about the Court's ruling, but at the behest of his friends, events took a strange turn. About two weeks after the high court decision, friends and supporters staged a nighttime rally at the town hall in Duluth, another community in Gwinnett County. The *Atlanta Constitution* reported that some five hundred people attended the March 12, 1992, rally. They wore blue-and-white buttons saying "We Believe" and listened to testimonials in support of Hill's character. "He always treated us with the utmost dignity and respect," declared one woman, a former high-school basketball player at Duluth High School, where Hill coached some years before coming to North Gwinnett High School. Ann Wadsworth, a friend of Hill's and an organizer of the rally, explained, "Someone has got to show the real side of Andy Hill." Hill attended the rally but did not speak.

The Supreme Court's decision was not the last step in the legal dispute. As a procedural matter, the high court's ruling sent the case back to the Eleventh Circuit. It wasn't until August 31, 1992, that the Eleventh Circuit issued a four-paragraph order, sending the case back to the U.S. District Court for further proceedings and trial. Weinstock then filed a new complaint in federal court, updating and amending the earlier allegations, and seeking at least $10 million in damages.

At that point, the Title IX lawsuit and the parallel state court lawsuit that was filed in 1989 disappeared from public scrutiny, never to reemerge. By January 1993, there were settlement discussions underway, and in April 1993, more than five years after Franklin's initial complaint, an agreement was reached and the two lawsuits were dismissed. Part of the agreement was that no one could talk about the terms of the settlement. Weinstock said he was only allowed to say that the matter had been "resolved to the satisfaction of the parties." A number of sources familiar with the case said, on condition that they not be identified, that the settlement included a cash payment to Franklin, although the amount will never be disclosed. In contrast to the high visibility of the case in its earlier stages, the settlement and dismissal of the lawsuit received no press coverage, either at the time of the settlement or in the months that followed.

One aspect of the case remained active, however—the third lawsuit, filed by Franklin's mother alleging violation of Georgia's obscure seduction law. It generated numerous decisions in the Georgia state courts, some of them rather bizarre. In particular, Gwinnett County Superior Court judge Richard Winegarden ruled in May 1991 that the Georgia seduction law only applied to women who were virgins at the time of the seduction. Since Franklin had engaged in sexual intercourse with Doug Kreeft prior to her encounters with Hill, Judge Winegarden said the law did not apply to her. On March 20, 1992, a few weeks after the U.S. Supreme Court ruling, the Georgia Court of Appeals ruled, three to zero, that virtue—the requirement that the woman be a virgin— was not part of the tort of seduction. The decision, by Judge Edward Johnson, sent the case back to the trial court. In a separate concurring opinion, appeals court Judge Dorothy Beasley explained that the reason that virtue is not an element of the tort is that the injured person, under the state seduction law, is the parent, not the daughter.

Before Judge Winegarden would let the case go to trial, he still had one more issue on his plate that was raised by Phillip Hartley, the lawyer for Hill. It turned out to be one that took Christine Franklin and Andrew Hill all the way to the Georgia Supreme Court. On June 30, 1993, Judge Winegarden, at the urging of Hill's lawyer, ruled that because the Georgia seduction law only punishes men who seduce women, the law discriminates on the basis of gender and violates the Equal Protection Clause of the Fourteenth Amendment to the U.S. Constitution. The U.S. Supreme Court has ruled that the equal protection guarantee prohibits sex discrimination by government institutions, unless the differential treatment is justified by an "important governmental objective" and is "substantially related" to achieving that goal. Judge Winegarden said he could find no substantial basis for punishing only men under the Georgia law. The lawyers for Nancy Franklin, Christine's mother, appealed to the Georgia Supreme Court, which was expected to hear arguments during 1994.

Technically speaking, Christine Franklin has had her day in court— many of them, in fact. But in practical terms, despite lengthy depositions, thousands of billable lawyer hours, hundreds of pages of briefs and numerous oral arguments, including one in the nation's highest court, no one has yet resolved—even for legal purposes—what went on between Christine Franklin and Andrew Hill.

Ironically, if it has been an ordeal for Christine Franklin to try to establish her veracity on the small stage of Gwinnett County, she has already left her mark on the nation. Sexual harassment and sex discrimination are a long way from being eliminated in American education; some studies would even argue that harassment is at an all-time high. Yet, public awareness of the extent of the problem and of the need for solutions has also never been greater, due in large measure to Franklin.

The *Franklin* decision provided a powerful new weapon to women to combat sexual harassment in education. As a result of the decision, schools throughout the country have been forced to adopt sexual harassment policies and grievance procedures. In 1993, lengthy articles in the *Miami Herald* and *Philadelphia Inquirer* focused on the significant attention being paid to sexual harassment policies in the public schools of Florida and New Jersey. In some places, these policies have enabled young women, for the first time, to be able to think of the pinching, groping, skirt-lifting, and other offensive activities perpetrated by young men as sexual harassment. In some places, students who were victimized by teachers who induced them into sexual relationships have been able to fight back.

Not everyone thinks these developments are all for the good of the country. Gwinnett County's Victoria Sweeny said that if the *Franklin* decision "prevents any student from being victimized by a teacher, that is a good thing." But, she said, "the expense to public education exceeds the deterrent effect of paying compensatory damages to an individual." Her fears were echoed by Los Angeles lawyer Larry Frierson in a July 1993 article in the weekly newspaper, *Legal Times.* "There is not a school in the country where you don't see adolescent boys teasing adolescent girls," said Frierson, who was representing a California school district in a harassment case. "The effect of [allowing Title IX suits] would be to open up a brand-new area of liability, and in financially troubled times for school districts, that's going to add to the problem," he said.

The effect of the *Franklin* decision is even broader than these concerns reflect. Although the *Franklin* case, itself, involved sexual harassment, Title IX involves virtually all forms of sex discrimination in education, including discrimination in opportunities and in employment.

The impact of *Franklin* has already been seen in some of these other areas. In June 1993 the Howard University women's basketball coach won a $2.4 million verdict from a Washington, D.C., jury. Although a judge later reduced the amount to $1.1 million, the verdict for Sanya Tyler was based, in part, on a Title IX complaint that, in contrast to the male basketball coach, she was paid a lower salary, had poorer office and locker room space, and had no assistant coach. Similar lawsuits were filed in 1993 by the women's basketball coach at the University of Southern California and the women's golf coach at Oklahoma State University.

Look, as well, for lawsuits under Title IX to redress employment discrimination in education, say experts in the field. The reason is that the traditional remedy for employment discrimination—Title VII of the 1964 Civil Rights Act—includes limits on damages, primarily the equivalent of back pay. Title IX has no such limitations and may become a more attractive vehicle for such lawsuits.

While women's rights groups view these developments in Title IX litigation as definite and long overdue progress, they hope that litigation will not always be required to drive the engine of social change. "For the sake of the entire community," said Ellen Vargyas of the National Women's Law Center in a 1993 law review article, "the far better course for educational institutions will be to eliminate the need for litigation by aggressively eradicating sex discrimination from our nation's schools, that is, to comply with the law and enforce Title IX."

CHAPTEN TEN

On days on which the Supreme Court is in session and hearing cases, any American willing to stand outside on the marble steps and wait in line for the doors to open may, if the line is not too long, ultimately gain admission to the public gallery and enjoy the drama of a Supreme Court oral argument.

To see an important case argued before the Supreme Court is to view one of the most *compact* exercises in self-governance one may witness in Washington, D.C. The entire business of arguing a major case before the Supreme Court is concluded in one hour.

This is an intense hour, in which all that has preceded and all that will come are funneled through a narrow, hourglass moment. Cases take years to work their way to the Supreme Court. Once the Court accepts a case for review, the case is normally briefed by the lawyers, considered by the Justices, voted upon, and resolved, with a written opinion, within the course of one Supreme Court term—the span of one year. At some point in roughly the middle of that one-year cycle a case will normally be presented for oral argument. Typically each side is given thirty minutes to argue. The lawyers are peppered with questions by the Justices. In some instances these exchanges are dry, technical, and boring. But often they are free-wheeling exchanges of view on all that makes for legal discourse at the highest levels: text, factual context, history, philosophy, policy, precedent.

For those moments in which the advocates are experienced and poised, and the Justices are "on," a Supreme Court argument can be a truly impressive event. The lawyers and Justices become wrapped up in debate over the critical issues of the day, exploring them with a wit, intelligence, and concentrated focus rarely matched in any other governmental forum.

But precious few Americans ever do stand in that line on those marble steps—nothing compared to the millions who tune in from time to time to watch congressional proceedings on C-Span, or hear the president's state of the union address, or watch members of Congress or the executive branch in the infinite array of press conferences, talk shows, or interviews, that form the daily parade of mass media information about government.

This quite naturally raises the question, why is there no television? Why doesn't C-Span or CNN carry the live broadcasts of important Supreme Court arguments? As Tony Mauro documents, there is no television in the United States Supreme Court because the Court refuses to permit it.

Tony Mauro takes the Court to task for what he describes as a "cult of secrecy," arguing that the Court has nothing to hide and should open its doors to the modern electronic culture.

Mauro is a seasoned journalist who has covered the Supreme Court and Washington, D.C., for years. He is also a zealous advocate of freedom of the press and open government. As his essay reveals, he is a passionate, unabashed, and unapologetic proponent of cameras in the Supreme Court. The reader should consider Tony Mauro's arguments, but at the same time seriously consider the arguments that the *Court itself* might advance, if it were defending itself on this issue.

Looking at the matter first from the side presented by Tony Mauro, why does the Supreme Court, guardian of a constitution crafted to ensure a free and open society, refuse to conduct its own business— which is, after all, the *people's* business—in a free and open manner? In an epoch in which court proceedings, legislative sessions, city council meetings, zoning board hearings—virtually every level of government high and petty—is now available for viewing round the clock on most American cable television systems, an epoch in which the future "electronic democracy" is *now,* why does the Supreme Court continue to conduct its business as if electrons were yet rumors of future invention? The Constitution belongs to the people, not to lawyers, law professors, and judges. Why has the institution at the very pinnacle of the legal system been so slow to let the people participate?

Wouldn't the televising of oral argument be a major educational resource? Wouldn't high-school civics classes, college and law school courses be enriched by the opportunity to see the issues studied in those courses crystallized in one-hour debates at the highest level? And wouldn't the televising of Supreme Court arguments actually improve the image and authority of the Supreme Court, by assisting a far wider circle of Americans in understanding the difficulty and complexity of many modern constitutional conflicts?

The essay presented here by Tony Mauro assumes that all of these questions should clearly be answered in the affirmative and concedes no countervailing interests in favor of maintaining the present system, in which cameras are not permitted.

Are there counterarguments, however, that merit serious attention? One of the first ironies that one must confront is the paradox that many of those who advocate cameras in the Supreme Court assert that the Supreme Court has nothing to conceal, because its decision-making process is, by comparison to many other governmental institutions, so rational. While the Court is not perfect, and the results of its deliberations *are* often controversial, the *process* does, on the whole, appear to function smoothly and rationally. But if that is the case, why tinker with success? At a more disturbing level, what if the secret is secrecy? What if the rationality of the Court's process is largely the product of the low profile the Court maintains? Perhaps the absence of cameras in the Supreme Court has actually helped to preserve the integrity of the process—assisting the Court to keep its head while all around are losing theirs.

It is worth contrasting, for example, the attitudes that most journalists express toward Supreme Court oral arguments with the attitude they express toward confirmation hearings for Supreme Court Justices held before the Senate Judiciary Committee. Conventional journalistic wisdom generally approves of oral arguments, finding them focused and intelligent, and generally disapproves of confirmation hearings, finding them meandering, posturing, made-for-television events in which the senators grandstand and mug and the nominees evade and dissemble.

The Supreme Court Justices, most of whom have gone through televised confirmation hearings, may well wonder if the television camera carries with it some virus that inevitably infects the proceedings it covers. If oral arguments before the Supreme Court were to take on the chemistry of confirmation hearings, it is difficult to believe that the quality of justice would be improved.

A second more complex question involves the role of celebrity in American life. Many Americans cannot name the Chief Justice of the United States, or perhaps any current sitting Justice. Many Americans may know most of the names, but would not recognize the Justices' faces. Indeed, it is not uncommon for Justices to take lunches with law clerks or friends in the Supreme Court cafeteria and go unnoticed by members of the public who are eating there. If Supreme Court arguments were regularly televised, the Justices would become mass culture personalities. Their names and faces would be recognized, their anonymity and privacy surrendered. Justices who are colorful and animated during oral argument, such as Antonin Scalia, would find themselves pilloried on Jay Leno or David Letterman; the whole Court would find itself parodied on *Saturday Night Live*.

Advocates for a more open Court might argue that this celebrity might make the Justices uncomfortable and cause personal embarrassment or inconvenience at times, but so what? The Justices should grow up, and accept this sort of scrutiny and ridicule as part of the cost of public service in modern times. All other public servants must endure it, and Supreme Court Justices deserve no special exemptions.

The Justices, however, are likely to perceive something more than personal inconvenience here; they are likely to question whether this sort of celebrity tends to somehow trivialize and denigrate the process of *judicial* decision making, a process that they might view as *different,* in important respects, from decision making in the more political branches of government. This returns us to one of the central themes of this book, the question of whether the Supreme Court's decision-making process genuinely is different from other exercises of self-governance in a democracy.

On this issue, Justices on the Supreme Court will certainly claim that it is—that the evolution of constitutional *law* as practiced in the United States Supreme Court is *not* an exercise in raw political power. Courts decide issues of *law*, the Justices might argue, and issues of *law* are not the same as issues of politics; Supreme Court Justices are bound to a fidelity to law that requires them to do more than simply vote their naked ideological preferences. What the Justices do, under this view, is decide disputes using the tools of textual interpretation, history, logic, and precedent that are unique to a well-ordered legal system.

The television cameras, the Justices might argue, would not understand this. The television cameras would tend to turn this dignified process of the interpretation of law into a more raucous, partisan, and political struggle for power. The Justices might see the Court's authority in American life as bound up in the respect that most Americans have for this "legal process." By making the Court too familiar, television might also make it too common, undercutting the respect for the Court's rulings that is vital if it is to maintain its position in the constitutional system of checks and balances.

The television cameras would also, the Justices might maintain, tend to elevate artificially the role of the oral argument in cases. Oral arguments rarely determine the outcomes of cases; they are just the visible tip of the litigation iceberg. The Justices are far more likely to be influenced by the briefs, the record, and their own jurisprudential inclinations and dispositions than any oral argument. Minds are more likely to be influenced and changed *by other Justices,* in the process of voting, positioning, and opinion writing that follows an argument than by anything the lawyers say during the argument itself. While occasionally oral argument will illuminate a critical point or sharpen an issue, rarely does it actually sway the outcome of a case. And the viewing public might often be frustrated by what it sees of oral arguments, because it might appear that the Justices and the lawyers are preoccupied with arcana peripheral to the heart of an issue pending before the Court. A case involving abortion, race discrimination, or freedom of speech might appear, superficially, to implicate profound and great questions of philosophy, but in the posture of the particular case, actually turn on a relatively fine factual distinction or interpretation of language. To the extent that these "technicalities" might appear to preoccupy the lawyers and Justices in a particular case, the public might come to the incorrect and over-simplified conclusion that the legal system is drowning in technicality and has lost sight of the larger issues of justice. Similarly, the Justices might be concerned with the possibility that because oral argument would be the only part of a case accessible to most members of the public, it would begin to take on, in public understanding of a dispute, a significance greater than it deserves, and in that sense would actually detract from a greater understanding of the Court and the issues before it.

These points in favor of secrecy—at least in favor of keeping television away from the Court—are substantial and worthy of careful consideration by thoughtful readers. Yet thoughtful readers might also wonder what to make, ultimately, of this battle of myths.

For in the end, it seems doubtful that putting television in the Supreme Court would be as important an improvement to our public understanding of the law or the education of students as television access advocates maintain. And it seems equally doubtful that putting television in the Supreme Court would damage the process as much as the Justices have traditionally feared.

While surely there is something to be said for maintaining the decorum of the present system, the idea that the Supreme Court's decision-making process is really removed from politics and ideology is, as this book has revealed, the stuff of myth. At the same time, however, this book has also helped show that the process is not *purely* political. Text, history, logic, and precedent *do* play important roles—they are the tools and language of argument and decision making. The intrigue of the Supreme Court and the study of constitutional law is the mix of "law" (which is never neutral or value-free, despite its ostensible language of objectivity) and "politics" through which this process is always evolving. Would television cameras dramatically change the essence of that process? It is hard to believe they would. The Supreme Court and the process of constitutional adjudication that we know today is the product of two hundred years of tradition and culture. The strengths and weaknesses of that tradition are unlikely to be washed away by television alone. As readers consider Tony Mauro's brief for television access and greater openness by the Court, they should ask whether the positive gain that might come from allowing more Americans to witness this process with their own eyes and ears (albeit through a television screen) is worth the sacrifice in institutional and personal privacy that the Court and its Justices would be forced to endure.

—Editor

The Supreme Court
and the Cult of Secrecy

TONY MAURO

The Bill of Rights was enacted against the backdrop of the long history of trials being presumptively open. . . . In guaranteeing freedoms such as those of speech and press, the First Amendment can be read as protecting the right of everyone to attend trials so as to give meaning to those explicit guarantees. . . . Free speech carries with it some freedom to listen.—Chief Justice Warren Burger, for the Court in *Richmond Newspapers, Inc. v. Virginia*

That the First Amendment speaks separately of freedom of speech and freedom of the press is no constitutional accident, but an acknowledgement of the critical role played by the press in American society.—Justice Potter Stewart, concurring in *Houchins v. KQED, Inc.*

Supreme Court Justices are fond of saying that the Court speaks only through its opinions. The rest of this book examines how the Court "spoke" through that medium during the 1992–93 term.

But the Court is an institution that speaks—or chooses not to speak—in many other ways. It is a place where approximately three hundred people work every day, nine of whom occasionally don black robes when they get there. It sets policy, it has an elaborate set of traditions and procedures, and it has a culture—a culture that communicates, as vividly as do its opinions, the Court's view of its place in the American scene.

The Supreme Court's current vision of itself is as an institution apart, a branch of government vastly unlike the other two. If asked to locate its place in the constitutional firmament, it would call itself coequal with the executive and the legislative branches, but somehow above them—not susceptible to temptations of media exposure and celebrity, not at all interested in laying bare its inner workings, and not inclined to win popularity contests by becoming familiar.

Rarely has the Court conveyed that vision more strikingly than in its 1992–93 term. A succession of events—its reaction to the release of the papers of the late Thurgood Marshall, its displeasure at the marketing of Supreme Court oral argument tapes, and its continued resistance to the broadcast of its proceedings—have spoken eloquently for the Court. Whenever the outside world began to close in, to scrutinize the ways in which it speaks other than through its opinions, the Court's initial reaction was to pull up the drawbridges.

The Court has functioned within this cult of secrecy for so long that its members may well have forgotten why.

Part of it, clearly, is a wistfulness for a bygone era, a pre-CNN and pre-C-Span period when public officials were less visible, and perhaps more revered. At an Eighth Circuit conference in August, 1993, retiring Justice Byron White candidly offered one reason why he is glad that television cameras, ubiquitous in the world of the other two branches of government, have been kept out of the nation's highest court. "I am very pleased to be able to walk around, and very very seldom am I recognized," White said. "It's very selfish, I know."

The Court's public information officer Toni House puts it slightly differently. "The Court is perfectly comfortable being in the public eye as an institution, but not as individual Justices. They simply don't wish to be personalities. They don't think that whether they play tennis or they are championship fox-trotters has anything to do with whether they are good Justices."

Still others give a more high-minded rationale for the Court's penchant for privacy.

In a 1990 speech, Justice Antonin Scalia spoke reverently of judges' "ancient reluctance to engage in public debate over the rightness or wrongness of their decisions and their ancient belief that by and large no news is good news." The Court has no duty or even self-interest in making itself more accessible to the public, Scalia suggested, because the Court's work is so difficult for the public to understand—and for the news media to report. "That is why the *University of Chicago Law Review* is not sold at Seven-Eleven," was Scalia's now-classic line.

University of Virginia law professor A. E. Dick Howard puts it another way. "The Court's mystique has its place. It probably enhances the public's view of them for the Court to be perceived as a little different from everyone else," Howard says. But, he adds, "What's so paradoxical about the Court's attitude is that they're the ones who have the least to hide. Their decisions are made through the most rational process you can find anywhere in Washington."

Whether or not Howard's complimentary view of the Court's decision-making process is correct, he suggests the right question: Does the Supreme Court really need its shroud of anonymity? It could also be asked, Does the Court deserve it?

It was like a thunderclap at the Court, one insider said, when the *Washington Post* began publishing the results of its research of the papers of the late Justice Thurgood Marshall in the last week of May 1993.

Inside stories of cases decided as recently as two terms earlier were exposed and well documented through the extensive paper trail the Justices appear to leave in every case they decide. The backstage maneuvering over *Roe v. Wade, University of California Regents v. Bakke,* even the more recent *Webster v. Reproductive Health Services,* were there for all to see.

"Collectively, the papers show the Court's decision-making process as a continuing conversation among nine distinct individuals on dozens of issues simultaneously," the *Post* wrote. "The exchanges are serious, sometimes scholarly, occasionally brash and personalized, but generally well-reasoned and most often cast in understated, genteel language."

Once the *Post* began its series, other media swarmed into the Library of Congress, unearthing fascinating nuggets from the 173,700 items in the collection. A petition from the Court's law clerks was found, asking for cancellation of the Court's Christmas party for fear of breaching the wall between church and state. Discussions of the use of Court limousines, chipping in for wedding gifts for a Justice's daughter, and how to handle interview requests from the press were all included.

Because the release came so soon after Marshall's retirement and death, the papers afforded an unprecedented window on the nearly current court. Ultimately, one scholar said, the papers would become a "secondary source," because Marshall took few notes during the Court's private conferences. But for now, they were a sensation. And soon, it became clear that for the Court they were an acute embarrassment.

The adverse reaction was swift. Marshall's widow, Cecilia, expressed dismay, as did former law clerks and longtime friends, including

William Coleman Jr. and Carl Rowan. None could imagine that the Library of Congress was doing Marshall's bidding by giving such unrestricted access to his papers so quickly after his death.

Within two days, the Court itself offered its view, in a letter addressed to the librarian of Congress, James Billington. "I speak for a majority of the active Justices of the Court when I say that we are both surprised and disappointed by the library's decision to give unrestricted public access to Justice Marshall's papers," wrote Chief Justice William Rehnquist. Noting that the library had not consulted with the Court or Marshall's family before making the papers public, Rehnquist added, "Given the Court's long tradition of confidentiality in its deliberations, we believe this failure to consult reflects bad judgment on the part of the library."

The last line of Rehnquist's letter seemed to reflect a realization that there was little the Court could do besides blow off steam: "Unless there is some presently unknown basis for the library's action, we think it is such that future donors of judicial papers will be inclined to look elsewhere for a repository."

The Court declined to state which, and how many, Justices, were in the majority joining Rehnquist's letter. But it was clearly not unanimous, and some in the know said that only five of the nine justices agreed to the letter. Indeed, Justice Byron White sent a separate letter to Billington containing these two sentences: "Whatever may be the reason for Justice Marshall's papers now being open to the public, I regret exceedingly that this has happened. As presently advised, however, I do not subscribe to the Chief Justice's May 25 letter." After White subsequently announced his retirement, it became known that White's papers would be shipped to the Library of Congress, made available by his permission during his lifetime, but after his death only after ten years. Sandra Day O'Connor has also lodged her papers at the Library of Congress, and the Marshall incident has not evidently changed her mind.

Within a week, after all the expressions of outrage, the controversy died down. What remained were the 173,700 documents neatly organized at the Library of Congress, a feast for researchers that is still being consumed.

In fact, the papers had been publicly available since a few days after Marshall had died in January. A handful of researchers—including David Garrow, at work on a book on *Roe v. Wade* and the right of privacy—had already begun plowing through the boxes and boxes of papers from Marshall's lengthy tenure on the Court. It was not until May that *Washington Post* reporters began to come around.

The Library of Congress had made them public matter-of-factly, confident that it was following the wishes of Marshall himself.

The library had been seeking to acquire Marshall's papers since 1965—even before Marshall joined the Court. At various times during his tenure, Marshall said he would follow the example of Hugo Black and burn his conference papers. An autobiography Marshall planned to write with the assistance of columnist Carl Rowan never got written, in part because Marshall was reluctant to bare his files for purposes of the research.

But Marshall never did burn his papers, and soon after he retired in 1991, the library renewed its request. Marshall indicated interest, and in October 1991 he met with Billington as well as several library staffers. "He was fully in charge and clearly told us to make his papers accessible after his death," recalls Billington. Other participants left the meeting with the sense that Marshall had considered placing restrictions on access but rejected them. The only one he stipulated was that during his lifetime, Marshall would allow researchers to see his papers only with his written permission. Based on the conversation, the library drafted an instrument of gift which Marshall signed.

The document said access would be allowed only for "private study on the premises of the library by researchers or scholars engaged in serious research." At the height of the controversy, some suggested that newspaper reporters couldn't possibly meet the definition of "researchers," but the library has always interpreted the word to include journalists.

Another cause for concern was the document's stipulation that after Marshall's death, "the collection shall be made available to the public at the discretion of the library." But Billington says "discretion" has always meant simply a determination by library staff about when the papers were organized enough to be made available—not a license to place restrictions on access that the donor did not envision. "Some have argued that opening Justice Marshall's papers now threatens the privacy of Supreme Court deliberations," Billington said at one point. "We have nothing but respect for the Court and its members. But we cannot serve as the Court's watchdog."

Marshall's true intentions will never be known. But it is hard to imagine that top officials of the Library of Congress would purposefully conspire to thwart his wishes.

What may have occurred, simply, is that Thurgood Marshall did not expect to die so soon. If, while he was talking to the Library of Congress, Marshall anticipated in some way that he would be around for ten more years, it would not have occurred to him that disclosure of his papers upon death would have made headlines or opened fresh wounds.

The Court's reaction to the release is also something of a mystery. Justices may have been pained to see Mrs. Marshall subjected to a new wave of publicity. More likely, the Justices reacted with disgust to seeing themselves in the headlines for their "private" deliberations. Law clerks and all Court personnel are sworn to secrecy about the behind-the-scenes vote shifts and debates that go on before a decision is released. Reading about their deliberative process in the newspapers would have a chilling effect on their candor, they seem to believe.

But as the controversy fades, it is fair to wonder if that is really true. Will the release of the Marshall papers change, even slightly, the Court's method of deliberating? In the end, the Court's pique over the Marshall release may just have more to do with its view of itself—that it speaks to the public only through its finished products, its opinions. Headlines about what goes before were unwelcome. No news, Scalia said, after all, is good news.

Fittingly enough the Marshall papers, which the Justices so fervently wanted to keep private, shed light on another aspect of the Court's aversion to publicity: its longstanding objection to television coverage of its proceedings. The Court's distaste for television was nothing new. But the Marshall papers offered the first inside glimpse of the Court's true feelings.

The occasion for the Court's discussion of the issue contained in the Marshall papers was the 1991 swearing-in of Marshall's successor, Clarence Thomas. Washington, D.C., lawyer Timothy Dyk, who has quietly campaigned for broadcast access for the better part of a decade, had petitioned the Court once again to allow coverage of any ceremony that might be scheduled. Dyk makes a similar plea with every new Justice—including, most recently, for access to the Ruth Ginsburg investiture at the Court on October 1, 1993. True to form, the Court turned him down.

Dyk's thinking has been that a one-time experiment, at a purely ceremonial event, might be a palatable way for the Justices to study the issue and hopefully overcome their fear of the television age.

Unknown to Dyk at the time, his September 1991 request for the Thomas investiture became the vehicle for an unusually political debate among the Justices, according to correspondence in the Marshall papers.

Always covetous of the Court's coequal status, most of the Justices were growing weary of the fairly recent practice of swearing in Justices at the White House as well as at the Court. The televised White House events were exploited fully by the president's political and public relations apparatus.

"The practice of having an oath administered in the White House lends further weight to the politicization of the appointment process," Justice Harry Blackmun wrote indignantly to his colleagues. "It certainly did not take place when Chief Justice Burger was sworn in, or when I took the oath, or when John [Paul Stevens] and Sandra [Day O'Connor] were sworn in. I refused to attend the White House ceremony the last time [for David Souter] and I shall not attend this time."

Stevens concurred: "The fact that the President's political advisors regard it as a useful photo opportunity emphasizes why I think we should do whatever we can to terminate the practice."

Scalia actually suggested, only partly facetiously, that broadcast access at the Court be offered to the president as a lure to cancel the White House ceremony. "The President's men are going to want good theater and attractive close-ups," Scalia wrote. "As far as I am concerned, an investiture ceremony, unlike an oral argument, is for show and not for go, and awareness of the cameras' presence is no problem." Lest anyone mistake his tactical suggestion for actual support for cameras in the Supreme Court, Scalia also wrote, "I believe in the camel's nose, and would not permit cameras for the investiture unless there is some offsetting benefit."

In fact, according to the correspondence, Stevens was the only Justice who unreservedly favored granting Dyk's request.

Blackmun was the only other Justice to come close, writing that "I am about where I have been, that is, to defer to any strongly expressed wishes of the chief justice (WEB or WHR). There is much to be said, however, in favor of the media's request to televise a ceremonial occasion. I could be persuaded to join John [Paul Stevens] on this."

All the others—including David Souter, who had spoken favorably about camera access during his confirmation hearing, and Marshall himself, who five years earlier had favored camera access—voted against it.

And what of Rehnquist? The Chief Justice politely dismissed Scalia's suggestion of a trade-off with the White House. "It is somewhat awkward to invite someone to your house on the condition that he not invite you to his house."

But on the merits of Dyk's request, Rehnquist took note of the recently begun experiment with broadcast access in the lower federal courts. "I think it would be a mistake for us to change our present practice with regard to televising our regular proceedings until the returns are in from these experiments," Rehnquist said.

Not exactly a stirring endorsement. But with Stevens the only certain vote in favor of access right now, Rehnquist's nod toward the lower court experiment appears to be the news media's only hope.

The experiment was authorized in September 1990, by the Judicial Conference, the policy-making body of the federal judiciary. It authorizes broadcast and still camera coverage of civil proceedings only in two federal appeals courts and six district courts across the nation. The media have grumbled about the experiment's exclusion of criminal proceedings but gradually have discovered that civil cases can be newsworthy too. Some access is better than none.

The federal courts have excluded broadcast coverage since at least 1937, when it was banned in the aftermath of the chaotic Lindbergh baby kidnapping trial. All but three states now allow some form of coverage, spurred on in part by the Supreme Court's own decision in *Chandler v. Florida,* which said the Constitution did not bar broadcast coverage per se.

But even the Judicial Conference's modest experiment might never have begun if not for Wisconsin congressman Robert Kastenmeier. Kastenmeier, now no longer in Congress, had considerable clout with the Judicial Conference in 1990 as chair of the subcommittee that oversees all federal courts. In May 1990, Kastenmeier announced that "the time has come for the federal judicial branch to allow cameras in the courtroom." He spoke of the "unchanged and still unmet need to provide the public with more information that will lead to a better understanding of the federal courts."

That, in turn, got the attention of Rehnquist, who wrote Kastenmeier that he was "by no means averse" to an experiment that would consider the idea. The Judicial Conference, taking the hint of its titular head, soon agreed to forge ahead.

In an institution that usually moves into new areas with glacial speed, Rehnquist's "by no means averse" formulation amounted to a major change.

It was Rehnquist's predecessor Warren Burger who, more than anyone else, had resisted the trend of society and the states toward the broadcast era. Warren Burger wrote the *Chandler* decision, which encouraged broadcasters at the state level. But Burger was determined at all costs to keep cameras and microphones out of his Court. They'd have to climb over his dead body to get in, he reportedly once said.

When broadcasters sought one-time access to listen to arguments over the constitutionality of the Gramm-Rudman law in 1986, Burger sent back a formal denial with this postscript penned in: "When you get Cabinet meetings on the air, call me!"

The analogy between private Cabinet meetings and public oral arguments was hopelessly flawed, but it was symbolic of Burger's nearly obsessive opposition to the idea.

Soon after he retired in 1986, I had the opportunity to ask Burger why he was so opposed to allowing cameras into his court. "Television in a short snippet is simply incapable of making a proper report unless you put the whole thing on," Burger said.

Anticipating such an answer, I asked how the excerpting done on television differed from that done by newspapers. Even the *New York Times,* I noted, does not print complete transcripts of oral arguments.

In a newspaper, Burger countered, "The words aren't coming right out of the mouth of the judge or the attorney. On television, you see the person and it's coming right out of his mouth."

At first, I thought Burger's point was that newspapers offered Justices "plausible deniability"—the ability to claim they were misquoted. Television images, on the other hand, could not be refuted, and were, in an odd way, too accurate for Burger's taste. I've since come to believe that Burger was really making a different assertion—that by having their images captured on television, Justices and lawyers would be aiding and abetting, in a more concrete way than in newspapers, the execution of an improper and undignified report on the Court's proceedings.

Television can go about its nasty business if it must, Burger seemed to be saying, but don't involve or implicate the Supreme Court. A variant, in short, on the view of the Supreme Court as different and apart.

Burger is not the only Justice whose judgment seemed clouded on the issue. His view that gavel-to-gavel coverage might be acceptable whereas garden-variety news coverage is not continues to shape the discussion—especially since C-Span has made it known that it would air all oral arguments, gavel to gavel, if they became available.   Even Ruth Bader Ginsburg expressed the view during her confirmation hearings. "If it's gavel to gavel then I don't see any problem at all in an appellate court," she said in response to a question from Senator Orrin Hatch of Utah. "The concern is about distortion because of the editing, if editing is not controlled."

In the context of print media, talk of "controlled editing" would be preposterous and downright unconstitutional, under the court's own decision in *Miami Herald Publishing Co. v. Tornillo.* Yet the same concept is bandied about freely in the context of broadcast media. There are some ways in which the broadcast and print media can arguably be thought of differently under the First Amendment, but this is not one of them.

As New York court administrator Matthew Crosson wrote in 1991, "If gavel-to-gavel coverage is acceptable but other coverage is not, then it is not the presence of cameras in court that is objectionable, it is what the media chooses to broadcast or publish. [But we should] not . . . evaluate the editorial judgments made by television statements and newspapers, however much we might disagree with some of those judgments."

Fred Graham, who has covered the Court for the *New York Times* and *CBS News,* recalls in his book *Happy Talk* another instance in which a Justice made comments about television that would never have been made about print. Byron White, Graham writes, once explained his opposition to camera access this way: "I can't see why the court should do anything to make CBS richer." The notion that CBS would be enriched by being able to report on Court proceedings was odd enough.

But using a broadcaster's profit motive as an argument for restricting access enjoyed by newspapers—not exactly eleemosynary organizations—was too much for Graham to bear. "When I tried to argue that newspapers had made money for years off their coverage of the Court," Graham continued, "all I got was a stony stare."

Graham, now chief anchor for the cable channel Court TV, observed that "in a world in which everybody else wanted to be on television, only the justices and the Mafia avoided it. The Mafia at least had a defensible reason, in that it had much to hide. But the Supreme Court's aversion to television seemed to grow out of an imperious resistance to change that took the form of judicial electrophobia."

In one sense, it seems refreshing that at least one Washington institution has no interest in televised publicity. It would even be admirable were it some private club or society, taking a solitary stand against today's talk-show culture. But this is the nation's highest court, an important and public institution, and it is still allowed to stay out of the public eye for what often seem like petty personal preferences.

Before he retired, Justice Lewis Powell was asked about camera access and he replied, "In fairness, I think you'd have to show little segments of each one's argument, and that would take more time than the nightly news would allow . . . so I doubt the feasibility of TV in the courtroom being fair." Fair to whom, asked Todd Piccus in a recent *Texas Law Review* article. He answered his own question: "Perhaps Justice Powell simply feared that selective coverage and the editorial process would be unfair to the justices themselves—the appointed-for-life public servants, whose official actions are unappealable, and whose actions ultimately and sometimes intimately affect every American citizen."

Not to belabor the point, any president or member of Congress who used the same words as Powell to argue against press access would be laughed at. Yet Justices can say it without apparent embarrassment.

Thurgood Marshall, who at one time supported camera access, joined the opposition as he grew older—some say it was because he grew older, and less inclined to see his gruff and sometimes disoriented manner portrayed on camera.

According to some at the court, Marshall was deeply pained by what he viewed as television's brutal treatment of Robert Bork during his confirmation hearings in 1987, and he decided the Supreme Court did not need that kind of scrutiny. Even though Marshall was at the opposite end of the political spectrum from Bork, he sympathized with him—as did other Justices. "They saw Bork and said, 'No camera is going to look up my nose hairs like that,'" said one court official at the time.

Marshall apparently had similar feelings about his successor. Soon after Marshall retired, he sat in a number of cases argued before the Second Circuit U.S. Court of Appeals in New York—a court where he had sat before becoming a Justice, and one of the courts that was permitting camera coverage under the experiment. But he vetoed the coverage for all the cases he sat on, telling the *ABA Journal* later, "After the Thomas hearing and seeing what TV did to the Senate, I said I'd not be a part of TV doing that to any court."

Rehnquist, though more willing than Burger to consider the idea, seems to come from the same basic school. In 1988, Rehnquist allowed Dyk to put on a private demonstration of how cameras would operate at the court. Rehnquist, White, and Anthony Kennedy attended, asking questions of Dyk as they would during oral argument, as two small cameras, using existing light, recorded the event.

The tape of the session was never made public, but apparently some of the questioning focused on ways in which the faces of Justices asking questions during real oral arguments could be kept off-camera. Evidently the Justices were interested in having the camera coverage mirror their practice with written transcripts of oral argument. When printed transcripts are made for the court, the lawyers are identified, but the Justices are not. Questions come from "the Court," not a named Justice.

How could cameras do the same thing? Regrettably, perhaps, the demonstration occurred before the advent of the "blue blob," used by broadcasters to obscure the face of, for example, the testifying rape victim in the 1991 William Kennedy Smith rape trial. In any event, nothing of substance came from the experiment.

Rehnquist's main comment on the issue came soon after he became Chief Justice. When asked about the possibility of cameras in the Supreme Court, Rehnquist said, "I hope we don't get to the time where the members of our Court are trying to get on the six o'clock news every night, and I think if they did, it would lessen to a certain extent some of the mystique and moral authority" of the Court.

If it all boils down to mystique, then how does one explain the court's angry reaction to Peter Irons?

Irons, a political science professor at the University of California at San Diego and director of that school's Earl Warren Bill of Rights Project, had come upon a new way to bring the Supreme Court closer to the people—without diminishing its dignity in the slightest. He wanted to bring to the public the drama of Supreme Court oral argument. How better to convey the Court's mystique?

Five years earlier, Irons had written *The Courage of Their Convictions,* a simply written book that told the story of sixteen individuals who had taken their cases, as the cliché goes, "all the way to the Supreme Court."

His new project took shape when he learned that the Court, in spite of its aversion to broadcast of its proceedings, has been audiotaping its oral arguments since 1955 for transcription and historical purposes. Irons saw the possibility of editing and reproducing those tapes to give teachers a new tool for educating students about the issues before the Court and how it resolved them.

The tapes originally were housed at the Court itself, but under circumstances that are still in dispute, the Court decided in the late 1960s to turn over the tapes to the National Archives, with the proviso that they be used only for "serious scholarly and legal research."

In the early 1980s, CBS's Fred Graham took it as his slightly mischievous mission to expand that definition and put an oral argument on the air. On the occasion of the tenth anniversary of the Pentagon Papers case in 1981, Graham obtained what even he described as a "bootleg copy" of the argument in the case. He put it on the air, and as Graham recalls, "the Chief Justice went into orbit." Burger stopped sending tapes to the archives for five years, and even tried to persuade the American Bar Association to pull back an award it was planning to give Graham for his report.

But eventually the archives resumed its role as repository of the tapes, and researchers—including Irons—were required to sign an agreement before they were allowed to copy the tapes. They had to pledge to use the tapes for "private research and teaching purposes" only, and to promise not to reproduce them.

Irons signed the agreement and made copies of twenty-three oral arguments—among the most historic and notable in the modern Supreme Court era. He planned to edit down the tapes—taking out the dull and confusing parts, of which there are many—and narrate them so they could fit neatly into a classroom period.

There was Thurgood Marshall, arguing passionately before the court in *Cooper v. Aaron* in 1958, a test of Little Rock's foot-dragging on school desegregation: "I worry about the white children in Little Rock who are told, as young people, that the way to get your rights is to violate the law and deft the lawful authorities. I don't worry about those Negro kids' future. They've been struggling with democracy long enough."

Irons came across New York University Law School professor Anthony Amsterdam's eloquent attack on capital punishment in *Gregg v. Georgia* in 1976: "The death penalty may be the greatest obstacle to adequate enforcement of crime in this country today because it sops public conscience and makes you think we're doing something about serious crime instead of devising other methods of dealing with it."

And Justice Abe Fortas's tone of righteous indignation in *Gideon v. Wainwright* about the notion that the federal Constitution does not guarantee the assistance of counsel to a state criminal defendant: "I may be wrong about this, but I do believe that in some of the Court's decisions there has been a tendency from time to time, because of the pull of federalism, to forget, to forget the realities of what happens downstairs, of what happens to these poor, miserable, indigent people when they are arrested and they are brought into the jail . . . and then later they are brought before a court, and there, Clarence Earl Gideon, defend yourself."

The material was rich, and Irons encountered nothing but enthusiasm as his project proceeded. He contacted many of the lawyers whose voices he planned to reproduce: Robert Bork, Laurence Tribe, Archibald Cox, Sarah Weddington, Erwin Griswold, and all endorsed his project. "Some of them did not even know the tapes existed and they were very excited about the project," Irons said.

The first sign of trouble came in April 1991, when the Court's marshal, Alfred Wong, responding to a query from Irons, reminded Irons of the restrictions contained in the agreement. That reminder did not slow Irons down, nor did it keep him from writing to Rehnquist seeking an endorsement of the project. Rehnquist himself did not reply, but on November 4, 1991, Rehnquist's administrative assistant, Robb Jones, wrote to Irons, "I applaud the concept and your efforts." Jones, apparently unaware of the restrictions, now reportedly regrets the letter.

Despite the mixed messages, it became clear to Irons that the Court was taking a decidedly dim view of his project. As a sort of preemptive measure in July 1992, Irons sent a memorandum to Jones arguing that for both legal and public policy reasons, the agreements could not and should not be enforced against him. He reminded Jones that the tapes were a rendition of public hearings, having nothing to do with national security or any other plausible justification for restricting their use. "Distribution of the oral argument tapes would, in fact, promote the national interest in education about the Bill of Rights," Irons wrote.

The next official word Irons heard from the Court came when his book-and-tapes package was already on its way to booksellers. Entitled *May It Please the Court,* it is handsomely assembled, with tapes in a book-like case, boxed with a companion book containing the transcripts of each tape. It sells for seventy-five dollars and was published by the New York Press in 1993, a not-for-profit publishing house in New York. On the cover, fittingly, is the famed 1935 photograph of the Supreme Court in session, taken secretly by photographer Erich Salomon—the only known photo of the sitting Court.

On August 3, 1993, the Court issued a terse statement noting that Irons had signed the agreement with the archives for every oral argument tape he obtained and was now selling. "In light of this clear violation of Professor Irons' contractual commitments, the Court is considering what legal remedies may be appropriate," the statement concluded.

By month's end, no "legal remedies" were announced, but Wong wrote a letter to the National Archives labeling Irons, in effect, a persona non grata. "In light of his actions and his willingness to violate the agreements he signed," Wong wrote, "future requests for copying audiotapes by Mr. Irons or by any project with which he is associated, should be considered a request for 'commercial use or broadcast' under paragraph (f) of the agreement between the Court and the National Archives and should be referred to me for consideration." For all the Court's buildup, it was a trivial response—especially since Irons has no intention of writing a sequel or ever requesting an oral argument tape again.

Yet the Court's action had the effect of transforming Irons into a minor hero, vastly heightening the level of publicity about his work and boosting its sales. By late September 1993, it had sold sixty thousand copies and the publisher was scrambling to print more copies. *New York Times* columnist William Safire attacked the Court for its reaction to Irons's project.

Clearly, the Court should have been able to forecast the public reaction to its threat of legal action against Irons. It could have punished Irons by ignoring him—the ultimate indignity. Yet the Court went forward. Why?

A primary reason, to be sure, was its lawyerly concern about the "contract" Irons signed and seemingly violated. For some lawyers that alone is enough to make a fuss, no matter what the consequences. But the Court could have afforded to let Irons's defiance go unnoticed. What could be the other reasons?

Another factor is a lesser-known facet of the Court's culture: its distaste for commercialism. This is a Court that won't allow even a charitable organization to auction off a Justice's doodling. The notion that Irons might be profiting from the Court's work was simply offensive to some, and the fact that his was a nonprofit publisher made little difference. Nor did the fact that a raft of legal publishers also make money from the Court's work through a dozen different newsletters and databases.

But when BNA or West Publishing (two major publishers of judicial decisions) profit from the Court's work, it is the Court's opinions they are selling—not the contents of the oral arguments.

It goes back, then, to the initial point: The Court chooses to speak only through its opinions. All the other parts of the process—the oral arguments that Irons sought to reveal and broadcasters want to air and the private deliberations that the Marshall papers exposed—are mere preliminaries, in the view of the Court. And those preliminaries may be somewhat untidy, perhaps too revealing, or misleading, the Justices seem to believe.

But if these controversies of 1993 prove anything, it is that the Court need not be so modest. The nearly universal verdict, after sifting through the Marshall papers, is that they ennobled the Court by making it clear to the public that each decision is preceded by careful, if not tortured, deliberation. The Irons tapes, as well, are already instilling greater understanding and respect for the Court among high-school and law school students alike.

The televising of oral arguments, as well, is unlikely to cast the Court in an unfavorable light. It may make the Justices somewhat more recognizable on the streets of Washington, but mostly it will enable television—the main source of news today—to cover the Court's proceedings with more precision. Television will cover the Supreme Court whether or not its practitioners have to leave the tools of their trade outside the Court's door. Why not enable them to make their coverage more real and more accurate? The Court's decisions would then be rendered, not by Justices brought to life only by courtroom sketches, but by real people on film who, increasingly, look like the diverse America they serve.

But whether or not these glimpses through the cracks make the Justices look better, they are an inevitable part of a process under way throughout the nation: a greater flow of information to the public about its government. The Supreme Court is neither well served by being, nor is it entitled to be, an exception to that trend.

As early as 1823, Thomas Jefferson foresaw the problem posed by a Supreme Court whose work is hidden: "There is no danger I apprehend so much as the consolidation of our government by the noiseless, and therefore unalarming, instrumentality of the supreme court."

APPENDIX

The Justices of the Supreme Court of the United States, 1992–93

William H. Rehnquist, Chief Justice
Appointed Associate Justice by President Nixon in 1972. Elevated to Chief Justice by President Reagan in 1986.

Byron R. White, Associate Justice
Appointed by President Kennedy in 1962. Resigned from the Court at the end of the 1993 term, replaced by Associate Justice Ruth Bader Ginsburg.

Harry A. Blackmun, Associate Justice
Appointed by President Nixon in 1970. Resigned from the Court at the end of the 1994 term, replaced by Associate Justice Stephen G. Breyer.

John Paul Stevens, Associate Justice
Appointed by President Ford in 1975.

Sandra Day O'Connor, Associate Justice
Appointed by President Reagan in 1981.

Antonin Scalia, Associate Justice
Appointed by President Reagan in 1986.

Anthony M. Kennedy, Associate Justice
Appointed by President Reagan in 1988.

David H. Souter, Associate Justice
Appointed by President Bush in 1990.

Clarence Thomas, Associate Justice
Appointed by President Bush in 1991.

Biographies of the Contributors

Paul Barrett covers the Supreme Court for the *Wall Street Journal*, where he has been since 1987. Before joining the *Journal*, he was editor and writer for the *Washington Monthly*. He has written on federal law enforcement and business regulation for numerous other publications, including the *Washington Post* and *Philadelphia Magazine*. He received his J.D. from Harvard.

Richard Carelli has worked for the Associated Press since 1969, covering the Supreme Court since 1976. Before joining the Associated Press, he worked as a journalist in New York, West Virginia, Ohio, Florida, and Washington, D.C. He holds a B.S. from Ohio University and a J.D. from George Washington University.

Marcia Coyle is the Washington Bureau chief and U.S. Supreme Court correspondent for the *National Law Journal*, which she joined in 1987. Ms. Coyle had worked before this for the Allentown Call-Chronicle Newspapers, first as a state capital correspondent and later as its Washington bureau chief. She holds a B.A. in English from Hood College, an M.S. in journalism from Northwestern University, and a J.D. from the University of Baltimore School of Law. Among other awards, Ms. Coyle has won the George Polk Award for Legal Reporting, the Investigative Reporters and Editors Award for outstanding investigative reporting, the Scripps-Howard Meeman Award for Environmental Reporting, and the Unity Award for investigative reporting about minority problems.

Lyle Denniston, a reporter for the *Baltimore Sun*'s Washington bureau, is the dean of American journalists who cover the Supreme Court. He is a regular columnist for the *Washington Journalism Review* and contributor to the *MacNeil-Lehrer News Hour*. Mr. Denniston is also an adjunct professor of law and lecturer at Georgetown. He has a B.A. from the University of Nebraska and an M.A. in American history and political science from Georgetown. Mr. Denniston is the author of *The Reporter and the Law: Techniques of Covering the Courts* (1980).

Aaron Epstein is a national correspondent for Knight-Ridder Newspapers covering the Supreme Court, the Justice Department, and related matters. He received his A.B. from Dartmouth and his J.D. from the McGeorge College of Law, University of the Pacific, and attended the University of Missouri School of Journalism. He was a member both of the *Philadelphia Inquirer* staff that won the 1980 Pulitzer Prize for Local Reporting for coverage of the Three Mile Island nuclear accident and of the Knight-Ridder team that won a 1988 Polk Award for coverage of the Iran-Contra affair.

Kay Kindred is a professor of law and Deputy Director of the Institute of Bill of Rights Law at the College of William and Mary, Marshall-Wythe School of Law, where she teaches education law and family law. She is also a member of the adjunct faculty of the college's School of Education. Professor Kindred received her A.B. in political science and sociology from Duke University in 1977 and her J.D. from Columbia University Law School in 1980. Before coming to William and Mary in 1989, she was a member of the offices of general counsel of the General Electric Company in Fairfield, Connecticut, and Old Dominion University in Norfolk, Virginia. She is the author of "When First Amendment Values and Competition Policy Collide: Resolving the Dilemma of Mixed-Motive Boycotts," *Arizona Law Review* (1992) and is a contributing author to *Corporate Fraud: Some Theoretical Examples and Responses* (Greenwood Press, forthcoming).

Tony Mauro has covered the Supreme Court since 1980 for the Gannett News Service and for *USA Today* since its creation in 1982. Since 1987, he has also written a column on the Supreme Court for *Legal Times* and the *American Lawyer* newspapers. Mauro is on the executive committee of the Reporters Committee for Freedom of the Press and serves on the Conference of Lawyers and Representatives of the Media, and the Freedom of Information Committee of the Society of Professional Journalists. He holds a B.A. from Rutgers University and an M.A. in journalism from Columbia. Before coming to Washington, he worked for newspapers in Massachusetts and New Jersey.

David Savage has been the Supreme Court correspondent in Washington for the *Los Angeles Times* since 1986. Before this assignment, he was an education writer for the *Los Angeles Times*. He has also covered Congress and the Supreme Court for a Washington weekly newspaper. He graduated with a B.A. in political science from the University of North Carolina at Chapel Hill and an M.S. from Northwestern University. He is the author of *Turning Right: The Making of the Rehnquist Court* (1992).

Rodney Smolla is the Arthur B. Hanson Professor of Law and Director of the Institute of Bill of Rights Law at the College of William and Mary, and a senior fellow of The Annenberg Washington Program in Communications Policy Studies. He received his B.A. from Yale and his J.D. from Duke. He was awarded the ABA Gavel Award Certificate of Merit in 1987. His books include *Suing the Press: Libel, the Media and Power* (1986), *Law of Defamation* (1986), *Jerry Falwell v. Larry Flynt: The First Amendment on Trial* (1988), *Constitutional Law: Structure and Rights in Our Federal System* (with Daan Braveman and William C. Banks, 1991), *Free Speech in an Open Society* (1992), *Smolla and Nimmer on Freedom of Speech* (1994), and *Federal Civil Rights Acts* (1994).

Stephen Wermiel joined the faculty of Georgia State University Law School in August 1992 after completing a year as the Lee Distinguished Visiting Professor of Law at the College of William and Mary. For twelve years, Professor Wermiel was the Supreme Court correspondent for the *Wall Street Journal*. He covered more than 1,300 Supreme Court decisions and analyzed trends on a broad array of legal issues. He received his B.A. in political science from Tufts University and his J.D. from American University. Currently, he is working on the authorized biography of retired Supreme Court Justice William Brennan. His article on Justice Sandra Day O'Connor's first decade on the Supreme Court appeared in the *Women's Rights Law Reporter* in 1992. Other articles have appeared in the inaugural issue of the *William and Mary Bill of Rights Law Journal* and in the *Northwestern University Law Review.* In 1995 he was voted Faculty Member of the Year at the Georgia State University Law School.

TABLE OF CASES

INDEX

Library of Congress Cataloging-in-Publication Data
A year in the life of the Supreme Court / by Paul Barrett
. . . [et al.]; edited by Rodney A. Smolla
p. cm. — (Constitutional conflicts)   Includes index.
ISBN 0-8223-1653-6 (cloth). — ISBN 0-8223-1665-X (pbk.)
1. United States. Supreme Court.   2. United States—Constitutional law.
3. Justice, Administration of—United States.   I. Barrett, Paul.
II. Smolla, Rodney A.   III. Series.
KF8742.Y43   1995   347.73'26—dc20   [347.30735]
95-4130CIP